Performing Cultural Tourisn

T0383047

While experiential staging is well documented in tourism studies, not enough has been written about the diverse types of experiences and expectations that visitors bring to the tourist space and how communities respond to, or indeed challenge, these expectations. This book brings together new ideas about cultural experiences and how communities, creative producers, and visitors can productively engage with competing interests and notions of experience and authenticity in the tourist environment.

Part I considers the experiences of communities in meeting the needs of cultural tourists in an international context. Part II analyses the relationships between individual cultural tourists, the community, and digital technology. Finally, Part III responds to new methodologies in relation to interactions between government and regional policy and community development.

Focusing on the way in which communities and visitors 'perform' new forms of cultural tourism, *Performing Cultural Tourism* is aimed at undergraduate students, researchers, academics, and a diverse range of professionals at both private and government levels that are seeking to develop policies and business plans that recognize and respond to new interests in contemporary tourism.

Susan Carson, Associate Professor, teaches and researches in the Creative Industries Faculty at Queensland University of Technology, Brisbane, Australia. She received her PhD from the University of Queensland, Brisbane, and now publishes in the fields of cultural tourism, Australian studies and postgraduate pedagogy. Susan's most recent publication in the tourism sector is 'Literature, tourism and the city: Writing and cultural change' with Lesley Hawkes, Kari Gislason and Kate Cantrell in the *Journal of Tourism and Cultural Change* (2016). She reviews submissions for international journals in the tourism sector as well as for creative industries journals, and is the co-author of a national Australian government Office of Learning and Teaching report into creative practice-led research in Australian universities (2014).

Mark Pennings is a Senior Lecturer in Art History and Theory in Visual Arts in the Creative Industries Faculty of the Queensland University of Technology, Brisbane, Australia. Pennings' research interests include visual arts, cultural tourism, the experience economy, cultural and political theory, social and sporting history and pedagogy in international learning. He teaches postwar and contemporary art, and runs study tours to New York City and Tokyo. Pennings has produced many art reviews, catalogue essays and articles in journals such as *Art Forum, Art Monthly, Art and Australia* and *Eyeline*. He has presented national and international conference papers in the field of cultural tourism, and is interested in the impact of corporate culture on the infrastructures of tourism in a global experience economy. He has studied art and art museums in experiencescapes, and has examined the role of Museum of Old and New Art (Hobart) and the Gallery of Modern Art (Brisbane) in Australian cultural tourism.

New Directions in Tourism Analysis

Series Editor: Dimitri Ioannides
E-TOUR, Mid Sweden University, Sweden

Although tourism is becoming increasingly popular both as a taught subject and an area for empirical investigation, the theoretical underpinnings of many approaches have tended to be eclectic and somewhat underdeveloped. However, recent developments indicate that the field of tourism studies is beginning to develop in a more theoretically informed manner, but this has not yet been matched by current publications.

The aim of this series is to fill this gap with high quality monographs or edited collections that seek to develop tourism analysis at both theoretical and substantive levels using approaches which are broadly derived from allied social science disciplines such as Sociology, Social Anthropology, Human and Social Geography, and Cultural Studies. As tourism studies covers a wide range of activities and sub fields, certain areas such as Hospitality Management and Business, which are already well provided for, would be excluded. The series will therefore fill a gap in the current overall pattern of publication.

Suggested themes to be covered by the series, either singly or in combination, include: consumption; cultural change; development; gender; globalisation; political economy; social theory; and sustainability.

For a full list of titles in this series, please visit www.routledge.com/New-Directions-in-Tourism-Analysis/book-series/ASHSER1207

39. Tourism Destination Evolution
Edited Patrick Brouder, Salvador Anton Clavé, Alison Gill and Dimitri Ioannides

40. Tourism, Travel, and Blogging
A Discursive Analysis of Online Travel Narratives
Deepti Ruth Azariah

41. Metropolitan Commuter Belt Tourism
Edited by Michał Jacenty Sznajder

42. Performing Cultural Tourism
Communities, Tourists and Creative Practices
Edited by Susan Carson and Mark Pennings

Performing Cultural Tourism

Communities, Tourists and
Creative Practices

Edited by
Susan Carson and Mark Pennings

Routledge
Taylor & Francis Group

LONDON AND NEW YORK

First published 2017
by Routledge

2 Park Square, Milton Park, Abingdon, Oxfordshire OX14 4RN

52 Vanderbilt Avenue, New York, NY 10017

Routledge is an imprint of the Taylor & Francis Group, an informa business

First issued in paperback 2019

British Library Cataloguing-in-Publication Data
A catalogue record for this book is available from the British Library

Library of Congress Cataloging-in-Publication Data
A catalog record for this book has been requested

ISBN: 978-1-138-04142-4 (hbk)
ISBN: 978-0-367-36912-5 (pbk)

Typeset in Times New Roman
by Taylor & Francis Books

This book is dedicated to our colleagues, at home and abroad, who make cultural tourism research so rewarding.

Contents

Figures

Tables

Contributors

Associate Professor Susan Carson (Australia) teaches and researches in the Creative Industries Faculty at Queensland University of Technology, Brisbane. She received her PhD from the University of Queensland, Brisbane, and now publishes in the fields of cultural tourism, Australian studies and postgraduate pedagogy. Susan's most recent publication in the tourism sector is 'Literature, tourism and the city: Writing and cultural change' with Lesley Hawkes, Kari Gislason and Kate Cantrell in the *Journal of Tourism and Cultural Change* (2016). She reviews submissions for international journals in the tourism sector as well as for creative industries journals, and is the co-author of a national Australian government Office of Learning and Teaching report into creative practice-led research in Australian universities (2014).

Dr Mark Pennings (Australia) is a Senior Lecturer in Art History and Theory in Visual Arts in the Creative Industries Faculty of the Queensland University of Technology, Brisbane. Dr Pennings's research interests include visual arts, cultural tourism, the experience economy, cultural and political theory, social and sporting history, and pedagogy in international learning. He teaches postwar and contemporary art, and runs study tours to New York City and Tokyo. Pennings has produced many art reviews, catalogue essays and articles in journals such as *Art Forum, Art Monthly, Art and Australia* and *Eyeline*. He has presented national and international conference papers in the field of cultural tourism, and is interested in the impact of corporate culture on the infrastructures of tourism in a global experience economy. He has studied art and art museums in experiencescapes, and has examined the role of Museum of Old and New Art (Hobart) and the Gallery of Modern Art (Brisbane) in Australian cultural tourism.

Associate Professor Sally Butler (Australia) is Associate Professor in Art History in the School of Communication and Arts, the University of Queensland, Australia. Her research focuses on cross-cultural and interdisciplinary approaches to contemporary Indigenous art and culture, contemporary aesthetics, and visual politics. Sally is also a freelance curator and arts writer and has organised cultural workshops and field schools in remote Australian Indigenous communities for the past 15 years. Recent publications include 'Radical dreaming: Cultural diplomacy and aboriginal art' (co-authored with Roland Bleiker) in *International Political Sociology* (2016), the Torres Strait Island volume of *Taba Naba – Australia, Oceania, arts of the sea people* exhibition catalogues for the Oceanographic Museum of Monaco (2016), and a chapter on "Indigeneity" in the forthcoming Routledge publication *Visual global politics*. Recent curated exhibitions include *Brian Robinson: Pacific crosscurrents* (2016), and *Cross pose, body language in Australian Indigenous art* (2015).

Ms Patricia Maria Santiago (Philippines) is an administrator and activist in the area of community, heritage and tourism in the Philippines. She is the Secretariat Head at ICOMOS, Philippines. She has acted as a research fellow at the Korea Culture and Tourism Institute, and was a research fellow of their Cultural Partnership Initiative Program in 2012. Patricia is also a member of the Philippines National Commission for Culture and the Arts, and is a facilitator for Cultural Mapping and Cultural Tourism, and Art and Cultural Education, at the Cultural Center of the Philippines. Patricia presented the paper 'Viajeng Cusinang Matua: A journey through the old kitchens of Pampanga' at the 2014 Third International Congress UNITWIN UNESCO Network, 'Culture, tourism, development' in Barcelona, Spain.

Dr Christine N. Buzinde (USA) is an Associate Professor in the School of Community Resources and Development at the College of Public Service and Community Solutions, Arizona State University, Phoenix, Arizona. Christine Buzinde's research focuses on two areas: community development through tourism and the politics of tourism representations. Her work on representations regards tourism texts as cultural repositories through which inclusion/exclusion, North/South and core/periphery can be understood. She examines texts as sites wherein entanglements of power and oppression as well as depictions of agency and resistance can be unveiled. Dr Buzinde's work on development adopts a grassroots approach and it aims to understand the relationship, or lack thereof, between community well-being and tourism development within marginalized communities. She conducts research in Tanzania, Mexico, India, Canada, and the US. She has published numerous articles in tourism, geographical and cultural studies journals.

Ms Vanessa Vandever (USA) has a BA in Political Science from Stanford University, USA. She is the Program Manager for the Grand Canyon Trust Native America Program where she is responsible for assisting communities with a variety of sustainable economic development projects. Ms Vandever also coordinates the General Management Plan (GMP) project for the Navajo Nation Parks and Recreation Department (NNPRD).

Dr Gyan Nyaupane (USA) is an Associate Professor in the School of Community Resources and Development at the College of Public Service and Community Solutions, Arizona State University, Phoenix, Arizona.

Dr Nyaupane's research focuses on two major areas: communities, public lands and sustainable tourism; and tourist behaviours and attitudes. The overarching theme of his research is to understand the complex relationships humans have with natural and cultural environments, particularly how tourism can transform those relationships. Dr Nyaupane's research aims to advance knowledge in the field of tourism, help managers in decision-making, and more importantly, empower communities that are most vulnerable to global environmental and economic changes. He conducts research in South Asia, Southern Africa, South East Asia and North America. He has published one co-edited book and more than 45 peer-reviewed papers and book chapters.

Professor Hilary du Cros (Hong Kong) is Associate Professor at the Hong Kong University of Education and teaches in the area of Cultural Tourism in the Department of Cultural and Creative Arts. Her key publications include: *Cultural tourism: The partnership between tourism and cultural heritage management* (with Bob McKercher, 2002); *Cultural heritage management in China: Preserving the cities of the Pearl River Delta* (with Yok-shiu F. Lee, 2007); 'World heritage-themed souvenirs for Asian tourists: A case study from Macau, in *Tourism and souvenirs: Global perspectives from the margins* (2013); *The Arts and Events* (with Lee Jolliffe, 2014); and *Cultural Tourism* (with Bob McKercher, 2014).

Professor Tim Middleton (UK) is Vice-Chancellor of Writtle University College, Chelmsford, Essex, UK. Professor Middleton has published respected research on a wide variety of writers, including D.H. Lawrence, Joseph Conrad, Iain Banks, Will Self, Patrick McCabe, Colm Toibin and Joseph O'Connor. He is co-author (with Professor Judy Giles) of *Studying culture: A practical introduction* (2007). His current research project is exploring the role of literary places in contemporary British culture via studies of real and imagined literary locations in cultural heritage tourism.

Dr Yang Zhang (China) is Assistant Professor of Faculty of Hospitality and Tourism Management at Macau University of Science and Technology, Macau, China. Zhang's specialization is cultural tourism and has published articles in *Annals of Tourism Research, Leisure Studies* and *Current Issues in Tourism*.

Dr Philip Feifan Xie (China) is Dean and Professor of Faculty of Hospitality and Tourism Management at Macau University of Science and Technology, Macau, China. His areas of specializations include heritage tourism, event management and the morphology of tourism.

Professor Ulrike Gretzel (USA) is a Visiting Professor at the Annenberg School for Communication and Journalism, University of Southern California. Before joining USC, she was a professor in the Business School at the

University of Queensland, Brisbane. She also held appointments at the University of Wollongong and Texas A&M University. She received her PhD in Communications from the University of Illinois at Urbana-Champaign. Her research focuses on persuasion in human-technology interactions, information search and processing, electronic decision aids, smart technologies, social media users, online and social media marketing, adoption and use of communication technologies, as well as non-adoption and digital detox.

Ms Joanna Hartmann (Australia) is a PhD candidate in the Creative Industries Faculty at Queensland University of Technology, Brisbane. She teaches communication subjects at QUT as a sessional academic. She is currently completing her doctoral thesis 'Arresting resistance: revealing cultures of girlhood, discipline, and defiance on Cockatoo Island', using a cultural studies approach to investigate the island's nineteenth-century institutions: the Biloela Industrial School for Girls and the Biloela Reformatory for Females. This research offers new approaches to examining historic sites and the ways in which marginalised histories are managed at such sites today.

Dr Evangelia Kasimati (Greece) is an economist at the Central Bank of Greece and head of the tourism research unit at the ATINER Institute in Athens. Prior to this appointment, she was a research fellow in tourism economics and applied econometrics at the Centre for Planning and Economic Research, Athens, and was a visiting Research Fellow at the Department of Economics at the University of Bath, UK. Her research and teaching interests lie in the areas of financial economics, tourism and sports economics, and macroeconomics. Dr Kasimati currently teaches a postgraduate course in the Department of Tourism Management at the Hellenic Open University.

Dr Nikolaos G Vagionis (Greece) has a PhD in Economics from the London School of Economics and his primary area of research is in planning and economics. In 1995 Nikolaos began to work with the Centre of Planning and Economic Research, KEPE, Greece, and is now a senior researcher at that institution. He has worked with the Technological Educational Institute of Athens, from 2001, lecturing on tourism economics, tourism policy and research methodology. He has also lectured at the Hellenic Open University and writes and presents papers and seminars on the subjects of regional and sustainable development, tourism, ecology and technology transfer.

Methodologies of touristic exchange
An introduction

Susan Carson

The field of cultural tourism studies is ever expanding as tourists desire an array of travel opportunities, and tourist providers and intermediaries provide experiences that are informative, entertaining and seek to meet community expectations. The term 'experience' is useful in tourism today but has almost become a cliché as tourist providers market the language of experience in their bid to attract tourist capital. At the same time, this term aptly describes the tourist search for an increasingly diverse and profound engagement with sites and events, while gaining access to expanded global and local transport and tourism networks. As scholars have noted for some time, many tourism sectors now promote *co-production*, that is an experience in which the visitor takes an active role in producing artifacts or directly engaging with events, as a means by which to access and enhance experiential knowledge. It is clear that today's tourists want to 'make' and 'do' as well as 'watch'.

Such engagement constitutes the many relationships involved in a cultural tourism experience: provider to consumer and vice versa; consumer to consumer. There are also the communities that support and encourage various cultural offerings. The goal of this book is to trace some of these emerging relationships in physical and virtual contexts, arguing that the agency demanded by tourists requires a greater sense of *cooperation* between various stakeholders in tourism locations. We use the term 'cooperation' for proposing new methodologies of cultural tourism because 'co-production' is quite a challenging term in that it presumes a balance of interests, and, as some of the chapters in this book indicate, that balance that does not always exist. A focus on cooperation recognizes the critical role that negotiation plays between consumer and producer, and acknowledges that the nature of performance in tourist activity is normally a temporary, and often transitory, agreement between provider and user.

Here we emphasize as well the relationship of *self-to-self*, because many travellers are seeking greater insights into self-knowledge by way of virtual, social media or physical activities. In this context, we draw attention to the notion of *performativities*, as discussed by Kevin Hannam (2006) and suggest how those performative enactments work to extend or re-draw tourism relationships in diverse environments. This framework of linking *cooperation* and *performativities* connects a desire for personal creativity, that is to actively 'do'; to participate in one's tourist experience, and a need to 'belong' to a host or peer group. In the process, we see new formations of tourist engagement that play with traditional 'mass', 'cultural', 'niche', or 'heritage' labels. For example, it is much more common today for group travellers to use online environments to source 'pre-trip' information and plan their travels with peers before leaving home. At the same time research indicates that tourists expect an element of surprise from travel experience. Other tourists such as solo-adventurers use both virtual and physical aids to go 'off the track' and entirely design their own itineraries. One of the interesting aspects of the changing tempo of cultural tourism is that 'cultural tourists', who may include artists or performers travelling for work or leisure, now recognize that at times they are also 'mass' tourists as they selectively engage in tours and travel that is aimed at large groups to major destinations, as Bill Aitchison's (2016) research into anti-tours has revealed.

In this, environment tourism providers, including community groups, are expected to manage diverse expectations and complement conventional tours with tailored events and specialized knowledge while seeking to protect familiar and long-cherished customs. Many Indigenous communities are searching for a way to present their locations and their cultural heritage to interested visitors without incurring environmental or cultural damage. They are also attempting to educate visitors about their culture, as Sally Butler identifies when proposing the framework of 'temporary belonging' in relation to Australian Indigenous tourism in her chapter. This desire for belonging is expressed in other domains scrutinized in this book. For instance Hilary du Cros's study of young Asian tourists visiting Hong Kong records that one interviewee wanted to be "a temporary resident" while there in Hong Kong, which suggests that what was once considered the 'backstage' of the tourism venture is now at the forefront of desirable experience for some visitors and providers. The concept of backstage here refers to the discourse around staging that has been studied by Erving Goffman, Dean MacCannell and others, noting in particular MacCannell's 2008 observation that 'stages' operate as a series of infinite regressions, and that these processes complicate notions of authenticity. As MacCannell cogently explained: "having a famous anthropologist as your tour guide; having him explain your experience to you in terms that go beyond and beneath the touristic representation is staged authenticity *par excellence*" (MacCannell, 2008, p. 337). The search for greater engagement complements the tourist's desire for participating in an authentic experience that is often individuated but can also be collectively expressed in virtual or physical domains. Here we begin to see a democratic sharing of communal cultural experience as well as a willingness to respect the privilege of admission to 'backstage' access sometimes provided by host communities.

This type of interaction flags new sites of exchange in which communities, creative producers, cultural representatives and visitors seek cooperative arrangements. We explore methodologies that prioritize how community interests can intersect with the desires of tourists who may want to engage more fully with the nuanced understanding of the backstage from the point of view, in part, of the *brokers i*n this ecology: from Indigenous representatives in communities to the social media forums that host peer-to-peer interactions as Hilary du Cros and Ulrike Gretzel reveal in their chapters. In examining the notion of cooperative spheres, the term *exchange* becomes crucial as a way of understanding a culture-led perspective of cultural tourism. This process takes place between people (on an individual level, in relation to communication) and concomitantly between cultures (watching cultural performances, listening to stories, eating local food, education); between people and sites/environments (getting there, airplane, car, bus, walking, the pilgrimage; seeing buildings of significance) and economic exchange (why governments support large cultural projects, and the way small towns and Indigenous communities prepare to attract tourists). Many of the chapters in this book consider the sites of exchange embedded in cultural tourism and the new methodologies associated with such arrangements that bring culture into focus in new ways.

In this shifting ground of cultural tourism there may well be transitions from co-production models that have been dominant in recent discourses on such topics, towards informed cooperative agreements, a process that is examined by Patricia Santiago in her chapter. In this context, the term 'community' can relate to a specific geography, social, or cultural practice, or a virtual landscape, as all of these sites enable the sharing of experiences between communities of producers and consumers in tourist cultures. There is the opportunity to mix the staged offerings for tourists with the tourist's desire for a performative experience and to think about the 'doing' of tourism as fluid and negotiable. The question of the interaction between a curated delivery of tourism experience and the potential to open up space for self-guided or even subversive activities (here we think of the anti-capitalist tour of London's banking district organized by Bill Aitchison) complicates and enlivens the tourism sector (Aitchison, 2016).

Our term 'performing cultural tourism' therefore acknowledges cultural studies' understandings of performativity that seem to best describe the current transition in tourist experience, and extends these notions to newly sought-after spaces where visitors and communities participate in cultural exchanges, which can function as cooperative spheres of interaction. Tourists are currently expecting to participate in and seemingly *co-create* their experience while accepting the transitory nature of this negotiation, and the 'staged authenticity' that often accompanies it, as MacCannell has identified. In this situation, new methodologies need to be developed to understand and explain the dynamics of community-to-tourist interactions. In this context, it is also timely to keep in mind the postcolonial legacies that are present when investigating the tensions between Eurocentric and other tourism traditions, and to recognize that the communal links between culture, landscape and Indigenous knowledge systems are critical in the types of interface that exist between local people and tourist cultures. These will surely have greater influence in future tourism configurations.

Given the growing importance of cultural tourism to many countries' economies, and the potential of cultural erasure, as outlined by Tim Winter, it seems opportune to investigate the ways in which distinct cultures are working to accommodate (or not) touristic expectations. It is imperative to identify a range of methodologies that are being developed or implemented to accommodate the increasingly complex crossover between host cultures and touristic product. The methodologies presented in this book are diverse. The connective tissue of these chapters is cooperation, creativity and *negotiation*: between tourist and provider, between different levels of government instrumentalities and between tourism organizations and residents.

The heritage sector is one area that illustrates the increasing attention to the processes of negotiation in tourism. Winter's analysis of UNESCO heritage applications (2016) concludes that forms of heritage tourism can become expressions of global power in which heritage has "emerged as an important form of spatial and social governance" (2016, p. 9). Winter also proposes that in this new orientation the strategic allocation of capital "raises important questions concerning new forms of cultural erasure and coloniality and the political violence they deliver" (2016, p. 10). These observations offer an informative context to the local and regional battles around heritage announced in the chapters by Santiago and Christine Buzinde, Vanessa Vandever and Gyan Nyaupane. As Santiago and Buzinde *et al.* indicate, some communities are attempting to protect and assert their historical cultural identity and practices while negotiating government legislation, commercial opportunities and tourist demands. The role of government is queried in a study by Evangelia Kasimati and Nikolaos Vagionis who examine the legacy of the 2004 Olympic Games in Greece. Their work draws attention to the local problems that ensue from large-scale international events designed as a flagship for a mix of sporting and heritage cultures.

This book concentrates on the way in which communities and visitors *negotiate* new forms of cultural tourism, offering methodologies that explain engagement in local and regional contexts. In this framework digital innovation is acknowledged as one of several approaches that are transforming the field of cultural tourism. No distribution channel has made a more significant impact on contemporary experience than the digital realm. Hilary du Cros's chapter is a significant addition to the assessment of the impact of virtual technologies in tourism given her aim to understand the 'whys' of such attitudes and the perceptions that have been revealed in her research. According to Ana M. Munar and Can-Seng Ooi (2012), there is a relatively small number of studies that examine virtual worlds and their effect on heritage in the tourism sector, therefore, the chapters by Ulrike Gretzel and du Cros add much needed scholarship by drawing on qualitative research to enhance our knowledge of this emerging field of study. Indeed, Gretzel extends this research in her consideration of the aesthetic and artistic qualities of selfies on Instagram. The acts of visual curation of the self for platforms such as Instagram, as Gretzel reveals, point to the quest for the extraordinary fuelled by social media. Gretzel analyses the content of selfies to identify how these images are constructed to make them 'share-worthy'.

Given the impact of the digital presence in tourism, Tim Middleton's finding that digital production, in this case for a literary trail, can limit rather than expand the type of experience sought is a valuable insight. In modelling an analytical autoethnographic approach Middleton reappraises and challenges prior assumptions about the self as researcher and consumer. Certainly, there is an "enhanced personal creativity" in the digital coverage of tourist adventures, but Middleton's research also considers the challenges in planning for an immersive literary trail that is delivered via a mobile phone app.

We find that each chapter, albeit in different ways, refers to the increasing focus on tourism as a *learning* experience (for Buzinde *et al.* a 'co-learning' experience) for consumers and producers. Many tourism providers supply accommodation, entertainment and tours, but some also wish to dispense cultural knowledge. This educative aspect is a feature of the chapters by du Cros, and Yang Zhang and Philip Xie. Zhang's and Xie's research describes tourist motivation that is attuned to both learning and entertainment. Du Cros documents the intense exchange of knowledge that is involved in the preparation for travel to a destination. Certainly, there is an "enhanced personal creativity" in the digital coverage of tourist adventures, as Ana M. Munar and Can-Seng Ooi proposed (2012, p. 257).

***

Part I of this book focuses on the shared needs of Indigenous communities and cultural tourists. In this context, Sally Butler's participatory research (Chapter 1) with Indigenous Australians is an important addition to the discourse of international cultural tourism. Butler adapts the concept of 'temporary belonging' (that relates to tourists' emotional attachment to place) to the growth of Indigenous community art centres in Australia, and proposes that the idea of temporary belonging provides an alternative model to authenticity debates in cultural tourism. In this chapter Anke Tonnaer's 2010 study of the concept of shared culture in Australian Indigenous tourism is examined and connections made with the performative-based methodologies that are a focus of this collection. A central feature of Butler's work is her inclusion of both virtual and physical sites: she shows how a digital site such as *Arnhemweavers* can support community-based immersive tourism, and also explains the processes involved in supporting student groups in a unique learning experience at the remote location of *Mäpuru* in the Northern Territory, Australia.

Patricia Santiago's contribution (Chapter 2) is important to this collection because it presents a study of an initiative in Sagada, Philippines, from the 'ground-up' in which communities argue for the development of a sustainable practice in cultural tourism that values spiritual and religious beliefs and practices. This tension between the secular and the sacred, as is evidenced in the negotiation between development and conservation, takes place in an environment framed by the opportunism of previous local and regional authorities. Santiago follows the efforts of some local leaders to develop efficacious systems of decision-making and communal and participatory processes, as well as the proposal to revive a tripartite system of decision-making in the face of local political tensions. In this instance, the way in which cultural tourism can be harnessed in a spirit of cooperation for the common good is an important factor for the community.

Similarly Christine Buzinde's, Vanessa Vandever's and Gyan Nyaupane's research (Chapter 3) focuses on socio-political conditions in the Navajo Nation reservation in the United States. These authors track local efforts to create multi-agency coalitions to devise a development plan that is inclusive of all residents of the Navajo Nation and is respectful of Indigenous culture. Using community-based participatory research (CBPR) the authors frame the Nation's desire for tourism products to alleviate the area's long-term underdevelopment and abject poverty, while at the same time indicating that communities are wary of being unfairly exploited by insensitive outside tourism investors. At the heart of the work by Buzinde, Vandever and Nyaupane, and by Santiago is a search for an equitable sharing of power in the context of wider economic pressures and opposition at times from within Indigenous community sectors.

In Part II, Hilary du Cros (Chapter 4) investigates the types of decision-making made by a group of Asian youth who travelled to Hong Kong. These decisions are informed by a particular sociability and by educational aspirations as articulated in blog sites, and also refer to the potentially exploitative nature of digital surveillance when information is analysed by those who 'lurk' on social media sites, including commercial providers of tourism and academics studying tourism. Like Middleton, du Cros notes the importance of self-reflexivity on the part of the researcher. This chapter discusses issues of narcissism, trust and self-censorship in the use of online sites proposing that an emerging culture of narcissism in some social media experiences can play a role in virtual peer support and travel decision-making. The findings indicate the importance of self-awareness and self-improvement in relation to travel, and how tourists can become more aware of travel impacts by sharing information and notions about the most valuable kinds of travel experience.

The quest for understanding via ethnographic principles of research immersion is taken up by Tim Middleton in Chapter 5. Here the author compares two self-guided literary tourist journeys: the first following a 'classic' autoethnographic account (Edward Thomas's literary tour of South West England); and the second focusing on the challenges of developing an app to follow in the footsteps of Scottish writer Iain Banks. Middleton finds a gap between a tourist's imaginative appreciation of a creative work and the identification of points of action in a creative work via an app. As an autoethnographer, the author compares the benefits of using long-established literary narrative techniques to deliver information about a novel's location with new technologies available for the enhancement of literary trails. In this process the author confronts his own position as a member of a research community and all that this entails for the performative engagement of cultural tourism. As Middleton argues, the challenge for heritage custodians and tourism agencies is to adequately translate personal experience into digital platforms that can be confidently used by individual and group tourists.

Yang Zhang and Philip Xie in Chapter 6 'Creating cultural tourism development: A tourist perspective' study the potential of creative tourism in Macau. This chapter provides new data on the ways local communities both produce and benefit from creative tourism. The authors use Greg Richards's definition of creative tourism, stating that its common components are "participative, authentic experiences that allow tourists to develop their creative potential and skills through contact with local people and their culture" (Richards, 2011, p. 1237), which makes the point that the creative tourist is essentially involved in a learning process. In their study of tourists to the Albergue Art Space in Macau the authors are, like du Cros, interested in understanding tourist perceptions and the concepts of creative tourism that are taken to a location. Zhang's and Xie's study supports this book's general thesis that tourists want to actively combine a range of diverse activities when visiting a location. In this enterprise tourists require greater access to culture and history and are seeking educative outcomes. As the authors state, the creative tourist is, in many respects, essentially involved in "a learning process".

Social media change and the search for the extraordinary is a focus in Chapter 7, in which Ulrike Gretzel explores selfies taken while travelling. Given that one of the goals of this book is to propose new methodologies for cultural tourism research, Gretzel's argument for a deepening of netnography (as a subset of ethnography) to allow for further immersion in the subject areas is important. Gretzel acknowledges the process of 'lurking' on social media to obtain public data captured via screenshots and argues that such photographs communicate a sense of the subject's travel identity. She also recognizes the significance of the 'selfie' as a social phenomenon that can tell us much, not only about tourist engagement with a visited site, but also about broader conceptions of selfhood in the contemporary era.

Part III presents three case studies that discuss new frameworks for the mixing of institutional cultural heritage and contemporary cultural production. In Chapter 8, Susan Carson and Joanna Hartmann consider re-framing issues around cultural tourism methodologies by thinking through a 'creative turn' in cultural tourism that involves managers, tourists, hosts and resident communities that re-work or fictionalize aspects of the past for contemporary visitor consumption. The authors are interested in the shifting power balance between stakeholders in today's tourism enterprises. With a focus on *overlapping*, and often *layered*, activities at Cockatoo Island (Sydney, New South Wales) and the Port Arthur Historic Sites (Tasmania), the chapter analyses management and visitor responses to cultural tourism programs as a way of revealing the nuances of visitor demands (including resident communities), and considers the challenges faced in managing historic locations that are also premier tourist attractions.

In their study of the 2004 Olympics, Evangelia Kasimati and Nikolaos Vagionis (Chapter 9) provide an account of the infrastructure gains in Greece that resulted from the Games, but also offer a critique of the role of the HOP (Hellenic Olympic Properties) for failing to make the most of the infrastructure that was built for the 2004 Games. Like many Olympic cities, Athens suffered from a top-down development approach that provided a much-needed transport system but failed to deliver sustainable sites for recreation, commerce and culture. In this context, the authors argue that there has been little extended cultural benefit for Greek society, and their assessment indicates the positive and negative effects of a 'top-down' management model for tourism.

Mark Pennings in Chapter 10 provides an alternative approach to cultural tourism development in his examination of a 'ground-up' model of museum development in his study of David Walsh's Museum of Old and New Art (MONA) in Tasmania, Australia. This locally inspired institution is now globally renowned. Pennings situates his study in the global context of art-museum led experiencescapes, such as Abu Dhabi's Saadiyat Island and West Kowloon's M+ that integrate art museums into national agendas for capturing a share of the global tourist market. Whereas global projects are often engineered via top-down governmental processes MONA is an eccentric addition to this process as it was inspired by the vision and funding of an individual, David Walsh. In this approach the high art mantel gives way in the face of the democratization of the museum experience. MONA appears to respect the diverse and individuated needs of its audience, and allows more freedom and agency in the way people want to perform their experiences. However, despite the inclusion of community and a privileging of personal 'performativity' Walsh continues to search for novel ideas that will mix interdisciplinary and international content in his museum structure. For example, MONA's latest exhibition, 'On the origin of art' described as "*wunderkammer*-esque experiences" (Do Campo, 2016, p. 1) will, according to Walsh, with characteristic tongue-in-cheek overstatement, "out-epic Ben-Hur and have more pathos than the crucifixion" (Crawley, 2016).

References

Aitchison, W. (2016) The emancipated tourist. In: Inheriting the city: Advancing understandings of urban heritage conference. Taipei, Taiwan. Ironbridge International Institute for Cultural Heritage, University of Birmingham. 2 April.

Crawley, J. (2016). On the Origin of Art exhibition is bigger than Ben-Hur, says MONA owner David Walsh. *Herald Sun*, [online]. Available at: www.news.com.au/national/tasmania/on-the-origin-of-art-exhibition-is-bigger-than-benhur-says-mona-owner-david-walsh/news-story/9dcaab0982dae2044c697dcb8ccb822f [Accessed 10 Nov 2016].

Do Campo, F. (2016). On the origin of art. *Art Almanac*, [online]. 31 October. Available at: www.art-almanac.com.au/on-the-origin-of-art/ [Accessed 10 Nov 2016].

Hannam, K. (2006). Tourism and development III: Performances, performativities and mobilities. *Progress in Development Studies*, 6(3), pp. 243–249. DOI: doi:10.1191/1464993406ps141pr.

MacCannell, D. (2008). Why it never really was about authenticity. *Society*, 45, pp. 334. DOI: doi:10.1007/s12115-008-9110-8.

Munar, A.M. and Ooi, C.-S. (2012). The truth of the crowds: Social media and the heritage experience. In: Smith, L. and Watson, S., eds. *The cultural moment in tourism*. London: Routledge, pp. 255–273.

Richards, G. (2011). Creativity and tourism: The state of the art. *Annals of Tourism Research*, 38(4), pp. 1225–1253.

Winters, T. (2016). Heritage diplomacy along the One Belt One Road. *The Newsletter*, 74, pp. 8–10.

Part I

Cooperation, exchange negotiation

The shared needs of Indigenous communities and cultural tourists

1 'Temporary belonging'

Indigenous cultural tourism and community art centres

Sally Butler

Introduction

Indigenous art centres located in remote communities in Australia are increasingly engaging in cultural tourism initiatives to diversify their income streams and advance the community's economic and cultural sustainability (Jones, Booth and Acker, 2016; Australian Government, 2016). This art centre momentum goes against the grain of a perceived lack of interest in Indigenous cultural tourism more generally. Early research into Indigenous cultural tourism in Australia found that attractions based on Indigenous culture ranked low relative to other activities (Ryan and Huyton, 2002). Surveys reflected that Indigenous cultural tourism appealed to a minority socio-demographic band of tourists. Furthermore, initiatives that promote Australian Indigenous culture as a tourism product "question their effectiveness in generating desired returns to Aboriginal communities" (Ryan and Huyton, p. 631). The data suggests a key problem pertains to tourist perceptions that they "see little of what is a developing Aboriginal cultural revival" (Ryan and Huyton, p. 631). 'Showcase' cultural tourism is clearly not the future, but more participatory models of community-embedded cultural tourism appear to have the potential to counter this problem.

A great deal of current scholarship surrounds debates regarding the benefits of Indigenous communities engaging in the tourism enterprise (Bunten, 2008; Butler and Hinch, 2007; Jones, Booth and Acker, 2016; Ryan and Aicken, 2005; Zeppel, 2001). Even more scholarship engages with questions over what constitutes an *authentic* tourist experience (Gmeich, 2004; MacLeod, 2006; Skinner and Theodossopoulos, 2011). Cultural tourism sits firmly at the intersection of these debates because it involves relationships between people and places; different perspectives of history and traditions; and appreciating the complexities of different lifestyles (Smith and Robinson, 2006). This chapter does not specifically address the tortured territory of defining an authentic tourism experience, nor does it attempt to weigh up the benefits and disadvantages of immersive cultural tourism for Indigenous communities. Instead it speculates on the idea of a tourism experience of 'temporary belonging' to provide some insight into the encounter between communities and visitors in the context of participatory indigenous cultural tourism. It takes an 'in-between' approach to a cross-cultural sense of community belonging in the context of tourism.

I have adapted this concept of 'temporary belonging' regarding communities from ongoing tourism discourse pertaining to tourists' emotional attachment to place (Kirshenblatt-Gimblett, 1998; Coleman and Crang, 2002b; Chambers, 2010). Indigenous communities represent a special case study of place in the tourism context because their very being is intrinsically related to place. Indigenous communities are people of a specific locality – they are the people of places (Butler and Hinch, 2007). The very word 'Indigenous' means belonging to a place. So there is an apparent corollary between tourists' emotional attachment to place and their emotional attachment to Indigenous communities. I want to explore this somewhat elusive emotional link through a tourism experience of what I call 'temporary belonging'.

The temporary aspect of this concept concerns the fact that people act differently in different contexts. They perform certain roles depending on the kind of event or activity they are participating in. We act respectfully at funerals, attentively at lectures, and are socially responsive at parties. The nature of the event in no small way determines how we act. This is crucial to tourism studies, of course, where the nature of the tourism event determines the tourism experience (Coleman and Crang, 2002b). The place of the tourism event is not a static element but a performer in its own right. Coleman and Crang's edited volume *Tourism: Between place and performance* is particularly relevant here in terms of how it approaches concepts of place in tourism as an interstitial dualistic 'performance' of tourism. Places and visitors perform tourism in this context, and this text particularly engages with ideas that defeat the oft-lamented dichotomy of place 'as either authentically experienced by locals or simulated and staged for visiting consumers' (Coleman and Crang, 2002a, p. 4). People and place are conflated within the terms 'local' and 'visitor', and thus place becomes animated through the activities that occur between the people of its spaces. The book attempts to hover around this local belonging and the tourism experience, and it offers a reference point, or mindset, for the situation of temporary belonging.

The idea of performance helps observers appreciate that tourism is a particular context of the social condition where, as previously mentioned, people 'act' in a certain way. This does not mean that they are necessarily behaving in a false or inauthentic manner, so much as responding to the conditions offered by place-based tourism encounters. I would argue that the temporary nature of our fundamental understanding of what cultural tourism is – a temporary inhabitation, or a temporary time-travel – is a significant, if subliminal, psychological aspect of tourists' encounters with host communities. Arguably the most successful cultural tourism experiences involve a sense that one belongs to a host community, no matter how temporary. 'Between' is a key term for *Tourism: Between place and performance* because the volume advances a dualistic model where 'cultures and belonging work in terms of a/not-a, inside and outside categories' (Coleman and Crang, 2002a, p. 5). This refusal to categorize 'performers' as either inside or outside helps in understanding a concept of performed, or temporary, belonging. In this chapter I am simply reconfiguring this performed oscillation between being inside and outside place to that of indigenous communities, and arguing that it engenders a tourism experience of 'temporary belonging'.

Temporary belonging is perhaps intrinsic to the concept of tourism itself, but it assumes greater significance in an age of global translocation (Smith and Robinson, 2006; Burns and Novelli, 2006; Zakin, 2015; Burns and Novelli, 2008). Diaspora, displacement, and dislocation in contemporary global lifestyles tend to diminish a sense of belonging to a community, or of being involved in a community. Even if we ourselves remain within one community today, these communities tend to change and move around us. We do not experience community belonging in similar ways to the more static global environment of the past. Within this mindset the participatory cultural tourism experience potentially offers a sense of community belonging that may be lacking at home. This (latent) desire to belong flowers within the temporary inside/outside conditions of the participatory cultural tourism experience.

Different kinds of tourism undoubtedly impact the condition of temporary belonging. It is important to emphasize that the precise nature of the relationship between host communities and visitors is crucial in determining the tourism experience. In this chapter I focus specifically on the growing trend of Indigenous community art centres that offer participatory cultural tourism initiatives. This aspect of the tourism industry is distinct to Indigenous cultural tourism that operates guided cultural tours of traditional homelands or culturally significant locations (Bunten, 2004; Aboriginal South Australia, 2016; Urban Indigenous, 2016). Whilst the latter are obviously participatory in terms of involving tourists in walks and various cultural activities, they are rarely embedded in communities for a period of time beyond one to three days. The point of my argument is not to ascribe value to different degrees of the immersive experience. Rather I aim to use the example of participatory art and cultural tourism to examine how this effect of 'temporary belonging' helps in new thinking about the future of cultural tourism. The tourism concept of temporary belonging also provides alternative models to the previously mentioned 'authenticity' debates surrounding cultural tourism.

The art centres discussed in this chapter offer more extended participatory cultural experiences than other attempts to temporarily involve visitors in community life. Before explaining the concept of Australian Indigenous art centres and how they initiate participatory cultural tourism, we should undertake a more detailed consideration of what temporary belonging might mean in spaces shared by visitors and Australian Indigenous communities.

Temporary belonging in Indigenous cultural tourism

The condition of temporary belonging obviously refers to the tourist perspective as opposed to that of the host communities, however the concept of place, and belonging to a place as a stage for the performance of the tourism encounter, intrinsically involves both perspectives. The ways in which these cross-cultural perspectives of place interact, in Australia and elsewhere, is very complex and difficult to articulate (McKenna, 2002). Coleman and Crang argue that within relationships between hosts and visitors:

> These multiple registers and framings may suggest we need to think not simply of semiosis but also the poetics of how these are strung together in the practices of visitors and performers – where neither side monopolises the right to define legitimate performances (Coleman and Crang, 2002a, p.15).

Coleman and Crang's appeal to a poetics of place in the tourism encounter reminds us that we are engaging with emotional, psychological, and thus elusive concepts that often resist empirical understanding. We are instead dealing with human sensibilities and sensitivities involving imagination, inspiration, motivation, reorientation, renewal, and pleasure. The authors argue that because the tourism experience place is as much about the local people as it is about the natural environment, it is perhaps best thought of through a poetics rather than rational approach. Rational approaches to emotional attachments often seem to dehydrate life's luscious textures, so to speak.

Rational understanding is also challenged by temporary belonging's obvious paradox: belonging suggests a permanence that is in sharp contrast to the temporary. Belonging itself is also an over-determined concept because it inevitably involves political issues and debates related to sovereignty, citizenship, nationalism and identity (Read, 2000). This is particularly the case with regards to Indigenous populations around the world who have been disenfranchised and disadvantaged by the political, social, and historical circumstances of colonization (Read, 2000). But belonging is also a universal human condition deriving from a sense of connection between various groups of human beings, and between people and place. Belonging is such a complex and multi-dimensional concept that it potentially overwhelms any effort to contextualize it. This is felt keenly in Peter Read's book titled *Belonging – Australians, place and aboriginal ownership*. The book's concluding statement in the Introduction addresses the impossibility of defining different Australians' sense of belonging: "In truth, I have no idea how this book will end. I confess to being a little apprehensive" (Read, 2000, p. 5). Read resorts repeatedly to cultural expression – a poetics of belonging so to speak – to work through concepts of belonging: art, poetry, film, and literature. He observes that Aboriginal art has profoundly changed the way that many Australians understand their sense of belonging:

> Bernard Smith observed that, a hundred years ago, 'To paint Australia you had to be Australian … Unless you were born with "Australian" eyes you could not hope to "see" the Australian landscape'. In the last

quarter-century many of us have substituted 'Aboriginal' for (Anglo-Celtic) Australian (Read, 2000, p. 4).

This mindset of course returns us to the authentic/ inauthentic dichotomy articulated in *Tourism: Between place and performance*, but it also demonstrates the pivotal role played by Aboriginal art as expressing a significant consciousness of belonging, and how art and other forms of cultural expression can prime visitors to a mindset of belonging, or to participate in a mindset of temporary belonging.

Following Coleman and Crang's appeal for a poetics of place in the tourism experience we might consider the poetics of temporary belonging in the tourism experience as expressed through cultural expression, rather than other types of theoretical discourse. We are looking for a psychological or emotional in-between-ness here that registers a global sense of alienation and an Indigenous community sense of belonging. Instead of ontological theory as such, let us consider two poems as a method of taking the measure of the in-between of temporary belonging. We begin with the characterization of the visitor as part of iconic alienated modernity (now globalism) in T.S. Eliot's 'The Hollow Men' (2016, 1925). 'The Hollow Men' is a poem that is universally recognized as an iconic expression of alienated modernity. Its imagery construes post-Industrial life in terms of an isolated human experience that is rendered lifeless through disconnection from the land and each other. The "dead land", "cactus land", dwindle under the "twinkle of a fading star" (stanza 111). Humanity walks alone and "Forms prayers to broken stone" (stanza 111). Globalization's hyper-modern diasporic mobility further reduces the sense of belonging and is arguably the psychology that makes tourists flee towards temporary belonging. The so-called authentic tourism experience is perhaps nothing more than a sense of connectedness, even if the connection is inherently on borrowed time. Eliot's is an extreme condemnation of post-Industrial life, but the sense of *not* belonging continues to resonate within advancing global mobilities.

Against the grain of this place of not belonging, we have a growing volume of indigenous poetry that grounds itself not only in belonging, but with an ontological identification with place. Twenty-first century indigenous poetry, in particular, attends to its global contexts by attempting to articulate how this belonging to place can be partially (and temporarily) shared with those who care to listen and learn. The Australian Aboriginal poet, Nola Gregory, creates the tenor of this shared belonging in a recent poem created for the 2016 National Aboriginal and Islander Day of Observance (called NAIDOC). In this poem we can sense the tenor of 'temporary belonging' that is potentially afforded to participatory cultural tourism initiatives:

'Songlines'

Come with us on a journey
Through land and sea and time
Follow down our dreaming tracks
Listen carefully, look for signs.

You will feel them in your spirit
As they weave into your soul
Songlines, our Ancestral story
Are alive and strong and bold.

They created for us the rivers
The trees and all their girth
Spreading out our storylines
As they walked upon the earth.

They are for us a legacy
Our connection to our land
They are seen through our existence
As we walk upon ochre and sand.

So listen very carefully now
As you walk upon our land
Let it seep into your spirit
As we take you by the hand.

We'll lead you to our dreaming
And sing you songs of old
As through dance and art recorded
Our Ancestral story is told.

For 60,000 years it's been
Our heart, our spirit, our song
Something for us to be proud of
It's our existence, its where we belong.

We follow in the footsteps
Of our Ancestral beings
We follow along our Songlines
And our journey to our Dreaming
　　Gregory, 2016, www.creativespirits.info/
　　　　aboriginalculture/arts/songlines.

'Songlines' was written by Ms Nola Gregory a Yamaji woman who lives in Geraldton, Western Australia, with her partner Grant Briggs and daughter Rashaan Briggs.

Shared cultural encounters as in the subject of this poem are the very basis of cultural tourism, and are often interpreted through an ontological perspective where a concept of 'being' determines the encounter culture. But as I discuss previously, this shared being is extremely difficult to understand. Scherrer and Doohan (2013, pp. 158–70) consider attempts to understand this kind of cultural exchange in the context of tourism in an article titled ' "It's not about believing": Exploring the transformative potential of cultural acknowledgement in an indigenous tourism context'. The authors arrive at a similar mindset to the in-between inside and outside of the *Tourism: Between place and performance* text, and argue for:

> the possibility of tourism operating in a mutually satisfactory hybrid space in which acknowledgement, tolerance and respect discharges the need for understanding different ontologies that operate within that space but provides the potential for learning (Scherrer and Doohan, 2013, p. 158).

Anke Tonnaer's 2010 study of the concept of shared culture in Australian Indigenous tourism modeled analysis along similar performative-based methodologies to those used in this text, and claimed that 'the tourist interaction gives rise to an intercultural space that is manifested through certain performative conventions that shape the meeting between tourists and Aborigines' (Tonnaer, 2010, p. 21). This study further concludes that the value is not about shared meaning so much as a shared performance or experience, "the actual enactment in which self and other become and be defined through their mutual entanglement" (Tonnaer, 2010, p. 21). I contend that this emphasis on shared performance and becoming or being with a (temporary) specific context of sharing, is precisely what is achieved as 'temporary belonging' in the participatory cultural tourism in indigenous communities. But enough of theorizing what 'temporary belonging' might mean – let us now turn to how it happens in the Indigenous cultural tourism industry.

Remote art centres and Indigenous cultural tourism in Australia

Despite the diversity of Indigenous cultural tourism there are relatively few initiatives that offer a community-based immersive tourism experience that works strategically against the showcase 'tourism product' mentioned previously. Participatory Indigenous cultural tourism is still a fledgling industry, but my own experience of engaging with existing and emerging initiatives over the past 15 years indicates that there are already sound models for further development of Indigenous tourism for both communities and visitor experiences. During this period I have helped organize small groups of university students, art enthusiasts, and international visitors, to participate in art and cultural tourism initiatives embedded in remote Australian Indigenous communities. The nature and degree of participation varies, but the key factor for determining a positive experience for both hosts and visitors is directly related to how much the community art and cultural centre, and through it the community members, control the tourism encounter.

As an art historian I am particularly interested in how participatory art and culture workshops effectively operate as cultural tourism, but art is by no means a discrete cultural activity for Australian Indigenous people. Art is inscribed within an all-encompassing epistemological framework that Nola Gregory describes in her poem through the concept of Songlines. Songlines are an Aboriginal cultural metaphor for the connectedness of all things, and the relationships between people and place (Rose, 1999). To participate in art making in an Aboriginal community, one must participate, and come to know, the breadth of cultural activity. This includes participating in traditional forms of harvesting art materials; hunting and food gathering; and performing song, dance, and storytelling. Participants are given guided tours of community homelands that often involve heritage-listed areas of pristine natural environment, rock art sites, spiritually significant landmarks, flora, and fauna.

The nature of the participatory tourism activities is contingent to the specific location of each community, and whether it has the means for organizing the implementation and delivery of these activities. Indigenous communities in Australia do not have the funds to run tourist information centres, but growing numbers do have community art centres that act as a kind of community hub (About Art Centres, 2016; Australian Government, 2016). In addition to engaging with the established success of Australia's Indigenous art market, these art centres support artists and art production by providing studio spaces, materials, and advice on art market requirements. The centres also manage the sale of the art and are thus involved in cultural awareness campaigns that help outsiders understand the cultural life that drives the art. Many of the centres maintain their own art galleries and cultural museums (or what Aboriginal people call 'keeping places') where both historical and contemporary cultural items are on display for community members as well as visitors.

Modern Aboriginal art is an intrinsic part of a cultural revival, whether the art is made from pre-contact materials such as ochre, wood, and bark, or from introduced materials like acrylic paint on canvas. The medium is not the message in this instance, so much as the desire to keep the Dreaming (stories that pass on important knowledge, cultural values and belief systems) alive after an era of assimilation attempted to extinguish it. The art movement of modern Aboriginal art, as such, commenced in the Central Australian desert in the early 1970s when the government policy of assimilation was overturned for a new policy of self-determination (Johnson, 2010). Thereafter art become a method for demonstrating rights to particular areas of land, differentiated kinship identities, and for passing on knowledge to younger generations of the Aboriginal population. Art centres actually predated the 1970s art movement as such with Ernabella (in South Australia) being among the first to initiate an art centre as early as 1948. These centres have blossomed to the extent that in 2004 the Australian government documented 94 Aboriginal art and craft centres in Australia, across urban regional and remote areas. Today the figure is estimated to be double that amount with most being owned by the Aboriginal community or Aboriginal Land Council (Australian Government, 2016). Art centres often play a pivotal role in small remote communities because they provide one of the few opportunities for employment, cultural regeneration and education, and also simply function as meeting places for communities.

Community art centres by definition are owned by Aboriginal communities, and are largely not-for-profit organizations whose mandate is to promote community employment, cultural sustainability, and a place for engaging with visitors interested in learning more about the local cultures. They are thus the prime site for implementing and controlling cultural tourism for the community. Over the past decade almost all of the art centres I have visited have expressed an explicit desire to diversify current income streams by offering more formally structured cultural tourism initiatives. Community members have expressed concerns about how to 'perform' cultural tourism in all of its various guises (Scherrer and Doohan, 2013), but there are existing models that have successfully serviced cultural tourism over many years. These initiatives also help in understanding how a condition of 'temporary belonging' is cultivated in the tourism experience.

Patrick Mung Mung, an internationally recognized artist and former Chairman of the Artists Council at Warmun, in north-western Australia, spoke of the significance of art centres in 2000, and their intrinsic relationship to place:

> the art centre is good to be a centre. It reminds the kids so they got to learn from this. Then they got strong. Then they know the painting. But the real thing. We should take them to the country
>
> (Mung Mung, 2016).

In instances where tourists participate in community cultural practices, such as art production, the community's conceptual frameworks for seeing and knowing their place in the world is shared temporarily with visitors who pay for the privilege to listen and learn (Scherrer and Doohan, 2013).

Case study: *Arnhemweavers*

One of the most successful art and cultural tourism initiatives run by a remote Aboriginal community ironically does not have a physical art centre as such. But this lack of a physical site only demonstrates how an online presence can support the infrastructure of community delivery of cultural tourism initiatives. *Arnhemweavers* (Arnhem Weavers, 2016) is the commercial name for an art and cultural tourism initiative that has operated in the very remote location of Mäpuru in Australia's central northern region of Aboriginal-owned land, called Arnhem Land. It has been running cultural workshops since 2003 and today continues to do so on an expanded scale. *Arnhemweavers* markets some of the finest weaving and other art forms produced in the region, but does so largely through a virtual gallery located on their website *Arnhemweavers* (2016). This website provides background information about the community, the artists, and the artwork, and it is also the platform for promoting their participatory cultural workshop initiatives.

In 2006 I organized a group of art history university students and art enthusiasts to participate in one of these cultural workshops. This community-embedded cultural workshop event remains my principal inspiration for a participatory cultural tourism experience of temporary belonging.

Our cultural tourism experience began with an acute understanding of what 'remote' means in terms of daily existence. We embarked on a two-day drive from Darwin to the Mäpuru community located 600 kilometres to the east. The drive takes in some of the most beautiful parts of the region, from dramatic gorges to lush swampland. Air transport to Mäpuru is expensive and infrequent. Due to its wetland location, there is no road access at all during the monsoonal summer season (called the Wet). The establishment of Mäpuru occurred as part of the Homeland movement principally in the 1970s when small communities of Aboriginal people returned to their traditional homelands, and often in very remote locations (Arnhem Weavers, 2016). The desire for cultural revival was one of the many imperatives driving this Homeland movement.

The idea to commence a weaving workshop originated from a desire by the Mäpuru community to re-establish self-esteem after several unsuccessful education initiatives (Arnhem Weavers, 2016). They wanted to create a situation where Yolngu (the local Aboriginal people) train outsiders. Workshops that could be provided by highly skilled local weavers were also seen as a method of promoting the market for fibre art. Financial return for woven art is poor relative to other art forms because the former requires more time and technical expertise relative to the time to create a painting for the art market. Staff from Charles Darwin University, led by academic John Greatorex, assisted the community in issuing notices of the workshops to every institution in Australia involved in textile production, and the first workshop was held in 2003. Annual workshops have ensued, and increased in 2016 to the point that three different workshops are offered at different times of the dry season.

The remote location and alien wetland environment of Mäpuru can give visitors a profound sense of alienation and vulnerability. Nothing is familiar and one relies almost entirely on someone else knowing where one should be, and how to behave. Mäpuru consists of less than 100 people so outsiders' presence is extremely obvious. The community provides accommodation by building traditional bark shelters raised from the ground, and visitors bring their own sleeping and cooking equipment. This visitor accommodation is located adjacent to a very large open-walled shelter that is the community's principal gathering place. Visitors are welcomed by community leaders and elders on arrival and then left to settle in.

Hands-on learning commences the following morning when the group is introduced to the first part of the weaving process, which is to obtain the raw materials. This involves excursions into dense mangrove habitats and woodlands to collect intensely coloured dyes from the roots of trees, and pandanus leaves for the weaving. Knowledge and practices are shared on these excursions about bush food, bush medicine, traditional practices of environmental sustainability, and an introduction to the spiritual understanding of how ancestors created the land. Visitors are also alerted to crocodile habitats and their capacity to cover a short distance in lightning-quick time. Our group learnt how mud mussels are found by walking with bare feet on the fibrous ground of the dense mangrove forests. Mussels situate themselves vertically in the fibres, and their sharp tip pushes into feet walking on the fibrous terrain.

Feasts of smoked mud mussels occur on the excursions and are an intrinsic part of the whole creative process.

Over the following week, the group continually works with the artists and community members, and learns about carving techniques, spiritual story-telling, and spiritual sites in country. Visitors also experiment with all kinds of bush tucker (food). These experiences take on an extremely hands-on dimension when collecting and harvesting resources for the weaving. Particularly subtle pandanus leaves are selected from the top of trees that are sometimes several metres in height. A long, hooked metal rod is used to pull a bunch of leaves over so that they can be cut away. This is not easy – the leaves have razor-sharp edges and are quite stiff and resistant to the harvesting process. Tree roots used for dyes are located well below ground level, and have an almost intractable connectedness to the earth. The point here is that the laborious nature of this process, and the requirement of expert direction from community members, creates a thoroughly absorbing context for learning about and relating to the local people and place.

Advice to be on the alert for stinging green ant nests in pandanus trees, crocodile slides on riverbanks that look like a 'path', and the possibility of hostile water buffalo, help develop deep respect for local knowledge. While the harvesting process might be arduous, for many visitors the weaving process itself is pure magic. Sitting alongside master weavers, participants watch in silence as techniques are demonstrated, or become involved in conversations on topics that range from everything from ancestral legends to favourite rock bands. This is the cultural tradition of 'yarning' – sitting down and telling stories – that is shared in a new cross-cultural context. Some visitors master various techniques, and others come to learn that they are intrinsically non-weavers, but for most there is little importance in such technical achievement or failure. This is because actual participation is the most important activity in the workshop: from chopping the mangrove trees to stripping the pandanus and collecting bush tucker. Some participants develop excellent skills in weaving techniques, but the workshop is really about a much broader cultural appreciation and an opportunity to learn about Aboriginal community life in general.

Cultural workshops developed over the years at *Arnhemweavers* cater for the variety of specialized groups interested in this experience. In 2016 two workshops were organized by the Centre for Education and Research in Environmental Strategies (CERES), which is a not-for-profit entity located in Melbourne. They organized a women-only and a mixed-gender group where women focus on weaving skills and men focus on bush survival skills. A former CERES Global Coordinator described the workshops as providing insight into an Aboriginal (Yolngu) sense of belonging: "These trips always leave people with far more than baskets, bark paintings and didgeridoos ... the gentle people of Mäpuru open our western eyes to a glimmer of the knowledge and wisdom of Yolngu culture" (Centre for Education and Research in Environmental Strategies, 2016). A 2012 participant is quoted on this website as saying: "I didn't just learn how to weave a basket in Mäpuru, I took a brief glimpse at my universe differently" (Centre for Education and Research in Environmental Strategies, 2016). This latter quote touches on the concept of temporary belonging as "a brief glimpse at my universe" that embodies the inside/outside sensation of being absorbed briefly into an Aboriginal worldview, and participating in cultural practices that allow one to see the natural and human environment differently.

A 2016 specialized group visit was instigated by the Nature Philosophy organization, an interest group focused on nature awareness, deep ecology, survival skills, and learning from indigenous communities (Nature Philosophy, 2016). CERES and Nature Philosophy have organized numerous workshops in Mäpuru (Nature Philosophy since 2008). Other cultural tourism initiatives in Mäpuru involve arts and crafts groups, universities, schools, and arts organizations. Most of these workshops are open to the general public and are advertised on the websites of *Arnhemweavers* and other relevant organizations. *Arnhemweavers* also advertises on their website that they will organize group workshops based on any of the following themes:

- Pandanus weaving, including pandanus collection, preparation, dyeing, and weaving.
- String making (using Banyan and Brachychiton barks) for bags and nets.
- Bush medicines.
- Harvesting of fruits and fish.
- Preparation of cycad bread (requires two weeks).
- House and shelter construction.
- Living on country.
- Trekking, following pre-contact paths across country.

The range of immersion in participatory Indigenous cultural tourism

Mäpuru is a very small, remote community in a location that resists any spontaneous tourist visits. There is no permanent tourist accommodation or all-weather roads, and only a very expensive, infrequent air service. These conditions alone allow Mäpuru to control their engagement with the tourism industry. The community controls the accommodation, programming, group size, and costs. This is an ideal model for Mäpuru, but there are a range of immersive cultural tourism initiatives offered by other Indigenous art centres whose participatory framework and tourism services relate to the diverse conditions of location, community size, accommodation and access, and most importantly, community attitudes towards tourism. The tourist experience of temporary belonging differs in each of these cases.

For example, Bula'bula Arts is an art centre located in the Aboriginal community of Ramingining, approximately 80 kilometres west of Mäpuru (Bula'bula Arts, 2016). I was involved in organizing annual participatory art and culture workshops hosted by Bula'bula from 2007 until 2014. The last of these trips transformed into a University of Queensland Art History course for student academic credit, but prior to this, groups involved a diversity of people including tertiary students from across the arts and sciences, artists, art enthusiasts, school teachers, and international visitors.

Ramingining is the community where the Cannes Film Festival Award-winning production of *Ten Canoes* was based, and many of the cast was involved in its art and culture activities. Cultural awareness events involved bush and boat trips on and around the heritage-listed Arafura Swamp wetland, learning about bush food, spiritual understanding of the country, and a great deal of other 'incidental' knowledge. Yolngu and visitors would share the four-wheel drive vehicles with children who often clambered over everyone. Hunting trips, fishing, eating water lily stems, and stalking (and being stalked by) crocodiles, all featured in the high-end participatory activities. Similarly to *Arnhemweavers*, the entire weaving process took place with gathering and preparing materials, and learning to weave over several days. This was accompanied by lessons in creating bark painting and wooden implements.

It is impossible to put into words the degree to which participants regard the visit as a life-changing experience for a full spectrum of reasons, and how much they felt 'at home' within a very short time. I believe that this temporary belonging is achieved principally because of the generosity, good will, and aspiring entrepreneurship of the hosts, and the participatory community-embedded nature of the visit.

Bula'bula Arts have embarked on a more formal cultural tourism enterprise over the past few years, and have secured and renovated a house (Mona Lodge) specifically for visitor/tourism accommodation. In 2016 I organized a trip to Australia's central desert based on art and culture workshops, which were hosted by the Ikuntji Artists art centre in the Haasts Bluff community. On this occasion the trip was offered as a University of Queensland Art History course for student academic credit, but the art centre regarded the visit as an experiment for their broader cultural tourism aspirations. Ikuntji Artists ran a very successful artists' festival in 2014 where tourists could stay in the (otherwise inaccessible) community over several days for a small fee and participate in the festival. Activities included a broad range of art and cultural events, and our more extended engagement with Ikuntji Artists built on the community's sense of success with this first cultural tourism initiative.

There are numerous Indigenous art centres and art communities across Australia (Maruku Arts, 2016,; Merrepen Arts, 2014) that involve art and cultural trips such as Mäpuru, Bula'bula Arts, and Ikuntji Artists, although they are not as embedded in the communities to the same extent as the three discussed above. From my own perspective, the experience of temporary belonging that I have witnessed in visitors is very much contingent on the degree to which artists and community members are involved, and the extent and nature of visitor participation. 'Community' in this sense of visitor experience is not a place but a state of mind that connects people and transforms them, even if only for a temporary duration.

References

Aboriginal South Australia. (2016). Aboriginal cultural tours South Australia. [online]. Available at: www.aboriginalsa.com.au/tours.html [Accessed 15 Jun 2016].

Acker, T. and Woodhead, A. (2014). The economies value chain reports: Art centre finances. In: *CRC-REP Research Report CROO6*. Alice Springs: Ninti One Limited. [online]. Available at: www.crc-rep.com.au/resource/CR006_AEVC_ArtCentreFinances.pdf [Accessed 1 May 2015].

Arnhem Weavers. (2016). [online]. Available at: www.arnhemweavers.com.au [Accessed 3 Dec 2016]

Australian Government. (2016). Indigenous art centre plan, Canberra: Ministry for the Arts. [online] Available at: www.arts.gov.au/g/files/net1761/f/indigenous-art-centre-plan-pdf [Accessed 2 Aug. 2016].

Brunton, C. (2004). Demand for nature-based and Indigenous tourism product. In: Brunton, C., *Report Prepared for Australian Government, Department of Industry, Tourism and Resources*. Report dated 15 Dec. 2004. Canberra: Colmar Brunton Social Research.

Bula'bulaArts. (2016). [online]. Available at: www.bulabula-arts.com/ [Accessed 15 May 2016].

Bunten, A.D. (2008). Sharing culture or selling out? Developing the commodified persona in the heritage industry. *American Ethnologist*, 35(31), pp. 380–395.

Burns, P. and Novelli, M. eds., (2006). *Tourism and social identities: Global frameworks and local realities*. Oxford: Elsevier.

Burns, P. and Novelli, M. eds., (2008). *Tourism and mobilities: Local-global connections*. Cambridge, US and Oxfordshire, UK: CAB International.

Butler, R. and Hinch, T. eds., (2007). *Tourism and indigenous peoples: Issues and implications*. Oxford: Butterworth-Heinemann.

Centre for Education and Research in Environmental Studies [CERES]. (2016). Arnhem Land – Mäparu. In *CERES*. [online]. Available at: http://ceres.org.au/global/arnhem-land [Accessed 15 Aug 2016].

Chambers, E. (2010). *The anthropology of travel and tourism*. Long Grove, IL: Waveland Press.

Coleman, S. and Crang, M. (2002a). Grounded tourists, travelling theory. In: Coleman, S. and Crang, M., eds., *Tourism: Between place and performance*. New York, Oxford: Bergahn Books, pp. 1–17.

Coleman, S. and Crang, M., eds., (2002b). *Tourism: Between place and performance*. New York, Oxford: Berghahn Books.

Crouch, D. (2002). Surrounded by place, embodied encounters. In: Coleman, S. and Crang, M., eds., *Tourism: Between place and performance*. New York, Oxford: Berghahn Books, pp. 207–218.

Desart. (2016). About art centres. [online]. Available at: http://desart.com.au/artcentres [Accessed 14 Jun 2016].

Eliot, T.S. (2016, first published 1925). The hollow men. In: *All Poetry*. [online]. Available at: https://allpoetry.com/The-Hollow-Men [Accessed 14 Jun 2016].

Gmeich, S.B. (2004). *Tourists and tourism: A reader*. Long Grove, IL: Waveland Press.

Gregory, N. (2016). Songlines. In: *Creative Spirits*. [online]. Available at: www.creativespirits.info/aboriginalculture/arts/songlines [Accessed 12 Aug 2016].

IkuntjiArtists. (2016). Events. [online]. Available at: https://ikuntji.com.au/events [Accessed 12 Sep 2016].

Iyer, P. (2000). *The global soul.* New York: Vintage.

Johnson, V. (2010). *Once upon a time in Papunya.* Sydney: University of New South Wales Press.

Jones, T., Booth, J. and Acker, T. (2016). The changing business of aboriginal and Torres Strait islander art: Markets, audiences, artists, and the large art fairs. *The Journal of Arts Management, Law, and Society,* 46(3), pp. 107–121.

Kirshenblatt-Gimblett, B. (1998). *Destination culture: Tourism, museums, and heritage.* Berkeley: University of California Press.

Leighton, A. (2007). *On form: Poetry, aestheticism, and the legacy of a word.* Oxford: Oxford University Press.

McKenna, M. (2002). *Looking for Blackfella's Point: An Australian history of place.* Sydney: University of NSW Press.

MacLeod, N. (2006). Cultural tourism: Aspects of authenticity and commodification. In: Smith, M. and Robinson, M., eds., *Cultural tourism in a changing world: Politics, participation and (re)presentation.* North York, Ontario: Channel View Publications, pp. 177–190.

Maruku Arts. (2016). Tours and workshops. [online]. Available at: https://maruku.com.au/tours-workshops [Accessed 14 Jun 2016].

Merrepen Arts. (2014). Welcome to the Merrepen Arts Festival. [online]. Available at: www.merrepenfestival.com.au/ [Accessed 31 May 2016].

Mung Mung, P. (2000). Aboriginal art centres. In: *Aboriginal Art Online.* [online]. Available at: www.aboriginalartonline.com/regions/art-centres.php [Accessed 13 May 2016].

Nature Philosophy. (2016). Mäpuru N.T. [online]. Available at: www.naturephilosophy.com/m%C3%A4puru-nt [Accessed 15 Aug 2016].

Plotnitsky, A. and Rajan, T., eds., (2004). *Idealism without absolutes: Philosophy and romantic culture.* Albany: State University of New York Press.

Plumwood, V. (2008). Shadow places and the politics of dwelling. *Australian Humanities Review,* 44, pp. 139–150.

Read, P. (2000). *Belonging – Australians, place and Aboriginal ownership.* Cambridge, UK: Cambridge University Press.

Rose, D. (1999). Indigenous ecologies and an ethic of connection. In: Low, N., ed., *Global ethics and environment.* London: Routledge, pp. 175–187.

Ryan, C. and Aicken, M. (2005). *Indigenous tourism: The commodification and management of culture.* New York: Elsevier.

Ryan, C. and Huyton, J. (2002). Tourists and Aboriginal people. *Annals of Tourism Research,* 29(3), pp. 631–647.

Scherrer, P. and Doohan, K. (2013). 'It's not about believing': Exploring the transformative potential of cultural acknowledgement in an Indigenous tourism context. *Asia Pacific Viewpoint,* 54(2), pp. 158–170.

Skinner, J. and Theodossopoulos, D. eds., (2011). *Great expectations: Imagination and anticipation in tourism.* New York: Berghahn Books.

Smith, M. and Robinson, M. eds., (2006). *Cultural tourism in a changing world: Politics, participation and (re)presentation.* North York, Ontario: Channel View Publications.

Tonnaer, A. (2010). A ritual of meeting: 'sharing culture' as a shared culture in Australian Indigenous tourism. *La Ricerca Folklorica,* 61, pp. 21–31.

Urban Indigenous. (2016). Private tours. [online]. Available at: www.urbanindigenous.com.au/ [Accessed 16 Jun 2016].

Zakin, E. (2015). Crisscrossing cosmopolitanism: state-phobia, world alienation, and the global soul. *The Journal of Speculative Philosophy*, 29(1), pp. 58–72.

Zeppel, H. (2001). Aboriginal cultures and indigenous tourism. In: Douglas, N., Douglas, N. and Derrett, R., eds., *Special interest tourism*. Chichester: John Wiley and Sons, pp. 232–259.

2   Saving Sagada

Patricia Maria Santiago

Introduction

Sagada is known to many travelers as a beautiful paradise nestled in the mountains of the Cordillera in the northern part of the Philippines. It is home to indigenous peoples known as Kankanaey one of the largest groups in the northern region, and still practices pre-colonial cultural traditions and rituals.[1] This small town is also known for its rich natural resources with forests full of towering pine trees and spectacular views of rice terraces interspersed with hiking trails that lead to majestic falls and natural springs. More active travellers can do spelunking (caving) to explore Sagada's popular caves. Unfortunately, all these activities are now threatened because of the sudden influx of greater numbers of tourists in recent times.

For example, from 2007–2008 Sagada experienced a three-fold increase in tourist numbers, and by 2014 (see Figure 2.1 and Figure 2.2) about 65,000 tourists were taking the nine-hour land route to Sagada from Manila, and passing through the winding roads and ravines of Halsema highway (one of the most dangerous highways in the Philippines).[2] Despite these challenges, many tourists visit Sagada to experience its cool climate and the natural beauty of its environment. This increase in the flow of tourists has placed considerable pressure on the resources and cohesion of the local Sagada community. This chapter examines, from the perspective of a participant in community activities, the strategies that this community is putting in place to recover some control over their economic and cultural destiny, and also documents the challenges confronting a participatory approach to tourism development. Here we also reflect on spirituality and religious practices as important motivations in community activism, and their contribution to the harmonizing of the secular and the sacred, which is of interest to those secular tourists who express a desire for a spiritual experience.

Methodology

Definitions of the term 'cultural tourism' are diverse but in the context of Sagada the statement that cultural tourism "has crystallized as a concept related to those who travel in search of culture, in its most general sense"

(Richards and Smith, 2013, p. 1) seems appropriate. The landscape surrounding Sagada is known for its caving and outdoor tourism, but this geographical draw is enhanced by the area's remoteness and its unique indigenous communities. Tourists coming to Sagada are often unaware of the fragility of the environment and the depth of community respect for local traditions. In this context tourism managers are faced with balancing tourist demands with community expectations, some of which are pro-development while others wish to see tourist activity regulated. In order to develop beneficial ways for the community to move forward so that there is a benefit from tourism without losing identity, the concepts of the PIC Model assist in framing this discussion. The PIC (Participatory, Incremental, Collaborative/Cooperative) Model, developed by Dallen J. Timothy and Cevat Tosun (2003) is one in which "participation in tourism planning, implementation and monitoring of tourism plans, and collaboration among stakeholders are the focus of the discussion" (Hung, Sirakaya-Turk & Ingram, 2011, p. 277). This model offers an insight into the type of tourism processes that are faced by a community such as Sagada. According to Hung et al. "the model suggests that community members' participation in tourism planning depends not only on power relationships but also on personal factors" (2011, p.277). Based on his adapation of the processes outlined in the 2003 model, Dallen J. Timothy writes that in many instances of heritage tourism disputation there has been "public opposition to policies and practices deemed unfair or inequitable, favouring elites and government agencies over lay people and local businesses" (2011, p.264). Timothy argues in favour of participatory development in communities that have heritage sites that are attracting greater numbers of tourists because "participatory development recognizes that destination residents, business people, local government and advocacy groups are all interdependent stakeholders, who must have a voice in the development process" (2011, p. 264). In this framework, 'true empowerment' occurs when community members and other stakeholders initiate their own goals, programs and projects (p. 265). The theorizing undertaken by tourism researchers draws attention to the complexity of planning with multiple levels of stakeholders in locations that have historic, heritage, cultural, and religious importance for diverse community sectors who must work with increasing numbers of tourists who want to access the area, often for a wide range of purposes.

The roads to tourism in Sagada

In 2007, 11,496 tourists visited Sagada. Twelve months later the figure had reached 31,456, which was almost triple the previous year's number of visitors.[3] This increase in tourist visits was enabled by the upgrade of the Halsema highway in 2008, which made Sagada more accessible.[4] This road improvement reduced the traveling time from Manila to Sagada from 12–14 hours to nine hours. Thereafter, tourist arrivals increased as more people used their own vehicles, or joined group tours with travel agencies in buses. As more people gained access to Sagada, its beauty became more widely known and the floodgates for budget package tours from local and national travel agencies soon opened, which brought income that assisted Sagada's local businesses to profit from the area's popularity. However, the profits that were gleaned from this newly popular tourism destination were not evenly distributed. According to an investigative study undertake by students from St. Scholastica's College in Manila only 27 percent of the total profits from tourism were going to a small number of local tourism stakeholders in the community, while 73 percent went to travel agencies operating from Manila or other places.[5]

Some local people, especially those who are not in the tourism sector, feel that this transition to greater tourism has occurred too fast for their small town. The great inflow of tourists has exceeded the capacity of the town to adequately cater for them in relation to accommodation, food and other services, yet the local government has not moved to regulate this situation. Of course, Sagada is not alone in facing this type of challenge. For example, some Greek islands and other Mediterranean islands are struggling to cope with tourists, especially those subject to cruise ship tourism.

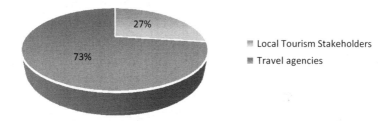

Figure 2.1 Tourism benefit distribution
Ctsy. Sagada Tourist Information Center

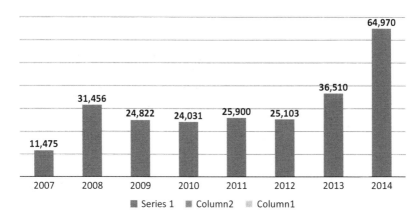

Figure 2.2 Tourist arrivals in Sagada
Ctsy. Sagada Tourist Information Center

Impact of tourism in the community

The package tour boom associated with tourism has offered some benefits to Sagada, for there have been dramatic increases in tourism fee collections and boosts to tourism-oriented businesses; notably guesthouses, restaurants, souvenir shops, and guides. All of these sectors and operators have experienced significant increases in sales and revenue. The gains in income however have been offset by negative impacts presented by increased package tour traffic, some of which threatens Sagada's continued viability as a tourist destination. Among these impacts are a very heavy traffic load exacerbated by the tendency of tour groups to use vehicle transportation for all trips, including short trips between hotels and restaurants. Many of the tour groups that ply the Baguio-Sagada-Banaue route usually only stay a day or two, and their tourist vehicles cause considerable congestion to Sagada's limited infrastructure and narrow roads. These roads require smooth traffic flow, which can only be maintained if on-street parking is strictly controlled, and this is a problem for many businesses that do not have their own parking spaces. Several roads leading to popular tourist spots have also been widened to accommodate visitors in the peak season, but this work is destroying the local community's natural resources, largely through the illegal logging of century-old pine trees in the mountain forests. The native forests are a major draw for tourists to Sagada who are attracted to the clean cool air of the pine trees that surround the walking trails, but they won't be there much longer if infrastructure continues to be built to accommodate the mass influx of tourists.

There are a number of other problems that have been caused by the increase of tourist visits to Sagada. For example, there are heavy visitation rates to key activity destinations such as: Lumiang Burial Cave, Sumaguing Cave, Mt. Kiltepan, and Bomod-ok Falls. This crowding not only has a detrimental effect on visitor satisfaction, but also compromises safety standards (particularly in the caves). In the long term, it is also having a negative impact on the environment. Local people are very concerned about the gradual destruction of their highly revered natural resources that are also sacred sites for the community, especially in relation to the Lumiang Burial Cave and Sumaguing Cave. These caves were formed thousands of years ago and many visitors entering them are touching the stone, smoking, and even urinating inside the caves. These activities present a grave threat to the sites and require protection. According to Joseph Rasalan, cave expert and ecosystem management specialist at the Biodiversity Management Bureau, people need to take into consideration that caves, unlike other areas that are open for tourism, are particularly sensitive habitats and ecosystems, and often have unique species inhabiting them. Once a person enters a cave, they are already changing the sensitive conditions of the area. Indeed, one person's footprint is enough to change the energy of a cave, or the introduction of oil from one's hands when touching the interior of caves can ruin the natural formation of stalactites and stalagmites that have thrived in these stable environments for hundreds, thousands, and millions of years.[6]

Some tourists are also insensitive or disrespectful towards local customs. For example, in 2015, a visiting couple held a pre-nuptial pictorial inside the Lumiang Cave. This greatly angered the locals, especially community elders. Jaime Dugao, one of Sagada's elders explained that the Lumiang Cave is not just any cave, it is a burial cave that has sacred value for the local community. Dugao hoped that visitors would treat the cave with appropriate respect once they understood how sacred the cave is to the local community and the important role it plays as a site where the spirits of the community's dead ancestors remain.[7] Tourists can also make unreasonable demands on local inhabitants. For example, it has been reported that locals are beset with questions like, "Where are the Igorots?" There is also the expectation that Igorots (Indigenous) community members in tribal garb will be ready and willing to pose for pictures on demand.[8] There is a trend toward the dilution of local culture, as tourists are crowding in on rituals, and sometimes attempting to join them, or are taking intrusive photographs at close range. According to Ezra Arinduque, a concerned local inhabitant who owns Sagada Weaving, Sagada's treasured culture and traditions are slowly changing due to tourism. 'Cultural shows' and other forms of cultural commercialization are becoming more common, but these violate long-standing community policies. It is valuable for visitors to watch and to learn about how the community dances and play gongs during rituals, but Arinduque believes there should be limits to the influence tourists have on local customs. For example, the very presence of outside spectators has an effect on the performance of solemn and age-old rituals, which at times are now only being performed for tourist entertainment in exchange for payment. Elders see this as a bastardization of their culture.[9]

In Sagada today, large parts of the natural landscape are changing due to the construction of new tourist amenities. Sagada was once surrounded by green fields, mountains, and towering trees, but the large number of tourist arrivals in recent times is beginning to threaten the beauty of this environment. Philippines Mines and Geosciences Bureau studies show that there is limestone under Sagada in an area known for its sinkholes. The heavy infrastructure built on the surface area, including roads and accompanying structures, will undoubtedly trigger ground subsidence. Several sinkholes in Sagada are located at the town center where most inns and businesses are concentrated, so continuing development may eventually threaten the safety of local inhabitants. The town and surrounding areas are also part of an irregular terrain, which requires high standards for building codes to protect the safety of tourists and local citizens. These are not currently in place and this lack of oversight means that many current dwellings might collapse if a strong earthquake were to occur. This lack of an enforced building code is another element that puts the safety of Sagada at risk. As Timothy argues, planning may work best when it is approached "bit by bit to achieve more specific goals and objectives" (Timothy, 2011, p. 266).

Other negative consequences of development include the distortion of local labor markets, as many businesses have been forced to bring in non-Sagadan workers to staff hotels and restaurants. There have also been reports of increasing numbers of students dropping out of school to make quick money guiding tourists, and many of these former students do not have proper training or accreditation. As well, local artisans have lost interest in creating souvenirs that evoke the artistic and cultural traditions of Sagada. Some continue to produce traditional objects that can instruct people about local customs, but many others are now selling more commercialized souvenir products that come from towns and cities like Banaue and Baguio City. It is rare to purchase hand-painted shirts or beautifully handcrafted traditional baskets made by local villages. Instead, most products in souvenir shops are mass produced, and are poorly made to keep prices low.

At the level of infrastructure, there is of course a generation of more waste that Sagada has no facilities to manage. According to former Municipal Councilor Eduardo Umaming, a substantial increase in the volume of waste has accompanied the boom in Sagada's tourism. He said that tourists have introduced a different attitude to the environment by bringing commercial goods, such as junk food wrappers and plastic bottles. Since there is no waste disposal system in the community, innkeepers and hostel owners burn garbage. The practice of burning plastic and other non-biodegradable materials however has produced so much pollution that it has been banned due to the heavy damage it has caused to the environment.[10] Further detrimental environmental impacts include water shortages, particularly during the summer season when tourism flow peaks. Tourists use so much water that there is often scarce supply for the daily needs of the locals, especially the terraces where water for fields of planted rice and vegetables is in high demand. Sigried Bangyay Rogers has claimed that during the summer season, when tourism is at its peak, tourists do not think about how much water they are consuming, as long as there is water flowing from the showers and faucets. Locals who suffer from tourists' excessive use of water have begun walking long distances to mountain springs to fetch the water they need and carry it back to their homes.[11]

There is a perception among many locals that today's package-guided tourists do not care and know little about Sagada's history, culture, and people. At the same time, independent tourists, who respect local customs and culture have been largely crowded out. Yet, when these tourists do visit they tend to stay longer and spend more money than package tourists. They are also often repeat visitors. These independent travelers, who have been visiting Sagada since the 1970s, now tend to steer away from Sagada as crowding becomes more serious and package tour agencies book rooms months in advance.

The culture bearers of Sagada

Long before Americans came to Sagada to establish the Episcopal Church, the Indigenous *Kankanaeys* or *Igorots* possessed a very rich culture that was upheld by the community and its elders. They carved the mountains to build majestic rice terraces. They created beautiful weavings for textiles and baskets.

Their music, played with gongs and bamboo, is some of the most beautiful in Southeast Asia. They have many rituals that celebrate life cycles, and have deeply embedded spiritual beliefs. They have also developed a unique system of government called the *Dap-ay*.

The *Dap-ay* refers to a group of elders who serve as the governing body in the community, and this pre-exists any modern-day form of government. In the *Dap-ay* rest legislative and judicial powers. As a socio-political unit, the *Dap-ay* gathers to settle disputes, resolve conflicts, issue laws, and direct customary conduct that binds the community, as well as making other decisions that involve and affect the general lives of the people. The *Dap-ay* served as the primary teacher of moral principles to citizens prior to the arrival of Christian missionaries. As a cultural center, the *Dap-ay* is also the seat of rituals like the *Begnas* or the rice harvesting ritual. This ritual symbolizes prosperity and is the cause for community celebration and merrymaking. When American Christian missionaries arrived, they did not impose a new religion. Instead, both Christian and Indigenous beliefs co-existed in the community with much mutual respect, tolerance, and generosity. The community gave portions of land to the Church, and in return, the Americans built schools, a hospital, and other facilities that provide social services to the community.

The *Dap-ay* elders are not paid to perform their function for the community. They are chosen because they have acted with courage and wisdom, and have gained the trust and respect of the community. The elders make decisions on behalf of, and in response to, the needs of the whole community. Their teachings have always been about what is best for the community rather than the individual. Unfortunately, in recent times, some of the elders' decisions have become corrupted by the system and operations of the national government. A national government agenda caused conflict among the elders and the community when they were forced to follow national and local government laws. This new system therefore undermined the roles and functions of the elders' social system. The erosion of the Indigenous social system attests to current challenges in the community. Leaders of the *Dap-ay,* the local government, and even the church have lost the sense of being able to work together for the good of the community. This is because the priority agenda of leaders has generally focused on tourism that promotes the commodification of culture and profit-raising enterprises, rather than a program that protects Sagada's culture and preserves the values of the Indigenous community.

The shift to cultural tourism

Package tourism has generated considerable problems and challenges for the Sagada community. Sagada needs to re-establish some control over the present and future circumstances of the community and its environment. One way to achieve this might be to develop measures that can reduce visits from large numbers of tourists and seek instead to attract visitors like independent and cultural tourists. However, the question then becomes: who will be responsible for steering the direction of the community towards a preferred form of tourism? Will it be the local government, the elders and the community, or the tourists themselves? In my opinion, it should be all of the above. This is indeed the perfect time to work collaboratively to enhance sustainability, the protection of the environment, and the preservation of Sagada's culture. In recent years, many members of the local community have failed in their responsibility to actively protect their culture and land. Moreover, it can be argued that any new form of government support or action is meaningless if the community does not cooperate in enforcing the implementation of laws and tourism policies that can assist them to take some control over their own destinies. Tourists should be encouraged to choose operators who run tours that will benefit Sagada's community, in more ways than simple economic efficiencies. The community also needs to ensure that their activities will educate visitors to be responsible travelers.

Declaration as a heritage town

A local ordinance declaring Sagada as a heritage site would be an initiative that could boost a sense of pride of place, and would encourage the community to acknowledge the value of the town's heritage value. This in turn would have an impact on visitors whose knowledge of Sagada would be informed by the values of heritage sites; this could positively shift the cultural awareness and sense of responsibility for tourists when visiting the destination.

A heritage declaration can also be used as the basis for implementing new policies to protect the cultural rights of Indigenous communities and their heritage, including their natural environment. Regulating tourist capacity and identifying important archaeological and heritage zones will improve the day-to-day lives of the people. Such decisions give priority considerations to the safety, peace, and order of the community. The best approach would involve a *three-fold system of governance*. Timothy outlines the importance of "collaborative, or cooperative planning" (2011, p.267) as an important approach to sustainable development (2011, p. 267). This includes collaboration between government agencies, different levels of administration, public and private organizations, and between private sector services such as heritage tours, as well as between political boundaries. The labeling of such a range of different stake-holders shows that the 'heritage' or 'cultural' product itself is only one aspect of a much larger logistical chain, although tourists are attracted to the location because of the cultural and physical environment.

Prior to the inception of greater tourism in Sagada there were three community sectors that managed affairs in the area: elders, the local government, and the church. This tripartite system of decision-making fostered positive communal and participatory processes. Municipal Councilor Dave Gulian observed that when the new local government leaders came to power in 2007, they proposed local policies that served their own rather than the community's interests. In this instance, tourism was used as a tool to convince people about the economic benefits of the so-called 'development' needs of the community, but this included the building of infrastructure that encroached on heritage sites; road widening that sacrificed century-old pine trees, and commercialized eco-tours led by unprofessional, divisive guides (Santiago and Gulian, 2016). In this instance, the lack of co-operation between administrative levels, together with intra-political dissent, resulted in local disputations. A new group of leaders were elected to office in July, 2016, and this presented an opportunity to return to the tripartite system, which may bring back a stronger sense of community. Indeed, the community has already begun to re-assert itself by creating a Tourism Council composed of a local government Tourism Officer, a representative from the guides associations, hostel and restaurant owners, church vestry members, environmental groups, and a community elder. This council will prepare a cultural tourism management plan to mitigate the negative impacts of tourism in Sagada. The council however must ensure that qualitative and quantitative cultural indicators are monitored periodically to verify the shift from mass or packaged tour tourism to independent and cultural tourism.

Cultural mapping

There are any number of initiatives the community can undertake to take back and protect their culture. Locally based teachers and community leaders can work together in documenting and re-assessing Sagada's cultural assets. They can then make information about local culture available to a wider audience via digital media and other means to promote awareness and appreciation of the natural and cultural heritage possessed by Sagada's community. It is clear that establishing a unique cultural profile provides an important means to understand a sense of place and identity for local peoples. For the most part, such profiles can substantiate and fortify existing knowledge as well as announcing new information about a culture that can be promoted on a global stage. Cultural information captures the uniqueness of a locale: its colors and shapes, textures and contours, sounds, smell and taste, beliefs, values, traditions, and a host of other tangible and intangible cultural treasures. Culture profiles can also provide valuable information to local governments, civil society organizations, the private sector, academe and other institutions. It is also evident that relevant and validated information is important for development planning, program and project implementation, monitoring and evaluation. Most importantly, culture profiles can be used as the basis for crafting local culture and arts development plans, tourism master plans, as well as providing inputs to Comprehensive Land Use Plans (CLUPs) and Local Development Plans (Antonio, 2014).

Developing creative industries

The development of sustainable creative industries can provide an important source of income while simultaneously improving the self-confidence of local artisans. Souvenirs and other local crafts are cultural expressions that are an excellent means by which to promote one's culture. Local artists can be encouraged to create and express their sense of spirituality through art works, often via contemporary patterns and designs specific to their culture, or by preserving the traditional crafts and styles of the community. Local creative products evoke the distinctive artistic and cultural traditions of a community. Therefore, a communication plan needs to be developed to clearly describe the specific message the community wishes to send to target groups of tourists. The type of message should be positive, and should cater to tourists who may be willing to pay more for unique, high quality, and authentic products that tell a story about a people's culture and Sagada's place as a heritage destination, rather than mass-produced, souvenir-objects that are not connected to its traditions. The establishment of a well-crafted design and entrepreneurial workshop would also be very useful and beneficial for local artisans, and could provide more sustainable employment opportunities for the community.

Experts from various government institutions and organizations have already begun to support these new endeavors. They are willing to share their expertise in cultural research and destination management to help prepare the community to move towards a more responsible and sustainable perspective in managing tourism. The National Commission for Culture and the Arts has approved a project grant to the local government for a workshop seminar to empower community leaders about the value of Heritage Conservation. The International Council on Monuments and Sites or ICOMOS Philippines has been providing consultations and free workshops on establishing a Cultural Tourism Management Plan for several tourism sectors in the community. Architectural Heritage Conservation graduate students from the University of the Philippines College of Architecture have undertaken studies for a possible conservation plan of the Mission Compound of the Episcopal Church. Establishing solid partnerships in tourism management will support the healthy development of the community's cultural tourism programs, and at the same time create a visibility platform for organizations, institutions, and corporations to be involved in the advocacy.

In the 1970s, elders created a set of guidelines for visitors, which they considered to be the 'ten commandments' for visiting Sagada. These were posted on the walls of hostels and homestays until the early 1990s, but were disregarded when tourism numbers grew substantially. In 2015, I collaborated with Steve Rogers, a long-time American resident of Sagada (and who is married to a local person), to write a new set of guidelines for visitors. This was necessary because of mass tourism's ongoing adverse impacts on the community, especially during holidays and long weekends. These guidelines were based on the earlier 1970s set written by the elders, and it is hoped that they will help alleviate the current problems being experienced by the community.

General guidelines for visitors to Sagada

1 *Please respect the culture.* Keep a distance from rituals or any sites you are told are sacred. Do not touch or disturb coffins or burial sites. Do not attempt to join or film any ritual without direct permission from the presiding elders. Do not disturb mass in the church or shoot videos/ photos in or around the church during mass.

2 *Please respect the people.* Sagadans are not exhibits in a museum or zoo. Ask permission before taking pictures or video of people, especially elders. Please don't ask us "where are the Igorots". We are the Igorots. We do dress in traditional clothing for special occasions, but please don't expect any of us to pose in traditional clothing for pictures, because we don't do that.

3 *Please secure necessary permits.* If you need to do field research, interviews in the community, conduct pictorials, or film anyone and any place in Sagada, please go to the Office of the Mayor and make sure you secure a permit and pay any necessary fees. This permit will deter- mine if your activity is allowed or not in the community. Guides are not allowed to secure any permit for such activities.

4 *Please manage your expectations.* Sagada is a community, not a museum. If you want to see the way we lived a century ago, there's an excellent museum in Bontoc; please visit it. Don't think, or say, that we have "lost our culture" because we no longer live in traditional houses or dress daily in wanes and tapis. We are indigenous people and we are deeply attached to our traditions and culture. We are also modern, well- educated people who are comfortable in any living or professional environment the world offers.

5 *Please walk whenever possible.* Walking is an essential part of the Sagada experience. The air here is cool and clean; you won't get all sweaty. The views are spectacular, and you'll enjoy them more on foot than crammed into a metal box. Sagada is a small town and places are close together. If you are going out to browse the shops, walk. If you are going from a hotel to a restaurant, walk. If your hotel is outside the town, drive to the edge of town and walk. If you're strong enough to walk through the caves, you're strong enough to walk to the caves. Walk. It's good for you, you'll see and enjoy more, and you'll help reduce our traffic problem.

6 *Please conserve water.* Sagada suffers from water shortages, espe- cially during dry season and periods of peak tourist flow. This can lead to diversion of water from our farms and rice terraces, where it is des- perately needed, to support tourism. If you are going hiking or caving, bathe after, not before. Please bathe quickly and with as little water as you can.

7 *Please manage your garbage.* Littering and tossing garbage outdoors is unacceptable and disgraceful: just don't do it. Sagada has no municipal

waste disposal system; every household and business has to manage its own waste output. Try to minimize the garbage you generate. As much as possible, what comes here with you should leave with you.

8   **Please be kind to the people in our kitchens.** Our restaurants are small kitchens that can only handle a few meals. When we say, we don't have food anymore, it means the stock we bought during the market day have already run out. We don't serve food frozen from weeks or months ago. To get better service, order your food at least 3 or 4 hours before your meal. That way, we have more time to prepare your food and serve it as soon as you arrive in the restaurant.

9   **Please use your vehicle responsibly.** Our streets are narrow, and on-street parking creates a serious traffic problem. Parking on the street is prohibited by local ordinance. Please follow the law, even when others don't or if someone tells you it's ok to park on the street. If you're asked to back up or pull to the side of the road to allow passage of a bus or other oncoming vehicles, please cooperate. If you are parked in a way that obstructs traffic, move. Do not load/unload in the middle of a road. Pull to the side so that other vehicles can pass.

10 **Please help us keep you safe.** Sagada is a mountain town filled with caves, cliffs, canyons, streams and forests. They are beautiful but people can and do get hurt or lost. We do our best to keep you safe, but we need your help. Guides are required in the caves for your safety, not for our profit. Please hire accredited guides and respect the prescribed guide to guest ratio. We do not allow children to guide, for their safety and yours, so please do not hire children as guides. We strongly recommend guides for hiking or exploring. If you choose to hike without a guide, please be responsible and tell your guest house where you plan to go and what time you plan to be back. Bring a mobile phone and make note of emergency phone numbers. If you go missing we will look for you, at any time of the day or night and in any weather. Knowing where to start is a huge help. If you plan to sleep somewhere other than your guest house, get in touch and let them know, because they will report you missing and we will go out looking for you.

11 **Please be modest.** This is a small, conservative town, and we like it that way. Please save the revealing clothing for the beach, and save the displays of affection for your private space. We are not known for nightlife: business in Sagada closes at 10PM. If you like to party all night that's fine, but you'll have to do it somewhere else. There is no commercial sex here, so please don't waste your time looking for it.

12 **Please give your share to help us preserve our environment.** All visitors (tourists, non-Sagada residents) must register at the Municipal Tourist Information Center and pay Php35.00 for the Environmental Fee. Your receipt will be checked upon entering caves and other tourist areas.

Conclusion

Cultural tourism has provided people all over the world with a better view of different cultures, access to stories about unique people, art objects, and landscapes that help define cultural identity. The people of Sagada hope that in the future cultural tourists in the Philippines will help us create more culturally sensitive approaches to local communities that safeguard both tangible and intangible heritage. Looking at tangible heritage in the context of the community will not only make us understand the functionality of things, but more so, its value in our everyday lives. Rituals, traditions, and artifacts must be viewed as part of a living heritage that protects, preserves, and promotes the values of people and their ways of life.

Mapping heritage to make conservation more tangible must be one of the goals of communities that wish to manage cultural tourism. While the value of tangible heritage is clearly manifested through conservation and restoration efforts, intangible heritage involves different experiential processes, which are often amenable to tangible forms such as recorded documentation and publications to preserve this type of heritage. This data can be used not just as a knowledge base from which to develop tourism policies, but can also be utilized as a library of heritage that can be passed on to ensuing generations. The most important players in safeguarding cultural heritage are the leaders of the community: its elders, local government officials, and church leaders. These are the people who have great influence in changing local culture for better or worse. Properly prepared and implemented, cultural tourism policies provide responsible guidelines for tourists and serve as important tools to preserve heritage. While we try to seek different ways of preserving heritage through tourism, it is inevitable that some heritage will be lost or destroyed through time. Natural calamities or unmanaged tourism however only exacerbates the loss of heritage.

Creative industries can be an important source of alternative income for the community, especially creative local inhabitants who have an association with traditional arts. These creative arts provide the message or branding of how local people want tourists to understand and appreciate the community's sense of place. It is important to recognize the human skill and talent required to produce such art to ensure that tradition and heritage will continue. Saving Sagada from the harsh realities of package tourism and bringing it in line with the more manageable platform of cultural tourism can be a long process, not just in relation to the demands of policy making and new management approaches, but also in the task of building a greater sense of pride and love for one's culture. When these goals are achieved, local communities will develop the confidence to own their decisions and be clear about setting directions for future generations. The broad principles of cultural tourism are therefore important for revitalizating values that enhance a sense of self and place for Sagada.

Notes

1 The Kankanaey people are a Filipino Indigenous group from the Northern Philippines. They are part of the collective group of Indigenous people known as the Igorot people. (Wikipedia.org)
2 This major highway was built by American Engineer E.J. Halsema in the 1920s. It is a 150 km stretch of road that connects Baguio City to Bontoc, Mountain Province.
3 Data provided by the Sagada Tourist Information Center.
4 *Strength and Experience of Bridging People and Progress*, 2008 Department of Public Works and Highways Annual Report, pp 9–10.
5 *Sagad na ang Sagada: A Call for Responsible Tourism in Sagada, Mountain Province*, Video Documentary, Mariah Karen Fulgosino, April 27, 2016.
6 Interview with Joseph Rasalan, *Sagad na ang Sagada: A Call for Responsible Tourism in Sagada, Mountain Province*, Video Documentary, Mariah Karen Fulgosino, April 27, 2016.
7 Interview with Jaime Dugao, *Sagad na ang Sagada: A Call for Responsible Tourism in Sagada, Mountain Province*, Video Documentary, Mariah Karen Fulgosino, April 27, 2016.
8 Ibid.
9 Interview with Ezra Arinduque, *Sagad na ang Sagada: A Call for Responsible Tourism in Sagada, Mountain Province*, Video Documentary, Mariah Karen Fulgosino, April 27, 2016.
10 Interview with Eduardo Umaming, *Sagad na ang Sagada: A Call for Responsible Tourism in Sagada, Mountain Province*, Video Documentary, Mariah Karen Fulgosino, April 27, 2016.
11 Interview with Sigried Bangyay Rogers, *Sagad na ang Sagada: A Call for Responsible Tourism in Sagada, Mountain Province*, Video Documentary, Mariah Karen Fulgosino, April 27, 2016.

References

Antonio, J.Jr. (2014). *Handouts for the profiling and mapping of towns and cities in the Philippines*. Manila: National Commission for Culture and the Arts.
Department of Public Works and Highways. (2008). Strength and experience of bridging people and progress. *Department of Public Works and Highways Annual Report*, pp. 9–10.
Fulgosino, M.K. (2016). *Sagadna ang Sagada: A call for responsible tourism in Sagada, Mountain Province*. Video documentary, [online]. Available at: www.you tube.com/watch?v=exbS5g9pJjU [Accessed 27 Apr 2016].
Hung, K., Sirakaya-Turk, E. and Ingram, L.J. (2011). Testing the efficacy of an integrative model for community participation. *Journal of Travel Research*, 50(3), pp. 276–288. DOI:doi:10.1177/0047287510362781.
Richards, G. and Smith, M., eds. (2013). *The Routledge handbook of cultural tourism*. Oxford: Taylor and Francis.
Santiago, P. and Gulian, D. (2016). *Personal communication. Municipal Councilor of Sagada,*State of Tourism Management in Sagada, 8 Jun 2016. Log Cabin Restaurant, Sagada, Mountain Province.
Timothy, D.J. (2011). *Cultural heritage and tourism: An introduction*. Bristol, UK: Channel View Publications.

Timothy, D.J. and Tosun, C. (2003). Appropriate planning for tourism in destination communities: Participation, incremental growth and collaboration. In: Singh, S., Timothy, D.J. and Dowling, R.K., eds., *Tourism in destination communities.* Cambridge, MA: CABI, pp. 181–204.

Wikipedia.org. Kanakanaey people. In: *Wikipedia the Free Encyclopedia*, [online]. Available at: https://en.wikipedia.org/wiki/Kankanaey_people [Accessed 5 Feb 2016].

3 Native American communities and community development

The case of Navajo Nation

Christine N. Buzinde, Vanessa Vandever and Gyan Nyaupane

Introduction

Communities worldwide are constantly imagining unique, innovative, culturally relevant, economically equitable, and environmentally safe community development ideas (see Buzinde and Mair, 2016; Timothy, 2002; Richards and Hall, 2003). Numerous community development success stories abound, but so do the failures. Arguably, the best practices are often characterized by well-thought-out processes that harness the collaborative power and expertise of local leaders and organizations, as well as external agencies such as universities to accomplish goals of import to the community. If well-organized, the collaborative dynamics that characterize coalitions comprised of various community representatives and outside experts can foster empowerment for members of the partnership and contribute to capacity building. It is however important to note that bottom-up approaches to community development that are led by various local experts are likely to yield more sustaining outcomes in comparison to top-down approaches to development that have little or no local involvement (Buzinde, Kalavar and Melubo, 2014; Mair, Reid and George, 2005).

Scholars have highlighted ways in which Indigenous knowledge augurs well for development studies and environmental conservation (see Brokensha, Warren and Werner, 1980; Brush and Stabinsky, 1996). The focus of this research has generally been on the value and relevance of Indigenous knowledge (see Semali and Kincheloe, 2002); the development approaches that can be beneficial for Indigenous communities (see Briggs, 2008); and the creation of awareness about Indigenous issues particularly within policy-related contexts (see Lalonde, 1991). Tourism scholars have also contributed to this body of literature by addressing host and/or guest related issues (see Butler and Hinch, 2007; Dyer, Aberdeen and Schuler, 2003; Johnston, 2000; Smith, 1996). According to Agrawal (2002), this recent research on Indigenous knowledge has been paralleled by the "valorization of allied social and conceptual formations such as community, locality, and subalternity" (Agrawal, 2002, p. 287). Such developments have opened forums within which to learn from the traditionally silenced voices of the margins, particularly those of Indigenous groups (Spivak, 1988).

Scholars have also noted that the dominant perception of Indigenous culture during the colonial era fostered the dismissal of Indigenous knowledge by classifying (aspects of) it as inferior, static, simple, and primitive (Nakata, 2002). This ideological perspective has been successfully countered by burgeoning studies that showcase "the complexity and sophistication of [for instance] many Indigenous natural resources management systems" (Warren, 1996, p. 83). In fact, over the last few decades, scholars have indicated that there is a strong relationship between successful sustainable development projects and Indigenous knowledge (Warren, 1996). This finding has provided support for community approaches, such as community-based participatory research (CBPR). Such approaches regard Indigenous knowledge as "the basis for grassroots decision-making" processes that involve local agencies in problem identification and solution generation (Warren, 1996, p. 84). Furthermore, the solution generation "is based on Indigenous creativity leading to experimentation and innovations as well as the appraisal of knowledge and technologies introduced from other societies" (Warren, 1996, p. 84).

Warren (1996) implies that there are collaborative partnerships where members work together with the goal of addressing community concerns by utilizing various knowledge bases. This micro-level analysis highlights development that is driven by local agencies that examine and solve structural problems that might prevent or thwart community well-being. Grassroots-based initiatives are vital to the growth of any community, and the narratives that characterize their journey offer invaluable lessons for other communities. In fact, interest in Indigenous narratives have become widespread as is evidenced by the existence of ubiquitous databases that document Indigenous knowledge, and much of this knowledge is recorded so that it might be shared amongst communities worldwide (Agrawal, 2002).

This chapter draws on the example of Navajo Nation, a Native American Indigenous group that is actively working on reversing decades of abject poverty through collaborative planning processes that inform sustainable development plans that make a positive and respectful contribution to tourism development. This chapter also discusses the socio-political structural conditions that have thwarted community development for many decades. This discussion is followed by an account of local efforts to assemble a multi-agency coalition to assist in the creation of a development plan that accounts for various concerns articulated by residents. These are plans that seek to both protect and nurture Navajo communities while simultaneously providing the foundations upon which successful tourism endeavours can be built. The efforts undertaken by the coalition are discussed within the conceptual framework of collaborative planning and the allied concept CBPR, which has been utilized extensively within tourism contexts (see Koster, Baccar and Lemelin, 2012; Stewart and Draper, 2009). The aforementioned accounts are complemented with discussions on the nexus between collaborative planning and community empowerment. Although the Navajo project is still in its early stages, it is hoped that the processes outlined will be useful to communities that may want to pursue a similar trajectory.

Navajo Nation

Located in the southwest part of the United States in the state of Arizona, Navajo Nation is home to the majority of the Navajo tribe. Navajo Nation tribal lands are situated in the "northeast quarter of the state of Arizona, and spill over into New Mexico and Utah" (NNPRD, 2016). Navajo Nation is the largest tribe in the United States with approximately 300,000 people living on or off the reservation (Discover Navajo, 2016). A large portion of the 17 million acres of Navajo Nation land is under the protection of the Navajo Nation Parks and Recreation Department (NNPRD), and contains beautiful natural red rock formations in the park's repertoire of sites to visit (Jett, 2009). The (NNPRD), much like similar agencies elsewhere, is tasked with protecting and managing the natural landscape (NNPRD, 2016). Within Native American culture, complex conceptualizations of nature are intertwined with cultural and spiritual dimensions that explain the tangible and intangible aspects of the environment. Accordingly, parks and recreation agencies in such contexts adopt a holistic approach that accounts for the connections between natural, cultural, and spiritual elements in the management, economic development, and creation of tourism agendas for the parks system. This is not an easy task as the spiritual aspects of Indigenous landscapes can either enhance or thwart park agency management plans.

Navajo Nation land abuts the world-renowned Grand Canyon National Park. A key distinction as one compares the two parklands is that the former is inhabited whereas the latter is dedicated to preservation that does not value the coexistence of humans within natural habitats. Navajo Nation is certainly not unique in this aspect because Native peoples inhabit many parks and protected areas around the globe. Poignantly, experiences of residing within parks and protected areas are often coupled with experiences of struggles with land ownership and protection of intangible sacred sites. Like most Indigenous groups, the Navajos have a tumultuous history connected to their land. In 1864, the Navajos were forcibly removed and imprisoned in Bosque Redondo, New Mexico for four years (Discover Navajo, 2016; National Public Radio, 2005):

> 8,500 men, women, and children were forced to leave their homes ... Along the way ... Navajos died of starvation and exposure to the elements. Navajos signed the historic U.S. Navajo Treaty of 1868 [that] allowed [them] to return [home] (Crow Canyon Archeological Center, 2016).

The Navajos attribute their release and return to the land they currently inhabit to the staunch spiritual belief that their requests for freedom were answered (Emmett Kerley, Navajo Medicine man, personal communication). A sustained level of commitment and responsibility to protect the land has characterized the Navajo habitation since their release. However, in 1966, a land dispute between the Navajos and the Hopi, a Native American tribe whose land is surrounded by Navajo land, resulted in a federal moratorium on development in the northeast part of the reservation. This had a severe and detrimental impact on communities in the locale for the moratorium (referred to as the Bennett Freeze) prevented Navajo communities from pursuing *any* development in their homesteads, even basic improvements like running water or electricity were prohibited. This led to a mass migration of people to other parts of the reservation and an exodus off the reservation, but a select few community members remained and persevered despite all the hardships caused by the federal moratorium.

In 2007, under President Obama's administration, the US government lifted the development restrictions on the area; however, the reservation still exhibits extremely low quality of life. The American Community Survey (ACS) found that 36.76 percent of the Navajo population residing on the Navajo reservation lives below the poverty level. Within the former Bennett Freeze area the rates are even higher, making the former Bennett Freeze Navajos some of the world's poorest citizens. According to the 2009–2010 Navajo Nation Comprehensive Economic Development Strategy, the unemployment rate for this area increased over a seven-year period from 42.16 percent in 2001 to 50.52 percent in 2007 (NNCEDS, 2010). The results have been devastating as not only do most homes lack electricity and running water, but the Navajo also have limited access to infrastructure, schools, and economic activities (Phelps, 2010).

The parklands on the former Bennett Freeze area were open to visitors during the moratorium, but only the most basic amenities were provided due to the constraints faced by the community. A number of tourists drive through Navajo Nation on their way to the Grand Canyon National Park, but the absence of established tourism products on the reservation means that the community has not been able to capitalize on this traffic, particularly in the (economically) underdeveloped parts of the reservation. According to the economic study conducted by C.B. Richard Ellis, Navajo Nation attracted 2.5 million visitors in 2002, but due to a scarcity of available hotel rooms, most visitors went elsewhere to spend money on accommodation, food, and shopping.

The lifting of the moratorium by President Obama's administration is to be celebrated, but it has led to some unforeseen circumstances. The community is currently facing an imminent threat from outside investors who want to impose development plans for tourism that exclude community involvement, and would have a negative impact on the cultural and spiritual landscape (Morales, 2014). Notably, most of the development plans proposed by outside investors require spiritually, culturally, and environmentally sensitive space and resources that are under the jurisdiction of the NNPRD. The NNPRD's goal is to preserve and protect the parklands for present and future generations, but it lacks the legal authority to prohibit the development that is perceived to be harmful to the natural, cultural, social, and spiritual fabric of the land. In decades past, the NNPRD had little need for legally binding jurisdictions, particularly in the former Bennett Freeze area. This was in part because the community was united against outsiders, whose previous contact had caused the community decades of social dislocation and abuse, and with the moratorium there was no imminent threat to local resources as any kind of infrastructure development was prohibited. With time, the traumatic history experienced by the community has partially faded in the minds of some members of the current generation. This has allowed them to envisage perhaps a new relationship with outsiders as visiting tourists, which may provide opportunities for the local community to share and educate tourists about Navajo spiritual beliefs that are associated with the natural landscape for which they are the custodians.

However, as the community is still experiencing abject poverty and is vulnerable to outside tourism investors who, lured by the lifting of the moratorium and the pristine natural and relatively underdeveloped environment, are pledging to end poverty in the area. These types of pressures have forced the NNPRD to begin work on creating a long-term culturally and ecologically sensitive development plan that is legally binding. The NNPRD refers to this development blueprint as the general management plan (GMP).

Other historical pressures on the community include memories associated with the impacts of decades of discriminatory federal policies (that is relocation, allotment, assimilation, termination, etc.) and the forceful enrollment of native children into Christian boarding schools, which stripped generations of tribal communities of their culture. The Navajo community is thus looking for healing through cultural sovereignty and decolonization. The GMP coalition and similar projects are enabling the Navajo community to harness, with alacrity and pride, the Indigenous knowledge that many members of earlier generations depended on for survival and community well-being. Furthermore, through the involvement of locals, the coalition aims to document the shared Indigenous knowledge, which will assist in empowering and educating the local community. The subsequent section presents a summary of how the NNPRD is approaching plans to create the GMP. The project is in motion, so even though the final outcomes are not yet available, the process is indicative of the many ways in which Indigenous communities are acting to instigate the change necessary to enhance long-term well-being on the reservation.

Collaborative planning

According to Gunn (1988) all planning related to tourism and economic development has to include collaboration with a variety of related organizations in order to be successful. Collaboration between various private, public, and/or non-profit organizations is a challenging (in part due to competing ideologies) but necessary step for all planners (Jamal and Getz, 1995; Hall, 1999). Within tourism, parks, and recreation contexts, collaborations between private and public organizations are increasingly prevalent (see Dredge, 2006; Gill and Williams, 1994; Ritchie, 1993). Similarly, in the case of Navajo Nation, a group of community leaders and community agencies assembled by the NNPRD came together to discuss the GMP and the ways in which the natural and cultural landscape could be protected and preserved for future generations. They also discussed how the natural assets of the community and its land could be managed to draw revenue from tourists while at the same time enabling those tourists to contribute to the continuing protection of the land. The group of convened leaders did not want the GMP to mirror plans created by other communities. Rather they wanted to develop a plan that drew on local Indigenous knowledge; respected local cultural beliefs; protected tangible and intangible cultural and natural community assets; incorporated an Indigenously informed approach to sustainability; and included the active involvement of locals. Armed with this philosophy the group leaders collabo-rated with the local state university (Arizona State University – School of Community Resources and Development) to secure a neutral player with expertise that was complementary to that of the community leaders. This collaboration represents an important multi-agency partnership that harnesses a broad range of expertise to aid in the creation and implementation of community initiatives (see Wolff, 1992).

Studies about community development indicate that there are three key functions enacted by community partnerships: creative collaborative capacity, building community capacity, and fostering change at the local level. *Creative collaborative capacity* is fostered amongst members of the partnership through a collaboratively devised project that aims to address a common goal (Foster-Fishman, et al. 2001). In the case of the NNPRD, the goal is to create a GMP that will act as the blueprint for development. *Building community*

Figure 3.1 GMP strategic planning meeting
Photo by Vanessa Vandever

capacity is accomplished through multi-agency partnerships, which strengthen the community's ability to pool resources to more effectively respond to social needs (Fawcett et al., 1995). For instance, the GMP coalition comprises a variety of government entities and non-profit organizations, including DinéHózhó, and various departments under the Navajo Nation Department of Natural Resources (NNDNR) (including the Historic Preservation Department, Fish and Wildlife Department, and the Parks and Recreation Department).

All partners who comprise the coalition (that is, a local institution of higher education and the various Navajo agencies) share resources (that is staff, funds, space) to facilitate the progression of the initiative. Given their geographical scope, which specifically delimits the focus on a local community, community coalitions are better poised, in comparison to external (to the community) agencies, to *foster change at the local level* (Fawcett et al., 1995; Wolff, 2001). Members of multi-agency partnerships are often local residents representing the various strata of the community as well as professional and grassroots agencies. In the GMP coalition, NNPRD and NNDNR are professional agencies, whereas DinéHózhó, a low-profit, limited liability company – L3C, is a grassroots agency. Members of the aforementioned agencies share a local lived experience that informs their understanding of community issues and this motivates them to contribute to the collective cause. These community coalitions are useful because they allow members to share tasks, responsibility, risks, expenses, and knowledge while jointly crafting community initiatives (Gunn, 1988; Fawcett et al., 1995).

Community-based participatory research

In order for the goals of the coalition to be accomplished according to the philosophical principles of the group, various research endeavors have to be undertaken to inform the social, legal, cultural, environmental, and economic dimensions of the GMP. Community-based participatory research (CBPR) is relevant to collaborative planning because of the premise that all research pivots on the relationship between research partners and collectively identified objectives for social transformation (Minkler and Wallerstein, 2003). The research endeavors that have and will continue to be undertaken by the GMP coalition are fashioned on the principles of CBPR, which is defined as a:

> collaborative approach to research, [that] equitably involves all partners in the research process and recognizes the unique strengths that each brings. CBPR begins with a research topic of importance to the community with the aim of combining knowledge and action for social change to improve community [well-being] (Minkler and Wallerstein, 2003, p. 4).

The GMP coalition needs to develop a legally binding development plan for the vast land managed by the NNPRD in order to inform future economic development; preservation/conservation efforts; and protect sacred sites and local homesteads. A well-crafted and legally binding GMP devised through a process that involves local residents is perceived as a necessary tool to enhance quality of life, particularly in the former Bennett Freeze part of the reservation. The involvement of local residents in the creation of plans for tourism and economic development can contribute to the enhancement of various community-related dimensions, especially if locals with sufficient expertise, power, and resources are recruited for the planning process (Mair and Reid, 2007; Scheyvens, 2003; Taylor, 1995).

There are a number of features in CBPR that have to be respected by members of any coalition. Israel et al. (2003) describe four key CBPR conceptions:

> (**a**) genuine partnership means *co-learning* (academic and community partners), (**b**) research efforts include *capacity building* (conducting the research ... [and] a commitment to training community members in research), (**c**) *findings and knowledge should benefit all partners*, and (**d**) CBPR involves *long-term commitments* to effectively reduce disparities (Israel et al., 2003 as cited by Wallerstein and Duran, 2006, p. 312).

The collaboration with NNPRD entails sharing knowledge, and allowing for *co-learning* to take place within a shared and safe space. The initial GMP coalition meetings involved a lot of co-learning as well as several site visits or reconnaissance trips (see Figure 3.2). First and foremost, members of the coalition acquainted themselves with the charters of each partnering organization in order to understand points of convergence that could be capitalized on. Other co-learning opportunities occurred during town hall meetings, when key development issues were canvased and residents were informed about the GMP coalition and its goals. A series of meetings were also held with members of the coalition to devise a mission and vision for the GMP, as well as to create an Indigenously informed definition of sustainability. A local medicine man and DinéHózhó representative, Mr. Emmett Kerley (in collaboration with Vanessa Vandever, one of the authors of this chapter), championed efforts towards this end, and he drew on cultural practices and local language to devise what the team unanimously regarded as a culturally appropriate and endogenously defined concept of sustainability. It is important to note that an articulation of sustainability that draws on Indigenous knowledge systems is an important process in decolonizing knowledge related to conservation (Simpson, 2004). During this process, all members of the coalition obtained new knowledge about aspects of the culture.

In many ways, the opportunities for knowledge exchange described above *contribute to capacity building*. The concept of capacity building in the NNPRD collaboration is encapsulated in the entire process of creating the GMP. For instance, there are five key stages to the GMP and each entails knowledge exchange between the NNPRD and various agencies. The four stages include environmental, economic, social, legal, and cultural aspects. Knowledge exchange at each stage will encourage the parties to broaden their

Figure 3.2 Co-learning through site visitation
Photo by Vanessa Vandever

respective areas of expertise as they collectively work on the GMP. Firstly, the focus on the environmental aspects will involve collaboration between a team comprised of Navajo Nation Natural Resources staff and NNPRD to obtain information on the geological make-up, and to establish an inventory of the plants and the wildlife within the region in question. Drawing on the data, the team will create a GIS mapping system of the area, and will determine the ecological carrying capacity of the land. A land use plan will also be created to determine zoning for various purposes, including flight zone areas; road and infrastructural development; trail development; protected areas; and tribal sacred areas, to name a few. The group will also account for climate change and address and implement a sustainable course of action.

Secondly, the focus on economic aspects will entail working with economists to examine the financial impact of the parks system on the community. They will seek to analyze and remedy any economic weaknesses, explore future revenue opportunities, and document any threats (economic and otherwise) that may affect the parks system. Thirdly, the social component will require parks officials to examine different uses of the parks' spaces and how the various uses align with existing zoning regulations. There are uses of the parks that will require zoning regulations, including ceremonial, agricultural, grazing, revenue generation, residential, and park infrastructure. There will also be an analysis of the function of existing zoning, and a needs-based assessment for future zoning regulations. An assessment of the permit system used by

NNPRD will be guided by best practices so that weaknesses can be rectified and transformed into strengths. Additionally, the various concessionaires that operate on parklands will be documented with the goal of aligning the spaces within which they operate with existing or new zoning regulations.

Fourth is the crucial legal aspect that will grant the community the legal authority to protect itself from outside threats, and will offer a legal blueprint for any future development ideas. Existing policies and regulations will be examined and updated, and criteria for allowing use or disuse of the landscape will be formulated. The long-term goal of this focus will be to ensure that the GMP is legally binding and recognized on and off the reservation by all national legal agencies. Equally important are designs for park protection and enforcement, as well as the mapping of all zones (that is, places where NNPRD will have full authority and places for co-management). All the above inter-agency exchanges incorporate training of NNPRD staff for capacity building purposes.

Last but not least, is the cultural dimension in which the goal is to document the life stories, memories, personal histories, attitudes, and values of residents residing in the former Bennett Freeze area. The process of collecting and documenting narratives from community members about cultural and natural resources will be undertaken via interviews and focus groups. The information will be used to inform economic and social development decisions within the framework of *cultural mapping*. Residents' life stories will serve various purposes. Understanding the cultural meanings residents associate with their natural landscape will inform processes to zone the area in a culturally appropriate manner. Residents' narratives will help to identify tangible and intangible sacred areas that should be protected; areas appropriate for foreign visitation and tourism; areas for private residential use; and areas for environmental conservation. Residents' life stories will also enrich efforts to create a world class Navajo Nation Parks system. With residents' approval, some of the documented narratives will be included in interpretive materials (signs, docent narratives, fliers, and audio files for visitors) showcased in Navajo parks to inform visitors about the land and local experiences related to resistance, suffering, innovation, and triumph. Interpretive materials of this nature will add a level of authenticity, which is generally valued by tourists, particularly those who frequent Native American parks (see Budruk et al., 2008). Prior to conducting interviews and focus groups, efforts will be undertaken to host town hall meetings with the goal of creating community awareness about the cultural mapping study as well as the larger GMP project.

The hope is that this activity will enable the community to become more knowledgeable about the GMP, and enable them to be cognizant of their collective responsibilities in contributing to its creation. In addition to town hall meetings, a column will be written in the local newspaper, a promotional piece will be featured on the local radio station, a link will be placed on the NNPRD Facebook page, and posters will be strategically placed at various locations on the reservation to raise further awareness. There is therefore a level of *capacity building* that organically emerges from the collaborative processes at the environmental, economic, social, legal, and cultural stages.

The *findings and knowledge* that emerge out of the process are of benefit to the coalition because they apply directly to the objectives of the GMP, which is to benefit the development process in the former Bennett Freeze area. One of the biggest dangers on the Navajo reservation is that many projects are initiated by outside investors with little or no involvement from locals, and are later abandoned by the investors (Bidtah Becker, Director NNNRD, personal correspondence). By contrast, the GMP coalition is led by Navajo agencies that have a vested interest in creating a *long-term commitment* to a community development plan that is sustainable, culturally appropriate, and economically innovative. Hence, the coalition espouses the CBPR assumptions proposed by Israel et al. (2003) to yield locally informed and use-inspired research directives that can be used in the creation of a sustainable development plan for the NNPRD.

Empowerment and collaborative planning

As illustrated earlier in this chapter, the concept of community-based participatory research (CBPR) is essential to discussions of empowerment and collaborative planning. This is because CBPR draws on community partnerships to foster co-learning amongst members; build community capacity; create mutually beneficial knowledge; and devise long-term plans that reduce disparities within communities (Israel et al., 2003). All of these factors can cultivate elements of empowerment (Laverack and Wallerstein, 2001).

Empowerment theory is in fact vital to discussions around community coalitions that are aimed at enhancing well-being through community capacity building. Empowerment theory explores the process of gaining influence over the conditions that matter to people who share communities, experiences, and concerns (Fawcett et al., 1995). According to Perkins and Zimmerman (1995), at "the community level, empowerment refers to collective action to improve the quality of life in a community and to the connections among community organizations" (p. 571). In the context of tourism, community empowerment allows for "a relatively equitable distribution of local benefits in terms of revenues and employment" and results in "a relatively high degree of control by local residents for administering tourism services" (Mitchell and Reid, 2001, p. 115).

Community empowerment can be regarded as a process or an outcome (Laverack and Wallerstein, 2001; Perkins and Zimmerman, 1995). When defined as an outcome, community empowerment is regarded as "an interplay between individuals and community change with a long time-frame, at least in terms of significant social and political change, typically taking seven years or longer" (Laverack and Wallerstein, 2001, p. 181). In the context of the Navajo GMP project one outcome is the implementation of policies at the Navajo Nation level and/or the federal level that support the emergent development plan. When defined as a process, community empowerment is viewed as a dynamic course in which some coalition members may experience empowerment during the planning process (Rappaport, 1987). Furthermore, members of the coalition:

> gain power as a result of a change in control over decisions in the inter-personal relationships that influence their lives ... [they] achieve these outcomes by seizing or gaining power through a process of identifying problems, finding solutions to these problems and then implementing actions to solve them (Laverack and Wallerstein, 2001, p. 182).

Drawing on theories of community health and community development, Fawcett et al. (1995) developed a framework that explores the nexus between empowerment theories and community coalitions. The framework entails five concurrent steps, is non-linear, and enables the flexibility required to meet complex challenges that communities and partnerships encounter. The various dimensions entailed in the model are interconnected and are part of the same dynamic. The framework is premised on the idea that members are motivated to join a coalition in direct response to pressing community issues. Accordingly, partnership endeavors undertaken on behalf of the community foster a sense of empowerment. The exchange of knowledge from various partner-ships also leads to skill development and capacity building which directly and indirectly contributes to individual and community empowerment. However, to ensure sustained empowerment throughout the planning process, the follow-ing five dimensions, (developed by Fawcett et al. (1995)) need to be accounted for in the coalition process, namely: *collaborative planning, community action, community change, community capacity,* and *outcomes, adaptation, renewal and institutionalization.*

Collaborative planning is one of the functions mentioned earlier in this chapter that coalitions engage in to create plans focused on enhancing commu-nity well-being. Much like the GMP partnership, members of the partnership represent diverse segments of the population and are thus able to advocate for changes needed by different constituents. Collaborative planning entails the use of various assessment tools that aid in obtaining information about com-munity concerns (Fawcett et al., 1995). In the case of the GMP partnership, town hall meetings were held in various communities to discern what devel-opment issues, tourism related and otherwise, were of concern to various constituents. Expert panels were also hosted to gain insight at the manage-ment level of development concerns. This information then informed the tasks that the partnership decided to pursue. Some emergent issues were related to vendors requiring more space and updated facilities; responses to trespassing by tourists onto private areas; the need for a local museum and other ame-nities to draw tourist dollars; and the need for locally managed development. All of these issues are relevant to the GMP and its development plans. Efforts were also undertaken to identify the mission and vision that governs the group's efforts, as well as identifying the resources needed to help bring the project to fruition. Although not as yet empirically explored, one can say that the opportunities for co-learning during the collaborative planning process cultivated a sense of empowerment amongst members of the coalition.

Community action refers to the various activities engaged in by members of the partnership in pursuit of the collectively defined goals identified by the coalition (Fawcett et al., 1995). With regard to this dimension, the GMP partnership will document all efforts and accomplishments brought about as a result of the collaborative actions. This documentation will allow for the identification of best practices that can be applied to other parts of the reservation. One of the key community actions proposed by the GMP coalition is the erection of interpretive signs strategically placed on trails within the park to tell the story of the land according to local residents. It can be argued that such a process will foster a sense of empowerment amongst locals because it will demonstrate how their lived experiences are vital to the understanding of the land. It also cultivates a sense of empowerment amongst members of the research team who gain unique insights into the diverse narratives associated with the land.

Community change refers to the outcomes generated by members of the partnerships (Fawcett et al., 1995). Some desirable community changes that will be welcomed by the GMP coalition after sharing the results of the project with the community might include: increased local awareness of the park's boundaries, mission, and charter; increased visitation to the park by tourists; increased commitment by locals to protecting the land; and, increased submission of competitive, culturally appropriate, and sustainability-influenced development proposals. The coalition will have to monitor changes and where they occurred, and whether they were a direct or indirect result of the actions of the group (see Fawcett et al., 1995). Such findings, if favorable, are bound to embolden members of the coalition an inspire them to continue working on the collective goals.

Community capacity and outcomes focuses on the long-term and highlights the community's ability to realize its own goals (Fawcett et al., 1995). The GMP coalition can address this dimension by evaluating whether actions undertaken to enhance the community's capacity to create a development plan were effective. If the intended actions were not effective, an alternative course of action needs to be identified and pursued. Recognition that community issues are complex and that they require flexible and amendable plans will allow the coalition to deal with any unfavorable outcomes that may arise. It can be argued that working together through the successes and the failures also adds an enabling facet to the collaborative process. The last dimension, *adaptation, renewal and institutionalization* refers to the partnership's ability to redefine its goals in the wake of new community related concerns while mediating negative effects (Fawcett et al., 1995). In the case of the GMP partnership this will be realized by ascertaining whether the group was successful in bringing the initiative to fruition. This also requires the group to disseminate information to the community relaying the results of the initiative. The community will thus be able to see how its input is connected to the actions and outcomes of the coalition, which will hopefully benefit the community at large.

Hence, this framework will allow for the emergence of what Fawcett et al. (1995) referred to as enabling circumstances resulting from collaborative planning processes that aim to enhance community well-being.

Conclusion

Community development initiatives are important endeavors that can enhance community well-being. To accomplish such goals requires a strategic task force that can work through a collaborative agenda that addresses local issues, involves local residents, and draws on shared resources through a multi-agency coalition. Research is utilized to aid the multi-agency coalition in making informed decisions. In the case study described in this chapter, research activities were governed by a community-based participatory research (CBPR) approach because its philosophical foundations resonate with the values of the coalition. Furthermore, the collaborative process engaged in by the GMP coalition provides enabling circumstances that encourage members to take ownership of the process and to continue devising innovative, culturally appropriate, locally informed, and sustainable approaches for community development. The GMP coalition is still navigating the early stages of planning, but the hope is that the plans collaboratively devised by the coalition will be informative for other communities that are contemplating similar tourism and economic development-related trajectories.

References

Agrawal, A. (2002). Indigenous knowledge and the politics of classification. *International Social Science Journal*, 54(173), pp. 287–297.

Becker, B. (2015). Personal correspondence with Bidtah Becker, Director of Navajo Nation Division of Natural Resources.

Borrup, T. (2012). Five ways arts projects can improve struggling communities. *Projects for public spaces*. [online]. Available at: www.pps.org/reference/artsprojects/ [Accessed 1 Aug 2015].

Briggs, J. (2008). Indigenous knowledge and development. In: Desai, V. and Potter, R.B., eds., *The companion to development studies*. London: Hodder Education, pp. 107–111.

Brokensha, D., Warren, D. and Werner, O., eds. (1980). *Indigenous knowledge systems and development*. Lanham, MD: University Press of America.

Brush, S. and Stabinsky, D., eds. (1996). *Valuing local knowledge: Indigenous people and intellectual property rights*. Washington, DC: Island Press.

Budruk, M., White, D.D., Wodrich, J.A. and Van Riper, C.J. (2008). Connecting visitors to people and place: Visitors' perceptions of authenticity at Canyon de Chelly National Monument, Arizona. *Journal of Heritage Tourism*, 3(3), pp. 185–202.

Butler, R. and Hinch, T. (2007). *Tourism and indigenous peoples: Issues and implications.* London: Routledge.

Buzinde, C.N., Kalavar, J.M. and Melubo, K. (2014). Tourism and community well-being: The case of the Maasai in Tanzania. *Annals of Tourism Research*, 44, pp. 20–35.

Buzinde, C.N. and Mair, H. (2016). Tourism and community empowerment: The case of the Tanzanian Maasai community. In: Sharpe, E., Mair, H. and Yuen, F., eds., *Community development: Application for leisure, sport and tourism.* State College, PA: Venture Publishing, pp. 193–200.

Crow Canyon ArcheologicalCenter. (2016). Peoples of the Mesa Verde region. [online]. Available at: www.crowcanyon.org/EducationProducts/peoples_mesa_verde/his toric_long_walk.asp [Accessed 1 Aug 2016].

Discover Navajo. (2016). [online]. Available at: www.discovernavajo.com/. [Accessed 1 Aug 2016].

Dredge, D. (2006). Policy networks and the local organisation of tourism. *Tourism Management*, 27(2), pp. 269–280.

Dyer, P., Aberdeen, L. and Schuler, S. (2003). Tourism impacts on an Australian indigenous community: A Djabugay case study. *Tourism Management*, 24(1), pp. 83–95. [Accessed 1 Aug 2016].

Ellis, C.B.R. (2003). *Economic impact study.* Report submitted to Navajo Nation. Window Rock, AZ.

Fawcett, S.B., Paine-Andrews, A., Francisco, V.T., Schultz, J.A., Richter, K.P., Lewis, R.K., Williams, E.L., Harris, K.J., Berkley, J.Y., Fisher, J.L. and Lopez, C.M. (1995). Using empowerment theory in collaborative partnerships for community health and development. *American Journal of Community Psychology*, 23(5), pp. 677–697.

Foster-Fishman, P.G., Berkowitz, S.L., Lounsbury, D.W., Jacobson, S. and Allen, N.A. (2001). Building collaborative capacity in community coalitions: A review of the integrative framework. *American Journal of Community Psychology*, 29(2), pp. 241–261.

Gill, A. and Williams, P. (1994). Managing growth in mountain tourism communities. *Tourism Management*, 15(3), pp. 212–220.

Gunn, C. (1998). *Tourism planning,* 2nd ed. New York: Taylor & Francis.

Hall, C.M. (1999). Rethinking collaboration and partnership: A public policy perspective. *Journal of Sustainable Tourism*, 7(3–4), pp. 274–289.

Israel, B.A., Schulz, A.J., Parker, E.A., Becker, A.B., Allen, A.J. and Guzman, R. (2003). Critical issues in developing and following community based participatory research principles. In: Minkler, M. and Wallerstein, N., eds., *Community-based participatory research for health.* San Francisco: Jossey-Bass, pp. 53–76.

Jamal, T.B. and Getz, D. (1995). Collaboration theory and community tourism planning. *Annals of Tourism Research*, 22(1), pp. 186–204.

Jett, S.C. (1990). Culture and tourism in the Navajo country. *Journal of Cultural Geography*, 11(1), pp. 85–107.

Johnston, A. (2000). Indigenous peoples and ecotourism: Bringing indigenous knowledge and rights into the sustainability equation. *Tourism Recreation Research*, 25(2), pp. 89–96.

Koster, R., Baccar, K. and Lemelin, R.H. (2012). Moving from research ON, to research WITH and FOR Indigenous communities: A critical reflection on community-based participatory research. *The Canadian Geographer/Le Géographe canadien*, 56(2), pp.195–210.

Lalonde, A. (1991). *African traditional ecological knowledge: A preliminary investigation of indigenous or traditional ecological knowledge and associated sustainable management practices in Africa and relevance to CIDA's environmental policy.* Hull: CIDA.

Laverack, G. and Wallerstein, N. (2001). Measuring community empowerment: A fresh look at organizational domains. *Health Promotion International*, 16(2), pp. 179–185.

Mair, H. and Reid, D.G. (2007). Tourism and community development vs. tourism for community development: Conceptualizing planning as power, knowledge, and control. *Leisure/Loisir*, 31(2), pp. 403–425.

Mair, H., Reid, D.G. and George, W. (2005). Globalisation, rural tourism and community power. In: Hall, D., Kirkpatrick, I. and Mitchell, M., eds., *Rural tourism and sustainable business.* Clevedon, UK: Channel View Publications, pp.165–179.

Minkler, M. and Wallerstein, N., eds. (2003). *Community based participatory research in health.* San Francisco: Jossey-Bass.

Mitchell, R.E. and Reid, D.G. (2001). Community integration: Island tourism in Peru. *Annals of Tourism Research*, 28(1), pp. 113–139.

Morales, L. (2014). Proposed gondola for the Grand Canyon's rim has community on edge. Transcript for National Public Radio. [online]. Available at: www.npr.org/2014/08/04/337144825/proposed-gondola-for-grand-canyons-rim-has-community-on-edge [Accessed 1 Aug 2016].

Nakata, M. (2002). Indigenous knowledge and the cultural interface. In: Hickling-Hudson, A., Matthews, J. and Woods, A., eds., *Disrupting preconceptions: Post-colonialism and education.* Queensland: EContent Management Pty Ltd, pp. 19–38.

National Public Radio. (2005). The Navajo Nation's own trail of tears. [online]. Available at: www.npr.org/2005/06/15/4703136/the-navajo-nation-s-own-trail-of-tears [Accessed 5 Aug 2016].

NNCEDS – Navajo Nation Comprehensive Economic Development Strategy. (2010). [online]. Available at: www.navajobusiness.com/pdf/CEDS/CED_NN_Final_09_10.pdf. [Accessed 1 Aug 2016].

NNPRD – Navajo Nation Parks and Recreation Department. (2016). [online]. Available at: http://navajonationparks.org/about-us/ [Accessed 1 Aug 2016].

OHP – Office of Health Policy. (2010). Developing a conceptual framework to access the sustainability of community coalition post-federal funding. Washington, DC: US Department of Health and Human Services, Office of the Assistant Secretary for Planning and Evaluation. [online]. Available at: https://aspe.hhs.gov/report/literature-review-developing-conceptual-framework-assess-sustainability-community-coalitions-post-federal-funding [Accessed 1 Aug 2016].

Perkins, D.D. and Zimmerman, M.A. (1995). Empowerment theory, research, and application. *American Journal of Community Psychology*, 23(5), pp. 569–579.

Phelps, W. (2010). Written testimony of Navajo Nation Council Delegate Walter Phelps. [online]. Available at: http://docs.house.gov/meetings/AP/AP06/20140407/101764/HHRG-113-AP06-Wstate-PhelpsW-20140407.pdf. [Accessed 1 Aug 2016].

Rappaport, J. (1987). Terms of empowerment/exemplars of prevention: Toward a theory of community psychology. *American Journal of Community Psychology*, 15(2), pp. 121–147.

Richards, G. and Hall, D. (2003). *Tourism and sustainable community development.* London and New York: Routledge Press.

Ritchie, J.B. (1993). Crafting a destination vision: Putting the concept of resident responsive tourism into practice. *Tourism Management*, 14(5), pp. 379–389.

Scheyvens, R. (2003). Appropriate planning for tourism in destination communities: participation, incremental growth and collaboration, In: Singh, S., Timothy, D.J. and Dowling, R.K., eds., *Tourism in destination communities.* Cambridge, MA: CABI, pp. 181–204.

Semali, L. M. and Kincheloe, J.L. (2002). *What is indigenous knowledge? Voices from the academy.* New York: Routledge.

Simpson, L.R. (2004). Anticolonial strategies for the recovery and maintenance of Indigenous knowledge. *The American Indian Quarterly*, 28(3), pp. 373–384.

Smith, V.L. (1996). The four Hs of tribal tourism: Acoma: A pueblo case study. *Progress in Tourism and Hospitality Research*, 2(3–4), pp. 295–306.

Spivak, G.C. (1988). Can the subaltern speak? In: Nelson, C. and Grossberg, L., eds. *Marxism and the interpretation of culture.* Basingstoke: Macmillan Education, pp. 271–313.

Stewart, E.J. and Draper, D. (2009). Reporting back research findings: A case study of community-based tourism research in northern Canada. *Journal of Ecotourism*, 8(2), pp.128–143.

Taylor, G. (1995). The community approach: does it really work? *Tourism Management*, 16(7), pp. 487–489.

Timothy, D.J. (2002). Tourism and community development issues. In: Sharpley, R. and Telfer, D.J., eds., *Tourism and development: Concepts and issues*, Clevedon, UK: Channel View Publications, pp. 149–164.

Wallerstein, N.B. and Duran, B. (2006). Using community-based participatory research to address health disparities. *Health Promotion Practice*, 7(3), pp. 312–323.

Warren, D.M. (1996). Indigenous knowledge, biodiversity conservation and development: A Keynote Address. In: Bennun, L., Aman, R.A. and Crafter, S.A., eds., *Conservation of biodiversity in Africa: Local initiatives and institutional roles.* Nairobi: Center for Biodiversity, National Museum of Kenya.

Wolff, T. (1992). *Coalition building: One path to empowered communities.* Amherst, MA: Community Partners.

Wolff, T. (2001). Community coalition building: Contemporary practice and research: Introduction. *American Journal of Community Psychology*, 29(2), pp. 165–172.

Zimmerman, M.A. (1995). Psychological empowerment: Issues and illustrations. *American Journal of Community Psychology*, 23, pp. 581–599.

Part II

The cultural tourist, social media and self-exploration

4 Investigating the role of virtual peer support in Asian youth tourism

Hilary du Cros

Introduction

This current investigation grew out of an interest in how social media platforms, such as travel forums and Facebook, influence the travel decision-making of young independent travellers in Asia. It is part of a larger study where research looks at how travel influences greater self-awareness and self-improvement and how tourists can become more aware of these travel impacts. This chapter, however, is principally concerned with how this knowledge is shared virtually, and the nature of virtual peer support that enhances the experience of novice travel for Asian youth tourists to Hong Kong. It will explore relevant theoretical and methodological avenues before outlining the study and its results in regard to travel decision-making and virtual communities.

Literature review

Decision-making theory

A review of tourism decision-making theory is useful in order to shed light on how tourists make decisions and what role peer virtual support is likely to have in the process. At its most basic level, a decision is the selection of an action from two or more alternatives. That presumes that two or more alternatives must be available.

It is important for this study to situate decision-making theories in relation to self-awareness and self-interest (sometimes even to the point of narcissism). This is becoming increasingly vital for tourism studies as tourists are becoming co-producers of some experiences (Sigala, Christou and Gretzel, 2012), particularly as we are increasingly living in an experience economy (Pine and Gilmore, 1999). Tourism services are seen as high-risk purchases, because they are a type of intangible experiential product (Kotler, Bowen and Makens, 2010), and they cannot be evaluated before their consumption. Costs involved in consumption and the perceived risk of dissatisfaction have meant that some tourists have become more aware of their needs and invest in their capacity to co-produce the experience they desire.

Meanwhile, two models of likely decision-making behaviour for tourism experiences are outlined here: Sirakaya and Woodside (2005) and Chen, Hsu and Chou (2003). Both studies have been questioned in relation to their efficacy for understanding peer virtual support in decision-making. The logical seven-step process envisaged by Sirakaya and Woodside (2005) is based on the presumption that a decision will be made in an orderly fashion, and is mainly based on the cognitive aspects of personal psychological perspectives. It avoids choice set-modeling used by some researchers because of its tendency to become inflexible and monolithic once initial choice-sets have been processed. Alternatively, Chen et al.'s (2003) work discovered four mutually exclusive tourist market segments in relation to how decision-making was undertaken:

- Pundit tourists – mostly free and independent travellers who are likely to recommend their decisions to others and will use the Internet for future trip planning
- Individualistic tourists, who are similar to pundits, except they do not use the Internet for planning
- Negative/neutral recommenders, who do not offer a positive report of their trip experiences (Internet or e-WOM)
- Those that have visited a 'must see' destination, but state they were dissatisfied with the experience

The first and the third segments may have the most relevance to this study given they are likely to be the highest users of the Internet as a medium of communication. What also needs to be ascertained is whether additional segments have developed since Chen et al.'s work in 2003, and what influence more acknowledged forms of e-WOM (e-Word of Mouth) are having on group decision-making and virtual peer support. The theories listed above have tended to focus on an individual unaffected by interaction with other individuals, before, during and after decisions. This is particularly problematic for studies of youth tourism where decision-making is likely to have a greater social context with both real world and virtual aspects.

e-WOM and virtual peer support studies

One of the earliest tourism studies that comprehensively examines interpersonal influence and e-WOM is that by Litvin, Goldsmith and Pan (2006). This provides a conceptual model including sources, mediating variables, and motivations for contributing and seeking e-WOM. Litvin et al. (2006) define e-WOM as "all informal communications directed at consumers through Internet-based technology related to the usage or characteristics of particular good and services, or their sellers" (p. 461). It has become an important issue for digital marketers who are seeking more understanding of the new dynamics of consumer-to-consumer (C2C) and business-to-consumer (B2C) practices (Kotler et al., 2010). Hence, the definition provided by Litvin et al. includes communication between producers and consumers (B2C), as well as those between consumers (C2C), as both integral parts of the e-WOM flow. They also encouraged future researchers to measure the dynamics created by e-WOM, and its implications for the cognitive, affective behaviour of travellers. When following this trend, this book chapter is principally concerned with C2C.

Studies have also been carried out that demonstrate that tourists' main concerns are initially the functional and practical aspects of employing e-WOM (e.g. De Bruyn and Lilien, 2008). That is, there is an interest in what information e-consumers can access and how easily they can access it via the Internet and websites, which is integral to how much e-WOM is utilized. Researchers have also deeply analysed factors that influence travel decisions and what were the most trusted e-WOM sources. Trust in other peer community members has been found to be a significant mediator for recipients of e-WOM (Xiang and Gretzel, 2010; Yoo and Gretzel, 2010; Yeh and Choi, 2011). Leung et al. (2013) found that consumers generally used social media during the research phase of their travel planning process; and trustworthiness is a key aspect in forming their decisions when using information from social media. The two main methodologies that have been used in the past for understanding e-WOM are either quantitative (Sotiriadis and van Zyl, 2013; Leung et al., 2013) or qualitative (Jimura, 2011; Martin and Woodside, 2011).

The main aim of Sotiriadis and van Zyl's (2013) study was to investigate the way users of one kind of social media (Twitter) employ e-WOM to make decisions about what tourism services to purchase, as well as the factors influencing the use of information retrieved from this social media (SM). The study combined two challenging issues: (i) the need to explore tourism services with a high degree of involvement for the purchase decision-making process within a digital environment; and (ii) the increasing popularity and expansion of Twitter indicating that it could be a form of SM that will provide an ongoing influence.

Sotiriadis and van Zyl's (2013) generated a series of hypotheses based on the key findings of available tourism literature and applied a quantitative methodology to test whether the hypotheses were valid or not. Their rationale was that a quantitative research methodology would allow for greater accuracy of results, and could summarize vast sources of information that assist in facilitating comparisons across categories and over time. The categories comprised: trust, messages' attitude (positive/negative), participation, intention to use e-WOM in decision-making, motivation, opportunity, ability, customer-to-customer know-how exchange, overall consumer value, loyalty and interpersonal/person-group connectivity. Findings once again confirmed that source reliability, expertise and trust were key factors. Trust appeared to roughly correlate with how often a person tweeted, though this required further testing for validation.

Hence, from a viral marketing perspective, Sotiriadis and van Zyl (2013) judged that source reliability and source expertise and knowledge were critical factors. They acknowledged that there were some limitations to their study, because it focused entirely on reader/recipient perspectives. Further research was required to explore the narrator/sender perspective in terms of motivations for engaging in review and recommendation activities, as well as the mediating factors of perceived source reliability and source expertise/displayed knowledge. Another problem for both kinds of study involve assessing the impact of social media feedback loops. It has been an ongoing concern in the discipline of public relations that the accuracy of study findings about social media interactivity can be affected by feedback loops that may distort the usefulness of information for later recipients (Smith, 2010; Xifra and Grau, 2010).

Despite these questions, Sotiriadis (2016) has further developed his quantitative work on Twitter. His article argues that further studies of SM could make a contribution to enabling new ways to enhance service experience for tourists. According to the findings of the 2016 study, tourist experience and innovation are important phenomena to take into consideration when tourism businesses and destinations use Twitter as a channel of interactive communication and constructive dialogue with tourist consumers. The providers of tourism services, however, need to adopt new approaches in the field of communications; such as, developing a multi-channel approach to communications with customers; embracing rather than resisting the influence of SM; and engaging customers in a mutually beneficial dialogue that builds awareness, increases web traffic and attracts new potential customers.

Meanwhile, there is an alternative qualitative methodology that has been deployed to study tourist interaction with SM. As Dennis, Merrilees and Jaya-wardhena (2009) outlined in their key study, the significance of opportunities for social interaction and provision of recreational motives in e-shopping can be revealed by virtual ethnography (webnography). This line of study is also known as 'netnography' (for example Kozinets, 2002; Martin and Woodside, 2011) and researches online blogs, social networking sites (for example, Facebook) and e-word of mouth (e-WOM) at websites such as TripAdvisor. In Asia, one of the first studies by Jimura (2011) to examine e-WOM adopted netnography to explore guests' expectations as developed by *ryokan* (small Japanese inns) websites. It closely examined how e-WOM, and guests' actual experiences at a *ryokan* met their expectations.

Jimura (2011) confronted difficulties understanding the role of product intangibility when conducting his research. He was concerned about how comprehensive tourists' views of a product were before purchase after using information from various sources, such as the product's website and e-WOM. Apart from displaying photographs, videos and souvenirs from their vacations, contributors to e-WOM also bring back memories, feelings and experiences. All of the latter are intangible, at least until they are communicated in online blogs, comments at social networking sites and/or tweets at Twitter.

The visual information that prospective guests of *ryokan* obtain before purchase likely had a great impact on their buying and decision-making processes. It also appeared that there was a risk that these impressions could be iterated through any number of feedback loops, before any of the *ryokan* guests could have encountered them. Jimura employed netnography – as did Martin and Woodside (2011) for a study of e-WOM for Tokyo hotels – to assess a large amount of data within a limited time (to avoid too many feedback loops). This also allowed him to interpret the contexts for e-WOM more clearly, which were available for a reasonable sample of *ryokan* guests.

Jimura (2011) found that global guests at the top three most popular *ryokan* in Japan were extensively using e-WOM on e-travel agents' websites, and that this information was more influential on decision-making than promotional information provided on websites by individual *ryokan*. Moreover, the *ryokan* websites lost ground to the e-travel agents' sites, because they provided no space for their own guests' e-WOM (Jimura 2011). In any event, even if e-WOM is provided, e-consumers are more likely to trust each others' views (C2C) on a seemingly independent website over that provided by a hospitality business (B2C).

Cultural distance and youth travelling styles inside Asia

Research on the nature of independent travel in the region is at an early stage, although the works of Ong (2005), Winter (2007) and Teo and Leong (2006) have given birth to further enquiry; such as, studies on Chinese independent youth tourists (Lim, 2009; Ong and du Cros, 2012; du Cros and Liu, 2013). These later studies have uncovered the communal nature of decision-making; intense use of Internet forums for socialization, and a stronger preference for short over long trips than traditional backpackers. These research efforts have coincided with increased scholarly interest in Chinese outbound tourism (Arlt, 2006; Chan, 2009; Cheng, 2007; Arlt and Burns, 2013). In particular, Arlt (2006) argues that Chinese outbound tourism in Europe shows that China's tourism industry has developed beyond its early heavily institutionalized beginnings, and has arrived at a stage of increased diversification of tourism motivations and practices. As such, this country's industry has a prominent role to play in regional Asian tourism.

Hong Kong is a city that has become a popular destination for tourists from China and elsewhere in the region. In 2012, when this research was largely undertaken, the city attracted 48,615,113 (representing an increase of 16 per cent over 2011). Of these arrivals, tourists who travelled to Hong Kong from China comprised 34,911,395, which was 73 per cent of the total number of arrivals (66 percent of this total arrived on independent visas, not as part of a tour group). Tourists from within the region made up an additional 19 per cent. According to these figures less than 10 per cent arrived from outside Asia. The key points of origin for Asian short-haul tourists to Hong Kong are Taiwan, Japan, Singapore, South Korea, Malaysia, Philippines, Indonesia and Thailand (in that order). The number of Asian visitors who stayed overnight in 2012 was 579,244 or 63 per cent (an increase of 3 per cent over 2011) (HKTB, 2016).

Given the above scenario where massive numbers of short-haul regional tourists are visiting Hong Kong, cultural distance was considered in the study as possibly having some role to play in the choice of destination and the responses of Asian youth tourists to the site once they had arrived. The notion of cultural distance has appeared regularly in the literature in regard to Western-centric studies of tourist-host relations, but rarely has the alternative been considered, probably under the erroneous assumption that it would not be a major factor. Comparative studies of Asian and non-Asian subjects illustrate that differences can be expected between these groups (Heine, 2001; Ng, Lee and Soutar, 2007; Moufakkir, 2011).

Tourism academics have adopted a variety of approaches to cultural distance in an attempt to understand more about the impact of contact between different cultures during travel. Cultural distance (CD) is defined as the degree to which the shared norms and values in one society differ from another society (Hofstede 2001). Moufakkir (2011) married the Foucauldian 'Tourist Gaze' first popularized in tourism studies by Urry (2002) to the notion of cultural distance. This brought to his study a more travel-orientated focus than that of Heine (2001), and is more specific than the work of Hofstede (2001) and his followers. In doing this, he wanted the gaze study to "go beyond the hows to uncover the whys of attitudes and perceptions. In this sense, the host gaze starts where perceptions' surveys stop" (Moufakkir 2011, p.77). As such, studies of the tourist gaze require more than speculative perceptions in order to move beyond the conventional gaze that Urry (2002) originally theorized.

One such study investigated post-Mao gazes of Chinese budget youth tourists to Macau (Ong and du Cros, 2012). Through attention to the virtual ethnography of a leading Internet forum, it was discovered that the forum members' post-Mao gazes were appropriate for the postcolonial spaces of Macau in a number of ways. The tourists (born and raised post-Mao) also presented views in this context that both confirmed and contradicted their pre-existing travel ideals when they reflected upon their experience of Macau's hybrid Portuguese/Asian landscape and community. The study also provided a new perspective on a group of tourists that had been largely ignored in the media and academic portrayals (Ong and du Cros, 2012).

Spontaneity and decision-making in Hong Kong

There have been expectations about the decision-making of Asian youth where it is assumed that they respond in the same way to travel-related variables (time, budget, familiarity with destination) as non-Asian or non-youth tourists. As a consequence, these tourists are often lumped together. For instance, one study examined how much spontaneity is allowed for in a trip. In relation to consuming the local culture of a city destination, McKercher, Wong and Lau (2006) have identified three main groups of variables: time budgets, personality and place knowledge in regard to how structured an experience a visitor may seek from a destination. It is generally argued that for 'time budgets', backpackers (think Western-educated) have more time to travel compared with conventional tourists who normally take shorter holidays. It was also found that the common assumption that they also prefer unstructured experiences was overturned when it was discovered that large number of these 'backpackers' preferred to take day tours, as they only spent a short time in the city. This would have been a good project to employ further analysis of the sample to see what difference youth and origin/background might have made to findings about spontaneity.

The culture of narcissism

Initially, common views about the culture of narcissism were derived from Christopher Lasch in the 1980s, as well as politicized opinions dependent on pre-social media discussions in the 1990s (Lasch, 1991). More recently, Scholz (2008) has commented that the Web is empowering many social movements in Western countries, and that social media is also extremely helpful in the pursuit of individual self-interest. At the same time, it should not be forgotten that, as Scholz argues, users are guests in the house of social media giants:

> Standing on their shoulders, we are entering their rooms; we are banking on the hospitality of their server farms, we are trusting that all the data that we are sharing through our conversations and on our profiles are not abused in scenarios of total control, barely imaginable today (Scholz 2008, n.p.).

Mascheroni (2007) has also posited that virtuality represents a site of mediation between relations and institutions. In the current capitalist system, social relations as they are communicated in social media are reified to some extent, and offer portals and possibilities for users to switch their emotions on and off in a self-indulgent sense, depending on the nature of their desire for interaction, or the conspicuous consumption of a particular experience in its virtual form. Narcissism is likely to be a foundational element of conspicuous consumption, because it is a form of deviant behaviour, which is often manifested to repair damage to the ego. Therefore, narcissists do not always understand the world as it is – narcissists see the world as they wish it to be. This is the primary basis of narcissism (Lasch, 1991). Hence, it is possible to see how an emerging culture of narcissism associated with some social media experiences can play a role in virtual peer support and travel decision-making, especially for the more escapist-minded research subjects who are following and competing with each other in their consumption of travel experiences as communicated in the digital realm.

Germann Molz (2012) and Germann Molz and Paris (2015) has long studied the relationship between travel and social connection. Her current methodology comprises a self-designed 'mobile virtual ethnography' that attempts to adapt ethnographic techniques to the study of the mobile and virtual social phenomena called 'flashpacking'. Her latest work also draws on social affordance theory where the concepts of 'assemblages' and 'affordances' are outlined in regard to several aspects of this new sociality: virtual mooring, following, collaborating and (dis)connecting. Intriguingly, Germann Molz and Paris (2015) discovered efforts amongst the non-Asian flashpacker sample to avoid psychological manipulation by peers and others by managing how accessible to their networks individuals were and to whom. It appears as if some individuals were resisting the teleology of technologically mediated togetherness. She wondered whether future studies should be less about the technology and more about the social desires and anxieties of being both mobile and connected (especially given the darker side of SM hinted at by Scholz 2008). How much anxiety Asian youth travellers have about the above is yet to be fully investigated.

In the midst of Germann Molz and Paris's (2015) investigation, however, the culture of narcissism comes to the fore in SM activities such as 'following', which include a sense of obligation to peers. For instance, if you visit somewhere first should others in your network automatically refer to your visit or virtual comments from those who visit it afterwards, so as to enhance the self-esteem of the first user? How effective or valuable are you as an opinion leader amongst your chosen social network if this does or does not occur? And what impacts does this have on perceptions of self-worth and social status? These questions haunt Molz's work, but unfortunately are not directly addressed in relation to virtual peer support.

Methodology

The approach for understanding this topic involves using an interdisciplinary focus and a multi-methods research methodology that has been piloted in the most recent research by the author for the study of youth tourism and personal growth in Asia. The methodology selected to study independent youth tourists borrows from anthropology, cultural tourism, creative arts, Asian heritage, geography, media studies, cultural studies and education. Asian youth tourists were interviewed in Mandarin or English. English as a second language is becoming more prevalent in an increasing number of Asian cities that contain an emerging and mature middle-class population, which has disposable income that can be spent on leisure travel and already possesses high standards of education or aspires to them.

As stated, previous studies have been either quantitative or qualitative on e-WOM and tourism decision-making. An innovative three-pronged multi-method research approach however deploys both quantitative and qualitative methods. The virtual ethnographic approach borrowed from anthropology (see also Adams, 2015) is also appropriate to this research, because it can bring the researchers closer to the individual consumption patterns and the social, cultural and political context of non-Western communities than previous approaches, such as structuralism (Saukko, 2003; Creswell, 2003; Crotty,

2003). It can also utilize both qualitative and quantitative methods and include a measure of empirical research of lived experience and decision-making for those preparing for travel. It also takes into consideration educational back-grounds, social and media influences and how these have shaped individual social and cultural development. A study of chatrooms and blogs and observed discussions of lived experiences in 'lurker mode' (Germann Molz and Paris, 2015) was also employed over a long period, and was combined with material from in-depth interviews and focus groups to supply qualitative data. Quantitative data collected from a larger sample of 271 face-to-face surveys provided additional evidence.

Virtual data collection and observation

Much has been written in the last ten years about the usefulness of tourism forums and online diaries for travellers. Pan, MacLaurin and Crotts (2007), for instance, have considered the usefulness and implications of travel blogs as destination marketing tools. Other tourism researchers, in turn, have looked to tourism blogs as research materials and spaces for understanding tourist characteristics, motivations and preferences (Carson, 2008; Wenger, 2008), tourists' decision making (Litvin, Goldsmith and Pan, 2006) and the ways in which destination images are framed (Pan, Maclaurin and Crotts, 2007).

Virtual ethnography in travel forums and web-blogs is meant to serve as a less intrusive platform for understanding the nature of Asian youth tourists' lived experiences. Internet forums are public domains so they are appropriate sites to conduct ethical research. Furthermore, as current research on inde-pendent Chinese tourists has shown, the Internet, through the development of Web 2.0 that supports social media networking platforms, now provides opportunities to form cybercommunities for these alternative travellers (Chan, 2009; Lim, 2009; Sparkes and Pan, 2009). In such forums it is hoped that Asian youth tourists will reveal themselves anonymously in a relaxed way – before, during and after travel.

This phenomenon led to the study of five cybercommunities (Douban. com; Qyer.com; Wanzi.cc; Uuyoyo.com, Freegapper.com and Thorntree on Lonelyplanet.com), as well as the individuals that contribute to them. Research was conducted into these sites to determine how instructive a resource they might be for understanding the nature of collectivity and spontaneity underlying Asian youth tourist travel decisions. For instance, Douban.com is a Chinese-language social media site that attracts mostly young Internet users with interests in cultural sectors, such as, (intellectual or independent) books, movies, independent music and travel. Except for major social media functions that allow people to share online resources, the website also has sections that allow users to participate in unique activities. These include, creating your own video, music clip and book database. Contributors can also form and join many groups based on users' interests, and create and join events for the same city. They can set up meetings while travelling; access an online radio service; read excerpts of cultural/lifestyle/IT/travel topics from diverse blogs; and create their own cybercommunity that matches their interests.

Previous research has indicated that Chinese-speaking/ethnically dominated chatrooms often exhibit very different characteristics to Anglo-American ones, particularly in regard to policing shared community values (Ong and du Cros, 2012). As such, this research is especially relevant to gauging youth tourists' sense of collective identity, and whether a pattern is as evident in similar travel discourses in English-speaking chatrooms dominated by non-Chinese speaking Asian participants.

In-depth interviews and focus groups

The study included 15 in-depth interview subjects (there were not the resources for focus groups) and used a mixed approach to source subjects. Some were interviewed at youth hostels, and others responded to an email request to travel forum contributors who visited Hong Kong in 2012. The subjects were mostly inexperienced and independent travellers, though a few more experienced ones were included and there were questions asked about their early experiences.

The selection criteria for the group of interviewees was that they should be Asian residents who are under 30 years old, have been largely educated in Asia, and who have undertaken some form of independent travel to Hong Kong (that is without the need of parental guidance or commercial tour operators). The interviews were conducted in English or Chinese, as the circumstances required. Resources were not available to employ Asian languages other than Chinese in the interviewing process. Eight males and seven females were interviewed, and they were in paid work or were studying.

Short structured face-to-face surveys

A preliminary project indicated that filter questions were necessary to target the right group that contained fully independent (of family and tour package) youth tourists whose main growth and development occurred in Asia. A sample of 150 subjects was tested with a preliminary questionnaire (a little longer than ideal) in Chinese and English to see which questions received the clearest responses.

The questionnaire was then revised and was aimed at elucidating and grounding the initial findings from the in-depth interviews and the digital ethnographic research. The study interviewed young Asian tourists to Hong Kong. The survey applied the Likert scale and used a range of open-ended, multiple choice questions to gather data about educational background, travel decisions and lived experiences of creative arts, intangible heritage and regional cultures. Initial analysis of the survey data was undertaken using Statistical Package for the Social Sciences (SPSS) statistical program package for frequencies, cross-tabs and means. Open-ended questions were analysed by using a simple spreadsheet and thematic reduction analysis method.

Types of decisions studied and results

The three main areas studied in relation to decision-making comprised: planning ahead/during trip; collective/individual modes and information sources used.

Spontaneity: planning ahead/during trip

More detail on this theme was garnered from in-depth interviews rather than semi-structured surveys. Respondent 7 from South Korea found posts from the popular English chatroom 'Thorntree' stimulating, "I always like to read people's travel stories. It always inspires me as different people have different experiences when they travel." She also noted that these narratives prompted her to try to explore Hong Kong more on her own after she arrived. However, the greater sample responses in the semi-structured surveys showed concern about leaving too much to chance in the pre-trip preparation (see Table 4.1).

A low level of spontaneity in trip planning was also evident in most of the in-depth interviewees. For instance, for the trip undertaken by Respondent 4, whose main purpose was relaxation, she did a lot of research through the Internet and also contacted a friend in the city (who is a local culture expert) for travelling tips. She travelled in a group with three friends, who came with her from Fujian Province. They all went together to popular tourist attractions, but for specific places only some of them were interested in, they went alone or in pairs.

Even so, she felt a sense of disappointment because her travel companions' frequent use of the MTR (Hong Kong's fast and convenient subway transport) meant that she missed the experience of walking around Hong Kong to absorb its ambience. She observed, "I felt that my trip lacked a sense of surprise – as in the concept of 'Slow Travel'." She is one of the few interviewees to directly mention this kind of tourist experience. However, it is also present in the Douban.com Chinese language chatroom group called 'Slow Travel' (started in 2010). The introduction page to guide the theme of the thread, states:

> (We should) become a temporary resident instead of a tourist. (We should) give up the idea of 'This is gonna be my only chance of trip in my life'. (We should) think: 'There are many opportunities for travel waiting for me.' Do not follow the traditional travel route, but live in a different place (Douban.com, 2013).

Table 4.1 Use of information sources before and during the trip

	Websites	Family and friends	Guidebooks	Other	Total responses
Before	112	127	114	32	385
During	76	62	97	21	256

Source: Author

The study found that there is some evidence of conflict in relation to views amongst interviewees regarding the importance of travel and the need for spontaneity and adventure. Respondent 11 from Taiwan was clear that he wouldn't be taking any more lengthy trips after the one to Hong Kong, because of family and work obligations. However, it is likely that youth tourists visiting a destination with a strong sense of purpose would have a different view about how important slow travel is to depth of experience and sense of adventure. For instance, Respondent 9 was visiting Hong Kong mostly for bicycling, and was avid to see what the city and its country parks offered for a keen cyclist given the destination is not known for its bike paths, unlike Taiwan (his home country). Even so, this interviewee was able to gain a sense of personal challenge by accessing places and experiences 'off the beaten track'.

Respondent 12 (also from Taiwan) provided the interviewer with the sense that he was very thoughtful about cultural issues and wanted to explore unique cultural sites at destinations. He observed that his travel philosophy is about "authentic travelling experience. It shapes my travel mode – more about making friends with locals, visiting hidden spots rather than shopping district/tourist attractions".

The more purposeful Respondent 6's original plan was to stay in Hong Kong for three days so as to watch the concert of a local stand-up comedian Wong Tze-Wah. She liked the performance so much she extended her trip to just within the visa limit for Chinese nationals. If she had stayed longer she would, "walk around a lot and measure Hong Kong with my footsteps!" She took the tram on Hong Kong Island a couple of times with an eventual destination in mind, but hopped on and off on the way. On one occasion, she visited the North Point wet market (fruit, vegetables, cold meat and live chickens) and enjoyed a spontaneous experience of local culture.

Collective/individual decision-making

In-depth interviews brought the most insight into modes ranging from highly collective to highly independent, as described by respondents before and during the trips. Some interviewees used chatrooms they were regular members of to ask for comments on the feasibility of proposed itineraries. Others solicited interest in gaining a travel companion or more by proposing to work together on a travel itinerary. Also, the possibility for loose collectivity as a decision-making mode was made possible through such chatroom discussions, even when participants had never previously met face to face. This use of the Internet for such collective decision-making was more prevalent in Chinese chatrooms than English-speaking ones. For instance, Respondent 1 noted that before arriving in Hong Kong:

> My original plan was to travel by myself. Later, I posted threads on Douban.com and found out several people who were also going to Hong Kong. Most of the time, it was just four of us hanging out together. The girl who came for shopping went back after shopping.

Regarding what happened during the trip this respondent also observed:

> The deal we made was: We share our own itinerary with others. If there were things in common, we could go together. If some places one wanted to go (and) could not match others, he/she could travel by himself/herself to those places, and call others to meet up and move to the next stops together, after he/she has finished visiting those places he/she wanted to go.

In this way, Respondent 1's travel companions could keep track of each other, but still retained some flexibility to explore in advance of the group. However, Respondent 15 uploaded an intensely detailed itinerary to one chatroom and expected the kind of response a travel agent would make. Needless, to say this approach was largely unsuccessful, as he had not visited the chatroom before and had no history of helping others. This example reflects the common view in the literature that trust is an important factor in social media relations.

Information sources used

All research subjects were asked about the types of information sources they used before and during their trip to Hong Kong. Multiple sources were used by most of those surveyed, and there was a strong response to the question about pre-trip planning (see Table 4.1). Key information sources before the trip included a combination of guidebooks, family and friends' advice and Internet websites (30 per cent Hong Kong-based; 70 per cent other). During the trip, guidebooks and websites remained strong sources of information (see Table 4.1). Therefore, personal sources such as friends and family and traditional guidebooks were clearly trusted and used by this group both before and during their trip.

The in-depth interviews found that social media had a role to play in many information sourcing and sharing experiences of subjects. For instance, Respondent 9, a Taiwanese slow travel/bicycle enthusiast, found it useful in this way:

> You know Facebook: If you post a nice snapshot taken during a biking trip, friends of your friends might see it and think this guy is cool. (Then) people will try to bike together if things work out. I've met a lot of friends in this biking circuit who share the similar value and vision. For example, this time, my friend lent me some biking accessories and taught me a lot of tips. (Respondent 9)

An examination of chatroom opinions on available apps and website information found that youth tourists were more likely to copy local practices (accessing local cultural and lifestyle websites) than seek advice from specific Hong Kong tourism websites, such as the Hong Kong Tourism Board.

Hopefully, local information availability has improved since the time Respondent 3's friend suffered an accident on Hong Kong's outlying island Pui O and had to use Weibo (mainland Chinese Twitter) to solicit rescue by helicopter.

In summary, most interviewees (semi-structured and in-depth) were not accessing Internet information as freely during the trip as before, although it is likely that many of these travellers use smartphones. There were a number who were writing blogs as they went. Respondent 9 found that the evenings in the hostel provided a good opportunity to write a trip blog and "contemplate everything, not only random things but also important national issues". The hostel with free wifi was also where Respondent 10 caught up with friends and family via WhatsApp and other means. It is likely that more hotspots with free wifi for tourists would benefit this group.

Feedback loops evident in social media

While specific questions about feedback loops were not asked, there seems to be some evidence that the virtual spaces that encourage these kinds of phenomena are most likely to be found in travel forums than other forms of social media. This is because people visit such websites specifically for travel information and opinions. There may also be a sense of shared experience or even history amongst members of forums who have repeatedly visited them to discuss more than one trip.

Narcissism, trust and self-censorship

Scholz (2008) is ambivalent about the 'freedom' of social media given that it is a technology that is part of a global marketplace that directly or indirectly exploit users for financial gain. Academics that lurk in forums or analyse social media may also be acting in an exploitative manner, and may face abuse, and may be seen as 'preying' on young adults when studying them (who may or may not be aware that they are exposed in this way). However, the Chinese travel forums that were studied were based in the People's Republic of China, and therefore some forms of self-censorship or awareness that more than fellow travellers could be viewing their comments led to some reluctance to be absolutely open. Some were able to overcome such ambivalence to agree to be interviewed by the author (self-interest or self-sacrifice?), however, it is advised that the impact of government censorship and/or the commercially exploitative nature of some platforms should be taken into account when designing future studies of digital discourse and marketing.

Self-censorship in terms of showing more respect to living cultures visited is unlikely to be found in conjunction with conspicuous consumption or narcissistic impulses in the case of Hong Kong. There were no overt examples (like those found elsewhere, particularly Myanmar) of respondents' boasting to others in travel forums of how they were able to get the better of local retailers and hoteliers, despite being able to pay well in excess of what was asked.

This kind of behaviour is more common in developing countries and is creating much ill feeling there (du Cros, 2016).

Conclusion

The interviewees were all chosen with the view that they would not have an intimate knowledge of local culture or language; that is, having lived in Hong Kong or Southern China and possessing Cantonese speaking skills. This would ensure some level of cultural distance even for ethnic Chinese from the region. The research subjects were also looking for information on more than just the best or cheapest hotels, flights and so on. They did not appear to be competing with each other on the cost of their travel experiences, as is sometimes found in less developed destinations.

Novice or less experienced travellers were also a feature of the sample interviewed. Accordingly, there was more reason for such a group to seek peer support regarding travel decisions. All subjects were younger than 30 years old and most had an understanding of the latest digital communication technology. Virtual peer support mostly occurred before the trip. However, this might change as Hong Kong establishes free wifi spots in more tourist areas.

One of the limitations of this study was that it was still not entirely clear from the face-to-face, semi-structured survey sample whether virtual peer support was preferred over real-time support from friends, or a pre-existing and superior knowledge of Hong Kong. Only Respondent 4 amongst the in-depth interviewees, who travelled with a friend, was in this category. A few others interviewed in depth also mentioned blogging and seeking information during the trip. This is definitely an issue that requires greater clarification in future studies of this kind. However, the results listed in Table 4.1 indicate that there was more virtual information sought pre-trip than during the trip. Free wifi/Internet access may have also been a factor in this result.

Despite these limitations, the methodology used in this study made it possible to discover that decision-making for Asian youth is largely semi-collective, as potential travellers needed to consult trusted information sources for travel decisions. Again, these impressions could be explored with more specific research on virtual peer support by other researchers, particularly those not primarily concerned with commercial gain in order for interviewees to truly open up for research on this topic.

Acknowledgements

I would like to thank my virtual "Smart Mob" of Kathleen Adams, Maximiliano Korstanje, Takamitsu Jimura, Marios Sotiriadis and Wantanee Suntikul for their invaluable comments on this study. The Hong Kong University of Education provided an internal grant to undertake part of the work for this study. Also, I would like to thank the University of New Brunswick, which contributed institutional support.

References

Adams, K.A. (2015). Families, funerals and Facebook: Reimag(in)ing and 'curating' Toraja kin. In: *Trans-local Times. TRaNS: Trans-Regional and National Studies of Southeast Asia*, [online] Available at: CJO 2015. DOI:doi:10.1017/trn.2014.25.

Arlt, W. (2006). *China's outbound tourism*. London and New York: Routledge.

Arlt, W. and Burns, P. (2013). China outbound tourism special issue. *Tourism, Planning and Development*, 10(2).

Carson, D. (2008). The 'blogosphere' as a market research tool for tourism destination: A case study of Australia's Northern Territory. *Journal of Vacation Marketing*, 14(2), pp. 111–119.

Chan, Y.W. (2009). Disorganised tourism space: Chinese tourism in an age of tourism. In: Winter, T., Teo, P. and Chang, T.C., eds., *Asia on tour: Exploring the rise of Asian tourism*. London and New York: Routledge, pp. 67–78.

Chen, Y.L., Hsu, C.L. and Chou, S.C. (2003). Constructing a multi–valued and multi-labeled decision tree. *Expert Systems with Applications*, 25(2), pp. 199–209.

Cheng, I.M. (2007). A comparative study of travel behaviour of single and multi-destination travellers from Mainland China in Macau. *China Tourism Research*, 3(4), pp. 449–477.

Creswell, J.W. (2003). *Research design: Quantitative, qualitative, and mixed methods approaches*. 2nded. Thousand Oaks, CA: Sage Publications.

Crotty, M. (2003). *The foundations of social research: Meaning and perspective in the research process*. Thousand Oaks, CA: Sage Publications.

De Bruyn, A. and Lilien, G.L. (2008). A multi-stage model of word-of-mouth influence through viral marketing. *International Journal of Research in Marketing*, 25(3), pp. 151–163.

Dennis, C., Merrilees, B., Jayawardhena, C. and Wright, L.T. (2009). E-consumer behaviour. *European Journal of Marketing*, 43(9/10), pp. 1121–1139.

du Cros, H. (2016). The Yangon tourism study. [online]. Available at: www.yangon heritagetrust.org/home [Accessed 3 Sep 2016].

du Cros, H. and Liu, J. (2013). Chinese youth tourists views on local culture. Special issue on outbound Chinese tourism. *Tourism, Planning and Development*, 10(2), pp. 187–204.

Germann Molz, J. (2012). *Travel connections: Tourism, technology, and togetherness in a mobile world*. London: Routledge.

Germann Molz, J., and Paris, C.M. (2015). The social affordances of flash-packing: Exploring the mobility nexus of travel and communication. *Mobilities*, 10(2), pp. 173–192.

HKTB. (2016). 2012 tourism statistics. [online]. Available at: http://partnernet.hktb. com/filemanager/intranet/ViS_Stat/ViS_Stat_E/ViS_E_2013/dec2012e1_1_0.htm [Accessed 28 May 2016].

Heine, S.J. (2001). Self as cultural product: An examination of East Asian and North American selves. *Journal of Personality*, 69(6), pp. 881–906.

Hofstede, G. (2001). *Culture's consequences: Comparing values, behaviours, institutions and organizations across nations*. Thousand Oaks, CA: Sage Publications.

Jimura, T. (2011). The websites of Japanese Ryokan and eWOM: Their impacts on guests' expectation and experience. *International Journal of Asian Tourism Management*, 2(2), pp. 120–133.

Kotler, P., Bowen, J. and Makens, J. (2010). *Marketing for hospitality and tourism*, 5th ed. London: Prentice Hall.

Kozinets, R.V. (2002). The field behind the screen: Using netnography for marketing research in online communities. *Journal of Marketing Research*, 39(1), pp.61–72.

Lasch, C. (1991). *The culture of narcissism: American life in an age of diminishing expectations.* New York: WW Norton & Company.

Leung, D., Law, R.van Hoof, H. and Buhalis, D. (2013). Social media in tourism and hospitality: A literature review. *Journal of Travel & Tourism Marketing*, 30(1–2), pp. 3–22.

Lim, F.K.G. (2009). "Donkey friends" in China: The Internet, civil society and the emergence of the Chinese backpacking community. In: Winter, T., Teo, P. and Chang, T.C., eds., *Asia on tour: Exploring the rise of Asian tourism*, London and New York: Routledge, pp. 291–302.

Litvin, S., Goldsmith, R.E. and Pan, B. (2006). Electronic word-of-mouth in hospitality and tourism management. *Tourism Management*, 29(3), pp. 458–468.

McKercher, B., Wong, C. and Lau, G. (2006). How tourists consume a destination. *Journal of Business Research*, 59, pp. 647–652.

Martin, D. and Woodside, A.G. (2011). Storytelling research on international visitors interpreting their own experiences in Tokyo. *Qualitative Market Research: An International Journal*, 14(1), pp. 27–54.

Mascheroni, G. (2007). Global nomads' mobile and network sociality: Exploring new media uses on the move. *Information, Communication and Society*, 10(4), pp. 527–546.

Moufakkir, O. (2011). The role of cultural distance in mediating the host gaze. *Tourist Studies*, 11(1), pp. 73–89.

Ng, S.I., Lee, J.A. and Soutar, G. (2007). Tourists' intention to visit a country: The impact of cultural distance. *Tourism Management*, 28, pp. 1497–1506.

Ong, C.E. (2005). Adventurism: Singapore adventure tourists in new economy. In: Ryan, C. and Aicken, M., eds., *Taking tourism to the limits: Issues, concepts and managerial perspectives.* London: Elsevier, pp. 173–183.

Ong, C.E. and du Cros, H. (2012). Post-Mao gazes: Chinese backpackers in Macau. *Annals of Tourism Research*, 39(2), pp. 735–754.

Pan, B., MacLaurin, T. and Crotts, J. (2007). Travel blogs and the implications for destination marketing. *Journal of Travel Research*, 46, pp. 35–45.

Pine, J. and Gilmore, J. (1999). *The experience economy.* Boston: Harvard Business School Press.

Saukko, P. (2003). *Doing research in cultural studies: An introduction to classical and new methodological approaches.* London: Sage.

Scholz, T. (2008). Market ideology and the myths of Web 2.0. *First Monday*, 13(3).

Sigala, M., Christou, E. and Gretzel, U., eds. (2012). *Social media in travel, tourism and hospitality; theory, practice and cases.* London: Ashgate.

Sirakaya, E. and Woodside, A.G. (2005). Building and testing theories of decision making by travellers. *Tourism Management*, 26(6), pp.815–832.

Smith, B.G. (2010). Socially distributing public relations: Twitter, Haiti and inter-activity in social media. *Public Relations Review*, 36(4), pp. 329–335.

Sotiriadis, M. (2016). The potential contribution and uses of Twitter by tourism businesses and destinations. *International Journal of Online Marketing*, 6(2), Apr.–Jun. 2016, DOI: doi:10.4018/IJOM.

Sotiriadis, M. and van Zyl, C. (2013). Electronic word-of-mouth and online reviews in tourism services: The use of twitter by tourists. *Electronic Commercial Research*, 13, pp. 103–124, DOI: doi:10.1007/s10660–10013–9108–9101.

Sparkes, B. and Pan, G.W. (2009). Chinese outbound tourists: Understanding their attitudes, constraints and use of information sources. *Tourism Management*, 30, pp. 483–494.

Teo, P. and Leong, S. (2006). A postcolonial analysis of backpacking. *Annals of Tourism Research*, 33(1), pp. 109–131.

Urry, J. (2002). *The tourist gaze*. London: Sage.

Wenger, A. (2008). Analysis of travel bloggers' characteristics and their communication about Austria as a tourism destination. *Journal of Vacation Marketing*, 14(2), pp. 169–176.

Winter, T. (2007). Rethinking tourism in Asia. *Annals of Tourism Research*, 34(1), pp. 27–44.

Xiang, Z. and Gretzel, U. (2010). Role of social media in online travel information search. *Tourism Management*, 31(2), pp. 179–188.

Xifra, J. and Grau, F. (2010). Nanblogging PR: The discourse on public relations in Twitter. *Public Relations Review*, 36(2), pp. 171–174.

Yeh, Y.H. and Choi, S.M. (2011). MINI-lovers, maxi-mouths: An investigation of antecedents to eWOM intention among brand community members. *Journal of Marketing Communications*, 17(3), pp. 145–162.

Yoo, K.H. and Gretzel, U. (2010). Antecedents and impacts of trust in travel-related consumer-generated media. *Information Technology & Tourism*, 12(2), pp. 139–152.

5 Doing literary tourism – an autoethnographic approach

Tim Middleton

This paper describes two instances of doing literary tourism, teasing out some methodological reflections via an autoethnographic approach that explores ways of performing acts of literary tourism. I begin with a concise account of autoethnography as a valuable research tool in the study and practice of self-guided literary tourism, and then move on to briefly discuss literary tourism as an instance of cultural and heritage tourism. I then offer analysis of two self-guided literary tourist journeys, drawing out implications for literary tourist practice. I begin my analysis via a reading of Edward Thomas's literary tour of South West England as recounted in, *In Pursuit of Spring,* high-lighting ways in which his study is something of a classic autoethnographic account of *doing* literary tourism. I then offer some reflections of my own literary tourism activity whilst in pursuit of the Argyll locations of Iain Banks's novel, *The crow road,* in 2008. The essay draws out the context of literary and heritage tourism activity in this region today and some of the lessons learned in terms of the study *and* practice of literary tourism.

Methodology

Autoethnography is a methodology that has begun to have more prominence in literary tourism studies (Grist, 2013, Brown, 2016). Coghlan and Filo (2013) have highlighted its value in the wider field since it enables access to the personal experience of tourists. Brown has argued that "it is also a highly practicable method because the accessible nature of tourism as an activity lends itself to autoethnography … using autoethnographic studies challenges a field that is still dominated by positivist and postpositivist research" (Brown, 2016, p. 138).

Autoethnography starts from an open acknowledgement of the contingent nature of research practice. What often frustrates readers of autoethnography is the apparent lack of critical distance between the author and subject – when the evidence is one's own experience how can something fleeting and personal be the basis for a contribution to an academic field? Auto-ethnography is, like other creative non-fiction, written from experience and as such is contingent on a variety of factors, many of which mitigate any sense of 'critical distance' or 'objectivity' (Hemley, 2012). Autoethnography can be criticised for being rooted in a kind of intellectual arrogance – begging the question, what makes my views/experience any more or less interesting/valid/ insightful than yours? The short answer is – nothing: they are my experiences, unique to me and who I am but, as Butler (1990) has suggested, who I perceive myself to be informs what I do. As Adams *et al.* argue, an autoethnographic approach provides researchers with 'a method for articulating their personal connections to – and their investment in – identities, experiences, relationships and/ or cultures' (Adams et al., 2015, pp. 15–16), and as Ellis et al remind us, it is approach which rests on contingency because:

> [M]emory is fallible, ... it is impossible to recall or report on events in language that exactly represents how those events were lived and felt; and we recognize that people who have experienced the 'same' event often tell different stories about what happened (Ellis et al., 2011, p. 7).

This doesn't make it an exercise in self-promotion, or a case of 'me, me, me', but it does require the writer to be open about who they are. I am a white, British-educated, middle-aged, male professor of English and Cultural Studies. I have written about, given papers, taught classes and examined PhDs on diverse topics across the field of modern and contemporary British literature and culture. As an educator, I have been trained to provide evidence for an argument, to establish the ways in which my insights relate to and depend on the work of others who have already written about the topic I am addressing. I make these declarations in the spirit of autoethnographic disclosure since it is "an approach to research and writing that seeks to describe and system- atically analyze (*graphy*) personal experience (*auto*) in order to understand cultural experience (*ethno*)" (Ellis, et al., 2011, p. 1).

For me, critical and cultural analysis has always started with my interest in a writer or cultural phenomenon. As an educator, I understand things by teaching them and writing about them: knowledge acquisition and develop- ment for me is a dialogic process. As I came to study and teach about literary locations, and then began to have a small input into tourism initiatives at a regional level via work on an advisory group for the United Kingdom's South West Tourism agency, I carried over this sense that knowing and doing were intimately connected. In developing work on literary tourist itineraries related to the work of Thomas Hardy I set about linking my personal experience as a reader and teacher of his work to that of my personal experience as a visitor to locations associated with writing, and working with organisations that sought to weave his legacy into their cultural tourism offerings such at the National Trust (Middleton, 2013a). Throughout this essay I am deploying what Adams et al. describe as 'analytic autoenthnography', "[i]n which a researcher acknowledges membership in a research community [and assesses] ... the theoretical contributions of research in distinct and separate moments of ... [their] narrative" (Adams, et al. p. 85). In this paper I am writing about and from my personal and professional experience of doing, teaching and writing about literary tourism – not anyone else's.

Literary tourism

Commentators such as Smith (2009) and Timothy (2011) locate literary tourism as a specialised instance of cultural tourism. UK national data, based on the International Passenger Survey 2006–2011, suggests that around 3 per cent of the circa 11 million inbound visitors coming to the UK on a holiday engage in visiting locations because of their literary or film and TV associations. Visit Britain's (2015) *Valuing activities* report, based on online interviews with 2,427 domestic tourists, notes that visiting a location associated with a TV series, film or work of literature was an activity engaged in by 2 per cent of day visitors and 4 per cent of overnight visitors. I write what follows from personal experience of a cultural activity – self-guided literary tourism – that a minority of tourists in the UK undertake.

Smith suggests that "visitors to literary places are ... more purposeful and have more specific reasons for making their visit ... than the 'general' heritage visitor" (Smith 1999, 64). Understanding the motives for instances of literary tourism activity is a complex business (Middleton, 2013a). Squire's study of visitors to Beatrix Potter's home at Hill Top in the English Lake District found that "visitors were actively negotiating and transforming the meanings of authenticity in attempts to fulfil expectations about what Potter's home, the setting for her books ... should be like" (Squire, 1994, p. 115). Literary tourists share with cultural and heritage tourists an interest in having an 'authentic' experience (Herbert, 2001). Debate continues about the relevance of this facet of the visitor experience, and this discussion is well-worn, with its roots in the argument between Boorstin (1961) and MacCannell (1973; 1976), and Urry's intervention correcting MacCannell's account of the tourist as dupe with the compelling argument that the "tourist finds pleasure in the multitude of games that can be played and knows that there is no authentic tourist experience" (Urry, 1995, p. 140). I adopt a constructivist view of the question of the authenticity of literary tourist experiences – this assumes that literary locations:

> have different meanings for different people [and that the] level of authenticity is negotiable between visitors, curators and service providers. Therefore authenticity is not inherent in the properties or characteristics of objects and places, but is simply based on judgements made about ... [literary tourism locations] by consumers (Timothy, 2011, p. 108).

Literary tourism is thus an activity in which "visitors make sense of their encounters with literary places" through the interaction of "private meanings ... with public forms and images" (Squire, 1994, p. 107). From this perspective, I would argue that writing about the literary tourist experience using more traditional qualitative methodologies, which tend to efface the researcher from the process, is in itself inauthentic since it involves aggregating the varied experiences of participants who are unique individuals. As such, I would suggest that literary tourism is an experience that can be very effectively explored via an autoethnographic research practice.

Edward Thomas as literary tourist

My focus is on self-guided literary tourism, which starts from an interest in a writer and their locales and then sets out to explore a region armed with knowledge of the work and just a map. The model that most speaks to my own experience and practice is Edward Thomas's *The South Country* (1909) in which he describes his approach as follows:

> And so I travel, armed only with myself, an avaricious and often libertine and fickle eye and ear, in pursuit, not of knowledge, not of wisdom, but of one whom to pursue is never to capture (1909, p. 6).

This methodology underpins his *In Pursuit of Spring* (2016: first published 1914) – a cycling odyssey across southern Britain undertaken in 1913 that traces his journey from Balham in SW London to the Quantock Hills on the Somerset coast. Thomas's journey is a literary one – his wide knowledge of the writing of Southern England informs his reflection on the locales he visits *en route* to Somerset, and his goal is to arrive in the Quantock Hills with the Spring, and to be in the region that the poet Samuel Taylor Coleridge inhabited:

> I would see Nether Stowey, the native soil of 'Kubla Khan', 'Christabel', and the 'Ancient Mariner', where Coleridge fed on honey dew and drank the milk of paradise (Thomas, 2016, 37).

My choice of this text as a guide to doing literary tourism is not, of course, random. My reading of Thomas is enriched for me because I have personal knowledge of many of the locations he visits. I was born, lived and worked in the South West for many years, and have visited, driven through, walked across and cycled around many of the locations Thomas mentions. When he describes the "dark trees of Grovely" wood near Salisbury, for example, I know the view up to the wood from the road (Thomas, 2016, p. 111). This means that as I read Thomas my own experience of these settings adds to my experience of his work – it is this that lies at the core of my interest in undertaking literary tourism: despite the gap in years one can still stand on the beach at Kilve and see the rock formations that Thomas saw in 1913. In fact, a recent *Guardian* essay on Thomas's book illustrates the interest of this 'then and now' aspect of literary tourism by allowing readers to compare photographs from his journey with contemporary images taken in the same locations (Sherratt, 2016).

I believe that this sense of a search for a shared experience of place underpins much literary tourism. As Smith has argued:

> Identifying and visiting literary places adds to the understanding and appreciation of literature ... and, conversely, ... a knowledge of literature sharpens our enjoyment of place (Smith, 1999, p. 47).

The role of personal experience in 'sense-making' strongly connects literary tourism as a practice and autoethnography as a method (Adams et al., 2015, p. 27). A challenge for heritage custodians and tourism agencies is that a personal experience tends not to be something that translates readily into the segmented data which tend to focus on setting out the broad range of touristic activity afforded by a literary location rather than the narrowly literary associations of the property. Croquet may have been played by Hardy and his guest as his Max Gate house, but one doubts that they indulged in Easter egg hunts. Hardy Country – www.hardycountry.org – is a concoction of the National Trust and regional partners, rather than the place that emerged from his fiction and poetry. However, standing in the writer's study at Max Gate on Good Friday reading his poem 'Unkept Good Fridays' written in the very room in 1927 creates an experience that is unique for the visitor, whether it is the first or fifteenth time they have read the poem (Smith, 2003). This is also an experience that has been curated by the National Trust property manager who arranges for appropriate poems to be displayed in Hardy's study.

Autoethnographic research is often structured around an epiphanic moment, curated or otherwise, when the writer describes a significant experience that changes the way they see the world (Adams et al., 2015). Less life-altering but nonetheless significant 'aesthetic moments' are also a key element of many autoethnographic studies (Adams et al. 2015, p. 48). I believe that it is this search for the 'aesthetic moment' that inspires much self-guided literary tourism. This hunch resonates with Urry's suggestion that the romantic gaze – "involving vision, awe, aura" – is a key element of this particular kind of touristic experience (1995, p. 191). Tellingly, recent UK research noted that 'emotional impact' was a key factor in visitors' perceptions of successful cultural tourism experiences. Visitors reported seeking this emotional engagement as part of what motivated them to visit locations related to heritage and culture (Visit Britain, 2016).

Thomas's journey is driven by a similar search for emotional impact. He begins in London's streets, oppressed by "the roar ... of the inhuman masses" (Thomas, 2016, p. 26) and the cold February weather, a place where glimpses of beauty and bliss are quickly "drowned in the oceanic multitude". He plans his journey as an escape from the winter city and its crowds, nostalgically imagining "travelling into one of the preludes to summer" (p. 33) such as the Springs of "five years, twenty years ago" (p. 33). Nostalgia seems to me a powerful catalyst for literary tourism, connected with complex motivations participants may have for undertaking aspects of heritage and cultural tourism, which is associated with the desire for a "temporary escape from a variety of external pressures: everyday life, modernity, and urban industrialization" (Squire, 1994, p. 113). In Thomas's book this search is overlain with an added religious symbolism since he begins his journey at Easter – on Good Friday – and there is clearly an element of secular reparation and resurrection through Nature in the work's trajectory.

Setting off in heavy rain after a stormy night Thomas picks his way through flooded streets. The rain becomes heavier and he seeks shelter in a bird shop – "not a cheerful or a pretty place" (Thomas 2016, p. 45), watching as another person sheltering from the rain buys a chaffinch "fluttering in a paper bag" (p. 46) and then cycles off. Thomas follows and notices that:

> Unable to bear the fluttering in the paper bag any longer; he got down, and with an awkward air, as if he knew how many great men had done it before, released the flutterer. A dingy cock chaffinch flew off amongst the lilacs of a garden saying 'Chink' (p. 46).

This is not presented as an epiphanic moment but is clearly a symbolic gesture of reparation and hoped for freedom. This other cyclist is a key aspect to Thomas's representation of his literary tour and as such functions as an interesting autoethnographic device. The other man is perhaps an amalgam of Thomas's actual travelling companions, but equally functions as "an inner voice externalised", which has exaggerated traits we know to be Thomas's (Harris, 2016, p. 18). It is the notion of watching and reflecting in experience as a means of developing self-awareness and deeper personal understanding that makes Thomas an autoethnographer. His use of 'the other man' as foil is a way of acknowledging and accommodating "subjectivity, emotionality, and the researcher's influence on research, rather than hiding from these matters or assuming they don't exist" (Ellis et al., 2011, p. 2). The formal structure of Thomas's narrative – its digressions, dialogues with the other man, acute observations of people and places encountered – are in and of themselves a means of doing his research and are illustrative of how he undertakes his literary journey. Writing from notes made and photographs taken on what were a series of journeys (Harris, 2016, p. 17), Thomas crafts a narrative that presents the trip as one continuous experience. He punctuates it with a mix of the quotidian and the humdrum set alongside moments of emotional impact: a mixture that may be part of many literary tourist's 'active negotiation' of the gaps between their preconceptions and what is actually before their eyes (Squire, 1994, p. 115).

As a case study in doing autoethnography Thomas has much to offer since his work foregrounds the ways in which literary technique is part and parcel of this method of inquiry (Adams et al., 2015). The other male figure enables him to "describe moments that are felt too difficult to claim" (Ellis et al., 2011, p. 4), or give voice to views that he cannot utter, which he articulates as "From Parents, Schoolmasters, and Parsons, from Sundays and Bibles … from Shame and Conscience … Good Lord, or whatever Gods there be, deliver us" (Thomas, 2016, p. 110). Whilst present throughout much of the narrative there are long sequences when he is absent (for example, pp. 49–94 then again between pp. 99–109, and pp. 110–168). When the two meet it is usually presents an occasion for a digression (for example, re clay pipes – pp. 94–99), or a means of allowing Thomas to take stock of the journey – "he reminded me ... of what I was engaged in forgetting" (p. 99). Later it is revealed that the other man is a writer and we hear him rant about the use of notebooks to record his observations. The notes become what is recalled, he laments, whereas:

> if he had taken none, then only the important, what he truly cared for, would have survived in his memory, arranged not perhaps as they were in Nature, but at least according to the tendencies is of his own spirit (p. 169).

With this self-conscious turn we see Thomas deploying another of the autoethnographer's devices: "using facets of storytelling (for example character and plot development), showing and telling, and alterations of authorial voice" (Ellis, et al, 2011, p. 4) to explain his experience.

In Pursuit of Spring deploys the tools of autoethnography in relating a literary tourist journey through Southern England in pursuit of Coleridge and a vision of Spring. The book ends as Thomas rides down from the Quantocks: pausing to look at the view "across the flat valley of the Mendips and Brent Knoll, and to Steep Holm and Flat Holm ... [and] the blueness of the hills of South Wales" (p. 227). He closes his account with a personal epiphany after spotting a discarded bunch of bluebells and cowslips left by the roadside:

> They were beginning to wilt, but they lay upon the grave of Winter, I was quite sure of that ... I had found Winter's grave, I had found Spring, and I was confident I could ride home again and find Spring all along the road ... Thus I leapt over April and into May, as I sat in the sun on the north side of Cothelstone Hill on that 28th day of March, the last day of my journey westward to find Spring (Thomas, 2016, p. 228).

He has told a story of his travels where personal memory and opinion are presented as being as valuable as hard facts. He mixes the mundane and quotidian with passages where he tries, by reference to the work of writers inspired by or writing from the places he is visiting, to evoke a deeper meaning to his experience without once suggesting that his experience is one his reader should be aiming to emulate. He doesn't attempt to offer a guidebook but rather presents a series of impressions based on his experience and illuminated by his wider reading and knowledge. The *Observer* newspaper favourably noted this impressionistic quality:

> [H]e thinks of other poets and writers, as he passes the places where they lived ... his thoughts on them are just and sincere as are his thoughts on the weather and the inns and the beauty of the country and the character of the people he meets (Sheratt, 2016).

By producing 'artful and evocative' thick descriptions of personal and inter-personal experience Thomas exemplifies good autoethnographic practice (Ellis, et al., 2011, p. 4) (see Table 5.1).

In pursuit of Iain Banks – reflections on doing literary tourism

Thomas's study had a clear goal – to follow the signs of Spring to the heartland of one of his favourite writers. I had begun to read the work of the popular Scottish novelist Iain Banks in my leisure time, but found that he dealt with themes and issues that I was covering in my classes and my writing. As a teacher, I spent some time in the 1990s leading seminars on national identity and contemporary literature. This work spilled over into critical essays and conference papers about Banks's work that began to take a focus on refuting the notion that he was one of Scotland's least 'place sensitive' writers (Patterson, 2002, p. 28). As part of a teaching related project in 2008 I created an opportunity to test this notion 'on the ground' when I undertook fieldwork in the Scottish region of Argyll with colleagues and a team of students to develop a literary tourism app based on the novelist's 1992 novel *The Crow Road*. My colleague Professor Martin Reiser has written about the technical aspects of this work (Reiser, 2012), and I have set out details of the way Banks uses the locales we visited for literary ends (Middleton, 2013b). In this paper, I offer an autoethnographic account of doing literary tourism high-lighting issues relating to authenticity and authorial intervention encountered during the fieldwork for our project. It is the lessons to be learned from attempting to do literary tourism in a technologically driven or overly rationalist fashion that I want to tease out in this paper, and it was by applying an autoethnographic lens that I perceived flaws in my approach to this field work. I have distilled my thinking into an account of two key aspects that shape my understanding of the experience.

Authenticity

The Crow Road isn't a guide to the region of Argyll between the village of Lochgair and the port of Crinan where much of the novel's action takes place. This region's significance in the history of Scotland however means that, in this novel, Scottish settings are far more than a mere backdrop to its action. The region is "in what had been the very epicentre of the ancient Scots kingdom of Dalriada" (Banks, 1992, p. 57). This is of particular significance for what Banks's novel does with that history by placing his villain Fergus Urvill's castle close to the Dark Age fort of Dunadd. The settings of key scenes are placed in the wider terrain of Kilmartin Glen, for it is in this area that the Scots as a race first arrived from Ireland in 503 AD under the lea-dership of one Fergus mac Erc. In a novel that plays out family history against the backdrop of world events the special significance of this region for the history of the Scottish nation is playfully interwoven (Middleton, 2013b).

Table 5.1 Common features in autoethnography and literary tourism practice as exemplified in Edward Thomas's *In Pursuit of Spring*

Autoethnographic facets	Thomas – Autoethnographer and literary tourist	Literary tourism facets
Epiphanies or 'aesthetic moments'	"I had found Winter's grave, I had found Spring, and I was confident I could ride home again and find Spring all along the road....." (Thomas, 2016, p. 228).	Visitors seek 'emotional impact' when visiting sites associated with books they have enjoyed
"Articulating … personal connections to – and …investment in – identities, experiences, relationships and/ or cultures" (Adams, 2015, pp. 15–16).	"And so I travel, armed only with myself, an avaricious and often libertine and fickle eye and ear, in pursuit, not of knowledge, not of wisdom, but of one whom to pursue is never to capture." (Thomas, 1909, p. 6).	Identifying and visiting literary places adds to the understanding and appreciation of literature … and, conversely, 'a knowledge of literature sharpens our enjoyment of place.' (Smith, 1999, p. 47).

The "tourist finds pleasure in the multitude of games that can be played and knows that there is no authentic tourist experience" (Urry, 1995, p. 140). |
| Written from experience | I travelled fast, in hopes I should
Outrun that other. What to do
When caught, I planned not. I pursued
To prove the likeness, and, if true,
To watch until myself I knew. (Thomas, 1918). | These places are 'consumed in terms of participants' prior knowledge, expectations, fantasies and mythologies generated in the tourist's origin culture rather than by the cultural offerings of the destination'. (Middleton 2013a, citing Craik, p. 118). |
| "subjectivity, emotionality, and the researcher's influence on research, rather than hiding from these matters or assuming they don't exist" (Ellis et al., 2011). | "if he had taken [no notes] … then only the important, what he truly cared for, would have survived in his memory, arranged not perhaps as they were in Nature, but at least according to the tendencies is of his own spirit" (Thomas, 2016, p. 169). | Literary tourism is thus an activity in which "visitors make sense of their encounters with literary places' through the interaction of 'private meanings …with public forms and images" (Squire, 1994, p. 107). |

(Continued)

Table 5.1 continued

Autoethnographic facets	Thomas – Autoethnographer and literary tourist	Literary tourism facets
Multiple perspectives - identities, experiences, relationships and/ or cultures' (Adams et al. 2015, pp. 15–16).	The Other Man – an alternative voice. Also citations from the authors who write about the locations he visits create additional voices and viewpoints.	Literary locations, "have different meanings for different people [and that the] level of authenticity is negotiable between visitors, curators and service providers. Therefore authenticity is not inherent in the properties or characteristics of objects and places but is simply based on judgements made about ... [literary tourism locations] by consumers" (Timothy, 2011, p. 108).
"Fleeting, fallible and feeling based accounts which accept that memories and histories 'are connected and differentiated, familiar and misrecognised" (Adams et al., 2015, p. 53).	Plans his journey as an escape from the winter city and its crowds, nostalgically imagining 'travelling into one of the preludes to Summer' (p. 33) such as the springs of 'five years, twenty years ago' (p. 33).	A "temporary escape from a variety of external pressures: everyday life, modernity, and urban industrialization" (Squire, 1994, p. 113).
Dialogic – "talking…sharing and learning about …everyday practices… beyond the 'rarefied atmosphere of the interview'" (Adams et al., 2015, pp. 52–53).	The other man figure enables Thomas to: give voice to views that he cannot utter provide the occasion for a digression take stock of the journey reflect on method and process – self reflexive	"Visitors were actively negotiating and transforming the meanings of authenticity in attempts to fulfil expectations about what … the setting for her books … should be like" (Squire, 1994, p. 115).

Source: Tim Middleton

We took what with hindsight was an overly literal or rationalist approach towards planning the itinerary by plotting the 'real' locations that feature in the fiction onto the map. In several cases this led to some dull treks to lochs where there was nothing to see but water surrounded by trees, but also up to Loch Glashen to film the scene where the hero's parents are spotted making love in a dinghy at the centre of the lake, or through the woods to Loch Coille Bharr to film the setting where – in a key part of the plot – a motor bike and body are dumped. The most telling lessons were not learned from the locations that worked – Carnasserie Castle as a double for the ruin Fergus's castle, running off the road in a rather too realistic recreation of the crash scene at Achnaba; filming at Connel airfield and catching a plane at take-off that perfectly matched a scene in the novel – but in fact the one that didn't work at all. Towards the end of the novel there is an atmospheric and emotional scene where Prentice (the novel's hero) looks down onto Kilmartin Glen while brooding on the landscape and its histories and his recent experience of loss. The novel tells us the exact spot we needed to film from, a dun or ancient fort site on the hill named Bac Chrom above the village of Slockavullin (Banks, 1992, p. 324). The marked-up map for our trip is shown in Figure 5.1.

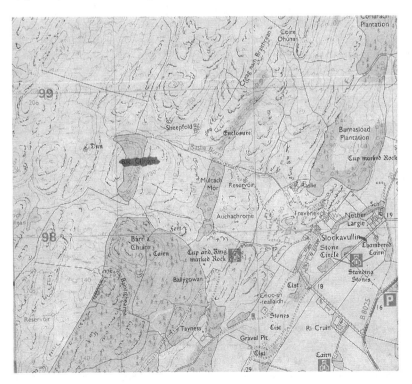

Figure 5.1 OS map (from *Explorer* sheet 358) showing the location of Bac Chrom Reproduced with permission from Ordnance Survey Limited – account number 10058299/ invoice number 92619077

We parked in the hamlet of Trevenek on the edge of Slockavullin and I led the party along a track through the hamlet of Raslie. We followed the track uphill as it ran along the edge of the burn and through the strip of woodland at the Mulach Mor. Our goal was the hill called Bac Chrom. The students were lugging camera equipment, tripods and sound recording gear. The technician was checking the GPS against the map and our location and was looking puzzled. I was 'the expert' on Banks and I'd planned the trip and our itinerary. My role here was 'leading' by deciding the route and taking a few still photographs to document our progress. Midges were bothering us as we passed through the woodland and came off the track onto the open hill. As we climbed it became apparent that the summit of the hill of Bac Chrom was so wooded that filming from it would really only present a view of trees and not the Glen below. It was also clear that the site of the dun (a hill fort) lay beyond the summit, and was in fact on the wrong side to offer a view down into the valley. Indeed, there were three duns – two on the wrong side of Bac Chrom and one half a mile below the hill's summit, and not in sight of the track to the village. Hot and tired we agreed that we had a good enough view from where Banks said the dun was, rather than its actual location, and filmed the scene from a point some 100 metres below the summit.

We had set out on this journey with a plan to capture images and video that would enable future visitors to explore the locations that inspired Banks, teasing out textual clues on the ground. We placed a premium on accuracy so brought GPS equipment to allow us to tag the locations we filmed. What we continually came up against was the gap between the text and 'the ground'. Inspired by the novel's rich evocation of the 'lived experience' of the region, I had overlooked the fact that the map represented the landscape whereas Bank's novel re-imagined it for creative ends.

Authorial intervention

As Ousby wisely reminds us, writers:

> frustrate the literal-minded researcher by moving real places across the county in obedience to imaginative requirements, by conflating several into one composite fictional entity, or simply by inventing a single place to epitomise the character of a whole terrain (Ousby, 1990, p. 9).

In his non-fiction travel book, *Raw Spirit,* Banks makes plain the ways that his literary imagination played fast and loose with Argyll's geography, writing that he had to cut the island of Jura in half to make *The Crow Road*'s imaginary west coast of Scotland work (Banks, 2004, p. 69). In attempting to follow the novel's locations using a map it quickly became apparent that what was more interesting were the ways in which this landscape's history was woven into the novel.

In attempting to follow the novel's locations using a map it quickly became apparent that what was more interesting were the ways in which this landscape's history was woven into the novel. This was something that was touched on in the book, but only by visiting the region and its museums did we gain an awareness of the ways that Banks's narrative playfully explores ancient Scots history alongside the McHoan's convoluted family history and the wider world events of its epoch. Visiting the region and learning more about its ancient sites sharpened my sense of the way Banks deals with a distinctively Scottish history to make this novel a potent description of the "imaginative possibilities of the *idea* of Scotland, or Scotlands, a matrix of myths, attitudes, possibilities, histories" (Gifford et al., 2002, p. 733). It is ironic that I only discovered this by leading a project that sought to pin down and frame something as fleeting, multi-faceted and subjective as a sense of place. By trying to film an epiphanic moment from the novel on the hill of Bac Chrom, and realising I couldn't, I gained insight into Banks's use of place, and about the role of unstructured and unexpected experiences as a key aspect in self-guided literary tourism.

Literary tourism in Scotland

Banks's use of the Kilmartin Glen locations in his novel directs readers to exactly the kind of cultural heritage tourism sites that Scotland's national tourism agency suggest should be central to the country's offer. It argues that tourism businesses "[m]arketing messages should showcase [the nation's] core assets – landscape, history, culture" (Visit Scotland, 2014a). Visit Scotland's *2015 Scotland visitor survey* found that 'History and Culture' was the second most highly cited reason for a tourist visit (32 per cent of 5,497 respondents). The survey included the question: 'Thinking broadly about your decision to choose Scotland for your holiday or short break, what first prompted you to consider Scotland for this trip?' Seven per cent of survey participants directly cited books set in or about Scotland as the reason for their visit. The most mentioned text was *Outlander,* and other books and writers cited were Walter Scott, *Harry Potter,* the Lewis Trilogy, *Blackhouse,* Ian Rankin, and *Kidnapped.* It is notable that this figure appears to be higher for the UK as a whole, where 4 per cent of overnight visitors cited this as a reason for their visit as a whole, but further research is needed to produce a secure estimate (Visit Britain 2015).

It may be telling that Banks is absent from this list, but I don't believe the idea of our literary tourism app was misplaced, for linking up a writer with a location could be an effective tourism growth strategy given the scale of visitor numbers with an interest in literary tourism. In fact, the current Visit Scotland site has a section on literary tourism which offers an e-book on Scottish Literature and brief details about 27 authors including Iain Banks (http://ebooks.visitscotland.com/scottish-literature/39/ accessed 14 Mar 2016). His presence in the *Visit Scotland* eBook implies that he is a writer whom the tourist agencies feel is worth citing when framing the country's offer. When we planned our field work we had in mind the way that a popular author can drive visitor behaviour, as is currently the case with *Outlander* tourism. It was also clear following our field trip that Banks's novel made particular use of a region of Argyll with very strong heritage tourism assets.

Argyll's economy has a reliance on tourism, which generated £92.3 million GVA (gross value added) to the regional economy in 2012 (Visit Scotland 2014). The most recent analysis of visitors to the Argyll region dates from 2011 and recorded 1.8 million tourists visiting Argyll, the Isles, and sur- rounding regions in 2010 (Visit Scotland, 2011). Within the region of Argyll where Banks's novel is set there are significant heritage tourism attractions managed by Historic Scotland: the ancient sites of Kilmartin Glen (including Carnasserie Castle), the Dunadd, and the Kilmartin stone circle. These are unstaffed sites and they are free to visit, and have estimated visitor figures for the year 2014–15 of 48,166:

> This is the total number for Kilmartin Glen – we do not have counters at the specific sites within it. We have previously simply divided this figure by the 15 sites within Kilmartin Glen in order to get an estimate at the visitors to each area but that is a very unreliable method. (Historic Scotland, 2016).

We simply do not know how many tourists have visited Dunadd, Carnasserie or the Stone Circle, but we do know that around 48,000 visitors are counted into Kilmartin Glen annually.

In designing the app we created a technologically mediated approach to this region via the locations cited in the novel.

It would be fair to say that prior to visiting the region we had not researched the ancient sites beyond the main hill fort of the Dunadd. Our approach to the region was to visit and log details of all the sites we could trace from the novel onto the Ordinance Survey (OS) map. At the time, we planned our project we were aware of the Dalriada Project, a heritage tourism initiative focusing on the same region that planned to use podcast walking guides, and we hoped that once we had developed our prototype we could connect the two.

The Dalriada Project was just getting underway when we undertook our fieldwork. It covered many of the sites and locations that feature in Banks's novel including North Knapdale, Kilmartin Glen, Carnassarie Castle and the Crinan Canal. The project aim was to "enhance people's access and under- standing of the outstanding natural and cultural heritage of mid-Argyll through a unique network of routes, sites and interpretation posts" (www. thedalriadaproject.org). Our app exists only in journal articles, but the Dal- riada Project final report details a highly successful collaboration that is operating at scale and successfully engages a local community:

> 3,560 people participated in our events, 150 school children participated in our community history programme and 90 local businesses got involved in our marketing initiative. In total, 5,187 people participated in

the project. This is significant from a small rural population of around 18,000 (Dalriada Project, 2011, p. 4).

The project was successful because it was open to being linked with other initiatives, and engaged people and communities via schools and conservation and heritage volunteer groups. It enabled local people to tell the story of their engagement with the area's heritage and landscape via oral histories, or creative projects such as making a stained glass window for a local hospital. It also tapped into an extant market for heritage tourism in the area.

Conclusion

In looking back on the literary tourism journey that shaped our fieldwork I'm struck by the sense of missed opportunity, but also by the fact that my failure to make a formal connection with the Dalriada Project was part and parcel of the rather simplistic basis for the field trip. In undertaking a literary journey through this region of Scotland in pursuit of Iain Banks's *The Crow Road* locations I had wrongly assumed that identifying the points on the map where the action took place would be a good basis for a tourist guide. This approach meant I had not thought deeply enough about the ways in which place is overlain with meanings (Agnew, 1993), and I failed to think through the way that associations between place and action that a novel deploys for its aesthetic purposes will not necessarily apply when a reader of that novel is trying to follow in the protagonist's footsteps. This is because the novel happens in your head, whereas your journey has to navigate the actual terrain itself as part of a process of doing. I had read the region through Banks's novel, but was forced to re-read it when the assumptions that informed the planned fieldwork were caught out by the inaccessibility of a location.

Looking back on this project in the light of subsequent work I can see that a stronger role model – such as Thomas – might've helped prepare me to manage a more nuanced and 'open' project. Literary tourism of the kind I have been examining in this essay yokes together the tourist's knowledge and curiosity with an active process of imaginative exploration. What the auto-ethnographic approach of a writer like Thomas has helped me to understand is that knowing and being are intimately connected – researching literary tourism means *doing* literary tourism and doing is an immensely complex business.

References

Adams, T.E., Holman Jones, S. and Ellis, C. (2015). *Autoethnography: Understanding qualitative research*. Oxford: Oxford University Press.

Agnew, J. (1993). Representing space: Space, scale and culture in social science. In: Duncan, J. and Ley, D. eds., *Place/culture/representation*. London: Routledge. pp. 251–271.

Banks, I. (1992). *The crow road.* London: Abacus.

Banks, I. (2004). *Raw spirit: In search of the perfect dram.* London: Arrow.

Bhandari, K. (2008). Touristification of cultural heritage: A case study of Robert Burns. *Tourism: An International Interdisciplinary Journal*, 56(3), pp. 283–293.

Boorstin, D. (1961). *The image: A guide to pseudo-events in America.* New York: Harper & Row.

Brown, L. (2016). Treading in the footsteps of literary heroes: An autoethnography. *European Journal of Tourism, Hospitality and Recreation.* [online]. DOI: doi:10.1515/ejthr-2016–0016, August 2016. Available at: www.degruyter.com/view/j/ejthr.ahead-of-print/ejthr-2016-0016/ejthr-2016-0016.xml [Accessed: 25 Oct 2016].

Butler, J. (1990). *Gender trouble.* London: Routledge.

Coghlan, A. and Filo, K. (2013).Using constant comparison method and qualitative data to understand participants' experiences at the nexus of tourism, sport and charity events. *Tourism Management*, 35, pp. 122–131.

Craik, J. (1997). The culture of tourism. In: Rojeck, C., and Urry, J., eds., *Touring cultures: Transformations of travel and theory.* London: Routledge. pp. 113–136

Dalriada Project. (2011). Final evaluation. [online]. Available at: www.thedalriadaproject.org/documents/dp-final-evaluation-web.pdf [Accessed 14 April 2016].

Ellis, C., Adams, T.E. and Bochner, A.P. (2011). Autoethnography: An overview. *Forum Qualitative Sozialforschung / Forum: Qualitative Social Research*, 12(1), Article 10. [online]. Available at: http://nbn-resolving.de/urn:nbn:de:0114-fqs1101108 [Accessed 24 Mar 2016].

Gifford, D., Dunningan, S. and MacGillivray, A. eds. (2002). *Scottish literature.* Edinburgh: Edinburgh University Press.

Grist, H. (2013). The Dennis Potter Heritage Project: Auto/ethnography as process and product', *eSharp*, 20, pp. 1–25. [online]. Available at: www.gla.ac.uk/media/media_279208_en.pdf [Accessed 25 Oct 2016].

Harris, A.(2016). Introduction. to Thomas, E., *In Pursuit of Spring.* Lower Dairy Toller Fratrum, Dorchester, UK: Little Toller Books. pp. 11–20.

Hemley, R. (2012). *A field guide for immersion writing: Memoir, journalism, travel.* Athens & London: University of Georgia Press.

Herbert, D. (2001). Literary places tourism and the heritage experience. *Annals of Tourism Research*, (28)2, pp. 312–333.

Historic Scotland. Personal communication 31 Mar 2016.

MacCannell, D. (1973). Staged authenticity: Arrangements of social space in tourist settings. *American Journal of Sociology*, 79, pp. 589–603.

MacCannell, D. (1976). *The tourist: A new theory of the leisure class.* New York: Schocken Books.

MacCannell, D. (1999). *The tourist: A new theory of the leisure class.* Berkeley & London: University of California Press. [First published 1976].

McCauley, S. (1996). Let's say. In Merla, P. (ed.), *Boys like us: Gay writers tell their coming out stories.* New York: Avon. pp. 186–192.

McKercher, B. and du Cross, H. (2002). *Cultural tourism: The partnership between tourism and cultural heritage management.* New York: Haworth.

Middleton, T. (2013a). Literary routes – walking through literary landscapes: Case studies of literary tourism itineraries in SW England. In: Bourdeau, L., Marcotte, P. and Habib-Saidi, M., eds., *Proceedings of the international conference: Tourism, roads and cultural itineraries.* Quebec City: Presses de l'Université Laval.

Middleton, T. (2013b). Landscape & imagination: Iain Banks' representation of Argyll in *The Crow Road*. In: Colebrook, M. and Cox, K., eds., *The transgressive Iain Banks: Essays on a writer beyond borders.* Jefferson & London: McFarland, pp. 63–75.

Ousby, I. (1990). *Blue guide: Literary Britain and Ireland.* London: A&C Black.

Patterson, A. (2002). *Scotland's landscape: Endangered icon.* Edinburgh: Polygon.

Reiser, M. (2012). Animating the archive. In: Andrews, R., Borg, E., Davis, S.B., Domingo, M. and England, J., eds., *The Sage handbook of digital dissertations and theses.* London: Sage, pp. 374–389.

Scottish Tourism Alliance. (2012). Tourism Scotland 2020. [online]. Available at: http://scottishtourismalliance.co.uk/wp-content/uploads/2013/03/Scottish-Tourism -Strategy-TourismScotland2020.pdf [Accessed 14 Apr 2016].

Sheratt, A. (2016). Edward Thomas's in pursuit of Spring – historic photo locations revisited. *The Guardian*, 7 April 2016. [online]. Available at: www.theguardian.com/ environment/2016/apr/07/edward-thomas-in-pursuit-of-spring-historic-photo-locations- revisited-little-toller?CMP=share_btn_tw [Accessed 14 Apr 2016].

Smith, K.A. (1999). *The management of volunteers at heritage attractions: Literary heritage properties in the UK.* Unpublished PhD thesis. Nottingham: Nottingham Trent University.

Smith, K.A. (2003). Literary enthusiasts as visitors and volunteers. *International Journal of Tourism Research*, 5(2), pp. 83–95.

Smith, M.K. (2009). *Issues in cultural tourism studies.* London: Routledge.

Squire, S. (1991). *Meanings, myths and memories: Literary tourism as cultural discourse in Beatrix Potter's Lake District.* Unpublished PhD thesis. London: University College London.

Squire, S., (1994). The cultural values of literary tourism. *Annals of Tourism Research*, (21)1, pp. 103–120.

Thomas, E. (1909). *The south country.* London: Dent.

Thomas, E. (1918). *Last poems.* London: Selwyn Blount.

Thomas, E. (2016). *In pursuit of Spring.* Lower Dairy Toller Fratrum, Dorchester, UK: Little Toller Books. [First published 1914].

Timothy, D.J. (2011). *Cultural & heritage tourism: An introduction.* Bristol: Channel View Publications.

Urry, J. (1995). *Consuming places.* London: Routledge.

Visit Britain. (2011). International passenger survey 2006–2011. [online]. Available at: www.visitbritain.org/activities-undertaken-britain [Accessed 15 Dec 2016].

Visit Britain. (2015). Valuing activities. [online]. Available at: www.visitbritain.org/ sites/default/files/vb-corporate/Documents-Library/documents/England-documents/ valuing_activities_-_final_report_fv_7th_october_2015_0.pdf – [Accessed 15 Apr 2016].

Visit Britain. (2016). Leveraging Britain's cultural heritage. *Foresight* (134), December 2014. [online]. Available at: www.visitbritain.org/sites/default/files/vb-corporate/ Documents-Library/documents/2014-12%20Leveraging%20our%20Culture%20and %20Heritage.pdf [Accessed 14 Apr 2016].

Visit Scotland. (2011). Scotland visitor survey. [online]. Available at: www.visitscotland. org/pdf/Visitor%20Survey%20-%20Regional%20Factsheet%20-Argyll%20and%20the %20Isles%20FV3_pptx%20[Read-Only].pdf [Accessed 14 Apr 2016].

Visit Scotland. (2014a). Visitor survey. [online]. Available at: www.visitscotland.org/ research_and_statistics/visitor_research/all_markets/scotland_visitor_survey.aspx [Accessed 14 Apr 2016].

Visit Scotland. (2014b). Scotland: The key facts on tourism in 2014. [online]. Available at: www.visitscotland.org/pdf/2015%200729%20Tourism%20in%20Scotland%202014_ Final%20draft.pdf [Accessed 14 Apr 2016].

Visit Scotland. (2014c). Tourism in Scotland's regions 2014 – revised. [online]. Available at: www.visitscotland.org/pdf/MAIN%20Regional%20Factsheet%202015_Revised %20Jan%2020161.pdf [Accessed 14 Apr 2016].

Visit Scotland. (2016). Scottish writers & literature. [online]. Available at: www. visitscotland.com/see-do/attractions/arts-culture/scottish-literature/   [Accessed   14 Apr 2016].

6 Creative cultural tourism development

A tourist perspective

Yang Zhang and Philip Xie

Introduction

Creative tourism is considered to be a new generation in tourism. It refers to an opportunity for tourists to "develop their creative potential through active participation in courses and learning experiences" (Richards and Raymond, 2000, p. 18). 'Courses' in this context refer to activities that tourists can learn to inspire their creativity. Creative tourism has been viewed as an extension of cultural tourism, and provides experiences for both host and tourists for the purpose of collective creation (Buchmann, Moore and Fisher, 2010; Richards, 2005). Creative tourism facilitates greater educational, emotional, and participatory interaction with the special character of a place, its living culture and heritage, and its community (UNESCO, 2006).

However, creativity is a loaded word. It is arguably not just an end in itself, but can be rather a means through which to develop distinctiveness, financial success, and authenticity (Zukin, 2010). In theory, creative tourism allows tourists to learn more about local skills, expertise, tradition and the uniqueness of the destinations they visit (Richards and Wilson, 2006). Thus, generating a social mix between visitor and local is crucial so that the lure of creative tourism produces valuable 'experiencescapes' (O'Dell, 2005), and stylish and aesthetically suitable consumption modes.

The creative tourist is often associated with the values of the "new cultural class" (Ley, 1994, p. 56) that has emerged in many destinations marked by gentrification. Many in this class represent an alternative cultural movement that is attracted to creative destinations that are accessible, have up-to-date amenities, contain a certain social diversity, and hold performance events and festivals that are experientially enriching. Creative industries have been built to accommodate these performative events, such as the "Pink Night" festival a co-performing tourism place in the Italian Romagna Riviera (Coleman and Crang, 2002; Giovanardi, Lucarelli and Decosta, 2014). These consumers (tourists, visitors, workers, residents) also "simultaneously consume and construct the place, co-creating the value that can be derived from the experience of these areas" (Pappalepore, Maitland and Smith, 2014, p. 237). Therefore, tourists' perceptions about creative tourism and the quality of the experiential products that stimulate their creativity through participation becomes a key factor in determining the sustainability of creative tourism in various destinations.

Mixed-use spaces in economic developments that encompass entertainment, retailing, food, and dining form a cluster of creative industries that establish experiencescapes for creative tourists. This transformation of vernacular architecture and local heritage into upscale tourism precincts demonstrates a complex interplay between adaptive reuse, gentrification, and creative destruction when catering to the new global tourist. For example, the establishment of Huashan 1914 Creative Park in Taiwan was built on a former distillery and rice wine brewery, and serves to reflect upon the slow and simple lifestyle that was part of the traditional culture of Taipei. The neighboring Songshan Cultural and Creative Park, which is a former tobacco factory located in a Japanese colonial era industrial complex, is used to house boutiques, cinemas, and restaurants. Despite the investments in these experiencescapes and the transformation of districts to attract tourist revenue, little research has been conducted about the perceptions of the actual tourists who visit these destinations, and what impacts they have on local communities (Xie, 2015). There is a particularly urgent need to understand creative tourists' profiles and preferences. For example, those who have expressed an interest in diversity and a gentrified experience, rather than an experience that is characterized by the kind of standardization prevalent in packaged tours and other forms of mass tourist entertainment.

This chapter ascertains tourists' perception of creative tourism in Macau, a former Portuguese colony located near the South China Sea. With the transfer of Macau's sovereignty to the People's Republic of China in 1999, this small enclave on the Pearl River Delta has become a gaming destination (Yeung, Lee and Kee, 2008). In recent years, creative tourism has been advocated by the Macau government's tourism bureau, which is seeking to diversify tourism options beyond the gaming industry. It is also providing more opportunities for locals to participate in tourism planning, and, as other global cities have done, to promote culture and heritage for public consumption within a 'creative industries' context (Lazzeretti, 2012). This includes sites in Macau such as the Ox Warehouse, which is an atmospheric former slaughterhouse that is run by a nonprofit organization that hosts contemporary exhibitions, workshops and performances by local and visiting artists. Several old districts, such as St. Lazarus, which once housed nursing homes for seniors, now contain restaurants, galleries, and art events.

The primary purpose of this book chapter is to investigate tourists' perception of 'product' in creative tourism destinations. This study surveyed tourists who visited the Albergue Art Space in Macau, a former Portuguese district located in St. Lazarus. This chapter begins with an extensive literature review in creative tourism. The research setting is then introduced and the methodology is detailed. The findings reveal diverse perceptions of creative tourism that includes the transformation of cultural heritage into intangible experience by way of material infrastructure for creative tourism production, and the concept of service quality as a potential factor which could influence tourists' experience and tourists' participation in creative production and consumption industries. A summary of findings is provided in the conclusion.

Creative tourism and experience

Many creative tourists want more than passive sightseeing, and wish to actively combine sport, theater, art, and lifestyle services, as well as having the opportunity to co-produce new products and services (Richards, 2011). The concept of creative tourism was first proposed in 1993 by tourism researchers Pearce and Butler, and has been gradually developed by a number of scholars and institutions (Raymond, 2007; Richards, 2011; UNESCO, 2006). The features of creative tourism include more access to culture and history involving more experience-centric activities, and offering an authentic engagement in the real cultural life of a destination. Therefore, the common components of creative tourism are "participative, authentic experiences that allow tourists to develop their creative potential and skills through contact with local people and their culture" (Richards, 2011, p.1237). In many respects the creative tourist is essentially involved in a learning process.

According to Richards and Wilson (2006, pp. 1217–1219), there are three basic types of creative tourist experiences: (1) creative spectacles, in which tourism sites produce creative experiences intended for passive consumption by tourists; (2) creative spaces, in which spatial changes occur to entice tourists to engage in active interaction; and (3) creative tourism, a convergence of creative spectacles and creative spaces that encourage active participation by tourists. All of the activities related to creative tourism allow tourists to learn more about local skills, expertise, traditions, and the unique qualities of the places they visit (Richards and Wilson, 2006). Alvin Toffler (1980) coined the term "prosumer" (professional consumer) to replace traditional consumers in the postindustrial era, and the essence of being a prosumer involves producing one's own goods and services. This is associated with the growth in prosumption – a process in which the consumer becomes a producer of the products and experiences they consume. This practice coincides with the emergence of a new breed of tourists aligned with skilled and creative consumption (Richards, 2014; Richards and Wilson, 2006), including postmodern travelers (Jelinčić and Žuvela, 2012; O'Dell, 2007), and creative tourists (Raymond, 2003).

Despite the growing popularity of creative tourism, Maitland (2008) suggests that there has been very limited research that explores what tourists want and enjoy, and these needs must be understood for those wishing to properly cater for this sector of the market. Raymond (2003, p. 3) segments creative tourists in New Zealand into three distinct groups: "the baby-boomers and newly retired", "those under 30, often students, backpackers, perhaps visiting New Zealand on a 'gap year'", and "New Zealanders themselves of all ages who are interested to learn more about different aspects of their country's culture".

These categories however were based on general demographic profiles and so remain too broad to be used effectively. Lindroth et al. (2007) in their study of Porvoo, Finland, argue that due to a mismatch between the perceptions of local communities and the needs of tourists, it has increasingly become difficult to delineate the profiles of creative tourists. Further, Gordin and Matetskaya (2012) suggest that a lack of adaptation to the needs of creative tourists causes a disconnection between public and private sectors, based upon a study in St Petersburg, Russia.

Many destinations have developed terms to refer to creative tourism, including 'Creative Tourism New Zealand', 'DIY Santa Fe' in New Mexico, 'Creative Paris', and 'Creative Life Industry (CLI)' in Taiwan. Examples of creative tourism include traditional craft making, porcelain painting, and dancing (Richards and Wilson, 2006). Destinations also have their own understanding of what activities appeal to creative tourists. For example, 'Creative Paris' categorizes the creative activities into "art, music, culinary, design, etc." (Creative France, 2013), 'Barcelona Creative Tourism' offers creative activities such as "performing art, theatre-related art, gastronomy, music, literature, etc." (Barcelona Creative, 2010), and the 'Creative Life Industries' of Taiwan uses six experience-types: food culture, life education, natural ecology, interior decoration, historic arts, and handicraft culture (Creative Life, 2008). However, all of these categorizations are supply-led (Tan et al., 2013), and it is important to ask questions such as: What does the creative tourist think of these creative activities? What factors influence the tourist's choice of activities during a vacation? What kind of experiential learning do these tourists want? At this time, these questions remain largely unanswered because research has not sufficiently identified what they want. This study therefore mainly focuses on the demand side of creative tourism and analyzes tourists who visited creative tourism destinations in order to explore their motivations and perceptions about creative tourism products.

Tourist perceptions

Perceptions or impressions of a destination held by tourists are directly related to anticipated benefits and consumption values (Tapachai and Waryszak, 2000, 38). These include the totality of impressions, beliefs, ideas, expectations, and feelings towards a place that accrue over time by an individual or group of people (Kim and Richardson, 2003). For a given destination, Murphy, Pritchard and Smith (2000) argue that the economic success of the tourism marketplace depends on how tourists perceive this complex amalgam of elements and experiences. By examining tourist perceptions and experiences, Cheang (2011) argues that positive perceptions are linked to experiences that exceeded expectations, and were based on cultural enrichment, host friendliness, and local hospitality facilities. There is a sense of personal fulfillment that is derived from such experiences, which was explained by Bowen (1998) as reflecting an embrace of creative activities through which a sense of autonomous and authentic personal identity can be constructed. In the context of historical and cultural destinations, many researchers (Garrod and Fyall, 2001; Poria, Butler and Airey, 2001, 2003) argue that a place's heritage and historical/cultural characteristics are often qualities that emerge. While tourists visit historical/cultural sites to observe historical landmarks and study the past, they also look for participatory experience; such as a desire to pray there, and become otherwise emotionally involved, and many feel a sense of obligation to immerse themselves in learning about a visited culture's past (Poria, Butler and Airey, 2004).

Vargas-Sánchez, Porras-Bueno and de los Ángeles Plaza-Mejía (2013) have analyzed these experiential qualities and conclude that tourists were influenced by other tourists' perceptions of the significance and value of that heritage. For some sites, this influence means that the heritage artifacts are designed and marketed to meet tourist expectations. Themes, products, and designs that mix modernity with nostalgia (for example, souvenirs that mix modern design with traditional patterns), are integrated into complementary local culture services and landscapes that are the central determinants of tourist experience of a certain destination (Cracolici and Nijkamp, 2009; Xie, Wu and Hsieh, 2012). In terms of tourist perceptions of creative tourism, a demand for sophisticated tangible creative products and intangible service are motivated by a desire for learning and entertainment that gives them significant emotional motivation. In other words, tourists expect to immerse themselves in "imagined, landscapes of experience" (O'Dell, 2005, p. 16).

The evaluative attributes of the present study draw compatible ideas from literature in the fields mentioned above. A set of attributes, including themes, programs, and designs (Xie, Wu and Hsieh, 2012) have been identified in typical creative tourism sites, and are thus the primary categories through which to gauge tourists' perception of creative tourism in Macau, which are further developed below.

Research setting

Macau has surpassed Las Vegas as "the largest gaming center in the world, and is poised to overtake the entire state of Nevada in total gaming revenues" (Culver, 2009, p. 1057). The development of casinos in Macau dates back to 1962, when the *Sociedade de Turismo e Diversões de Macau* (STDM) was launched, however, there was a huge surge of new casinos after the territory was transferred to Chinese administration in 1999 (McCartney, 2005) and it became Macau's pillar industry. Multiple cultures are also represented in specifically themed environments throughout the territory, ranging from casinos to smaller-scale shopping and entertainment precincts (Cheng, 2002). In addition, Macau represents the integration of two cultures – Portuguese and Chinese – and has been a cultural melting pot for East and West since the sixteenth century (Li, 2005). This cultural heritage therefore has considerable potential for creative tourism development.

In some respects, creative tourism depends on the resilience of communities (Ahern, 2011), and in Macau's case, the resilience of a gaming city. Macau's reliance on gaming has made it prosperous, but it will need to diversify its economy if it wants to avoid the adverse impact of a major financial crisis. Creative tourism is seen as an important element in a diversified economy, and can play a "crucial role in both China's economic reforms and its utopian desires" (Simpson, 2008, p. 1053). Creative tourism development in Macau has gained attention from local government and communities, and in 2003 the Civic and Municipal Affairs Bureau established the Macau Center of Creative Industry, and the Macau Creative Space to encourage the growth of local creative industries.

Macau experienced a very compact development and contains many organic and mixed-use neighborhoods, which are mainly centered on the former Leal Senado Square. As Mai (2006) argues, Macau has great potential for creative tourism although the current development of this industry is still in its infancy. Firstly, the majority of its built heritage is old and rich in patrimonial value, and has been accepted into the World Cultural Heritage List, which has attracted international esteem. Secondly, Macau is a free social environment that attracts many cultural creative talents, and already has a sizeable local group of creative people that it can draw on as a resource. It is also a member of CEPA, "9+2" Cooperation (Mainland and Hong Kong Closer Economic Partnership Arrangement), and is a bridge between Chinese and Portuguese speaking countries.

This study has chosen Albergue da Santa Casa da Misericórdia Macau as the case study site. It is located in the typical S. Lázaro Neighborhood, and was renovated and restored in 2003 under the supervision and vision of Brother Carlos Marreiros, and the altruistic collaboration of engineers Gilberto Gomes and José Silveirinha. According to the Macau Government Tourism Administration, this precinct has served as a base for the development of Macau's cultural and creative industries in recent years. Albergue SCM features a small courtyard with two 100-year-old, yellow-hued Portuguese buildings. Two old camphor trees tower over this tranquil courtyard. Many of the local poor and refugees lived here during World War II so it became known as the 'Shelter of the Poor'. It was also known as the 'Old Ladies House' as it once served as a refuge for elderly females. Nowadays, its galleries house various local art and creative design exhibitions, and a nearby Portuguese restaurant draws tourists from around the world. Albergue SCM also holds poetry-reading sessions and art seminars to enhance local art, cultural and creative development. These sites and activities imbue this historical monument with a unique vitality.

Methodology

Since this study is context-specific in its examination of Macau, scales adopted from literature have been slightly modified to suit a local situation. A 14-

Figure 6.1 Pic Albergue da Santa Casa da Misericórdia Macau

item scale measured on a five-point Likert scale was generated from the research (Baloglu and Mangaloglu, 2001; Chi and Qu, 2008) to measure the destination perception construct. In addition, questions requiring demographic information were directed at creative cultural tourists at the end of the questionnaire.

The measurement scales have been adopted and slightly modified from the extant literature, and a pre-test of the measurement instrument was deemed necessary to validate the items in the scale. This pre-test was conducted in two stages: initially, the survey questionnaire was circulated to a pool of tourism scholars, creative industry officials and the Macau tourist office requesting feedback on the wording, the questionnaire layout, and their understanding of the measurement items. Their feedback was recorded and taken into account when the survey questionnaire was revised. The questionnaire was then pre-tested using a sample of creative cultural tourists in Albergue da Santa Casa da Misericórdia (N=50) to ascertain the reliability and validity of the measurement items. Cronbach's Alpha reliability scale of tourism perception is 0.860, which suggests that this questionnaire is suitable for an extended survey of large sample sizes. The final version of the questionnaire survey was administered in Chinese (Mandarin) as the majority of tourists in Macau are from China. The survey was undertaken in various travel seasons in Macau from January to April 2016. Tourists were approached on a next-to-pass basis within and around the site, and researchers explained the purpose of the study. A total of 412 valid questionnaires were collected. Frequency analysis of the respondents' social demographic characteristics was conducted to explore their assumptions and a mean value analysis of tourist perception was used for obtaining tourists' attitude within this variable. Finally, exploratory factor analysis was employed to identify the dimensions of tourists' perception towards this creative tourism destination.

Findings

Social demographic characteristics of tourists

The demographic variables of respondents are listed in Table 6.1. Of the total respondents, 63.3 percent were female and 36.7 percent male, which indicated that females form a disproportionate number of visitors to this creative tourism destination. The majority of respondents were between the ages of 21 and 30 (51 percent), and between 31 and 40 (23.2 percent). In terms of occupations, 43.2 percent identified themselves as white collar (often working in the business sector), and 18.9 percent as students. With respect to educational attainment, 68.5 percent of respondents claimed to have earned a college degree and 16.4 percent reported completing a graduate degree. In terms of monthly income, 46.1 percent of respondents are at the level of 10,000 Macau Pataca (US $1,200) and above. The overwhelming number of visitors, 90.4 percent came from the neighboring regions of Macau, such as Hong Kong (44.3 percent) and Taiwan (46.1 percent), while Mainland tourists only comprised 7.8 percent of the total. The data shows that 23.6 percent of respondents stated they visited St. Lazaro after seeing information about it on the Internet. Receiving recommendations from friends and relatives was more popular with 30.3 percent of respondents claiming they went to Macau for that reason.

These characteristics reflect a viable sample and demographic pattern of tourists who visit the creative tourism destination of Macau, and these match typical cultural tourists (Orbasli, 2000; Richards, 2001; Richards and Wilson, 2006). More importantly, they match the characteristics of "Bobos" ("Bourgeois Bohemian," a term coined by David Brooks in 2000) that refers to a new knowledge elite. "Bobos" are prevalent in globalized cities and adopt lifestyles and political attitudes that stand in contrast to that of conventional tourists. They tend to have a rewarding and well-paid occupation with high income, and above average educational attainment. They exhibit enthusiasm for contemporary arts, alternative rock concerts, and so forth (Saint-Paul, 2015). From a demand perspective, the many female tourist respondents demonstrate a new form of creative tourism market where gender is an important consideration. On the other hand, the relatively low number of Mainland Chinese tourists suggests that traditional group tourists are not visiting sites like Macau. Instead, it is more appealing to a generation connected to social media and the Internet that plays a key role in disseminating information about creative tourist destinations. Word-of-mouth recommendations from friends and relatives are also crucial for decisions made by creative tourists.

Table 6.1 Profile of sample respondents (N=412)

% of the sample		% of the sample	
Gender		Education	
Male	36.7	Less than high school	2.0
Female	63.3	High school	13.1
Age		College graduation	27.3
<20 years	7.8	Bachelor's degree	41.2
21-30	51.0	Graduate degree	16.4
31-40	23.2	Information source	
41-50	8.6	Internet	23.6
51-60	7.0	TV program	5.9
>61 years	2.5	Relatives and friends recommend	30.3
Occupation		Tourism magazine	10.0
Students	18.9	Others	30.1
Business	7.8	Monthly income (MOP)	
Civil servant	5.9	<2000	16.8
White collar	43.2	2001-4000	10.9
Teacher	4.7	4001-6000	8.2
Doctor	1.8	6001-8000	8.8
Blue collar	2.3	8000-10000	9.2
Attorney	0.6	>10001	46.1
Retired/others	14.8		
Tourist source			
Mainland China	7.8		
Hong Kong	44.3		
Taiwan	46.1		
Others	1.8		

Source: Authors.

Perception of creative tourist destination

Table 6.2 presents the mean ratings of tourists' perceptions about the creative tourism destination they visit. On a scale ranging from 1 (completely disagree) to 5 (completely agree), tourists were asked to describe various aspects of their attitude towards the destination. A total of ten description summaries

Table 6.2 Tourists' perception of creative tourism destination

Characteristics	Mean	S.D.
Old architecture is filled with local specialty	4.487	.587
Inner decoration has an exotic flavor	4.288	.663
Architectural painting represents local flavor	4.358	.638
Spatial planning is comfortable	4.084	.713
Whole ambience is artistic	4.116	.708
Signage is clear and convenient	3.557	.929
Service instruments are suitable and comfortable	3.784	.731
Overall environment is clean and tidy	4.073	.727
Creative product/performances are interesting	3.821	.787
Service is warm and friendly	4.065	.752
Service is timely	3.751	.714
Watch the process of creative products	3.314	.822
Experience the production of creative products	3.299	.841
Participate in creative performances	3.334	.844

Source: Authors.

Note: Features were rated on a Likert scale ranging from 1 (completely disagree) to 5 (completely agree).

seemed to reflect positive perceptions of typically popular events and sites in a creative tourism destination. The three most commonly cited viewings of their visiting experience were old architecture representing a local specialty (4.487), inner decoration with an exotic flavor (4.288), and architectural painting with a local flavor (4.358). These results demonstrated that tourists gained strong visual impressions from the interior and exterior design elements on display at Albergue SCM.

Table 6.3 demonstrates the result of exploratory factor analysis that was used to identify the latent factor structure. The Kaiser-Mayer-Olkin (KMO) measure of sampling adequacy value was .874 and the BTS was 1829.832 (p < .001). This indicated that the sample was appropriate to conduct an exploratory factor analysis. As a result of population attributable fraction (PAF) with varimax rotation, three factors within the 14 items were identified, explaining 61.67 percent of the variance, which are vernacular heritage (five items), service quality (six items) and participatory experience (three items).

The findings suggest that vernacular heritage, service quality, and participatory experience promoting authenticity and originality in creative tourist destinations may be particularly successful in attracting tourists. The significance of vernacular architecture (both interiors and exteriors) is due to tourist perceptions that old architecture is exotic and represents a significant departure from their everyday lives. In addition, they paid close attention to

Table 6.3 The result of tourists' perceptions

Factors	Factor loading	Explained variance	Composite mean
Vernacular heritage		22.076	3.091
Old architectures are rich in local specialty	.611		
Inner decoration has exotic flavor	.843		
Architecture color matching is full of local flavor	.834		
Spatial planning is comfortable	.696		
Whole planning is artistic	.694		
Service quality		20.507	2.871
Signage is clear and convenient	.556		
Service instruments are suitable and comfortable	.664		
Overall environment is clean and tidy	.646		
Creative products/performances are interesting	.698		
Service is warm and friendly	.776		
Service is timely	.547		
Participatory experience		19.083	2.672
Watch the process of creative products	.853		
Experience the production of creative products	.875		
Participate in creative performances	.857		

Source: Authors.

service quality in which a fun and comfortable atmosphere is perceived as valuable. Participatory experience is also ranked, which demonstrates that tourists have a desire to gain hands-on experience with creative products. Those who seek learning experiences wish to participate in cultural performances, arts shows, and food tasting. The findings resonate with Kao, Huang and Wu's (2008) study that categorized the quality of tourist experiences according to immersion, surprise, participation, and fun.

Conclusion

This chapter describes tourists' perceptions of creative tourism, and in particular, the roles that vernacular heritage, service quality, and participatory experience play in attracting tourists. The research consists of analysis from a demand and consumer perspective, using quantitative data to collate tourist's creative perception through their interactions with the environment, people, product, and service. The study suggests a number of valuable findings that can assist in developing creative tourism, and highlights the importance of the three major factors as core appeals in a creative tourist destination.

This research demonstrates that the sustainability and viability of creative destinations should be considered during macro tourism planning. The success of creative tourism relies on local endorsement and ownership of the sites, including the involvement of communities to foster a sustainable cultural heritage. The development, management, and communication of creative tourism sites requires optimum modes of interpretation and service, whereby tourists are encouraged to participate, interact, and engage with some aspects of creative culture, such as drama performance and handicraft production. In the interim, vernacular heritage still plays a key role in enhancing the creative tourism experience.

From an academic perspective, this study contributes to the literature on creative tourism systems, especially the demand side by exploring creative experience from the tourists' viewpoint. It is evident that in order to have creative experiences, tourists care about more than a well-decorated or restored architectural edifice. Rather, the key element that contributes to the creative tourists' perception of destination is the opportunity to learn and participate in creative production. From a marketing perspective, this study has implications for practitioners such as creative shop owners, tourism planners, and policy makers who are seeking to further develop creative tourism in Macau. For example, respondents in this study have high income, good careers, and are well educated. This indicates that they are actively involved with creative tourism, but by different standards in comparison to the mass tourist. Indeed, the creative tourist may exemplify a trend towards a more professional consumption capacity for creative products and services. Moreover, although tourists from Mainland China are the largest group in Macau, the percentage of Mainland Chinese tourists in Albergue da Santa Casa da Misericórdia is relatively small. This suggests there is huge potential to expand creative tourism in the Mainland Chinese market. Tourism officials and destination marketing organizations should therefore pay more attention to marketing efforts to promote visits from mainland Chinese tourist groups. Regarding the promotion channel for Chinese tourist groups, building up online marketing platforms in China could be a potential option for younger clientele. Meanwhile, vernacular cultural heritage should be the core element of Macau's creative tourism products, which is distinct from the many creative tourism attractions in Chinese cities, such as Xintiandi in Shanghai, and the 798 Art District in Beijing.

Importantly, creative tourism cannot be simply derived from mass tourism without considering that it best serves experienced consumers who actively pursue unique learning and participative experiences. For example, social media as a popular marketing tool has been widely used by destination marketing organizations, especially online media which shared 23.6 percent of the total proportion of respondents as the information source for visits according to this study. However, with regards to the specific online media choice for Mainland Chinese tourists, there is potential to promote Macau on Wechat, which is now the most popular social media site in China.

While this exploratory study of tourists' perceptions toward creative tourism relates to Macau, results reinforce the need for tourism planners to deliver positive, memorable experiences for any site wishing to attract those who have an interest in creative tourism. The most appealing experiences are often surprising in nature for they exceed tourists' baseline expectations. Focusing on participatory experience, such as cultural events or craft making helps generate self-expressive creativity (Ivcevic and Mayer, 2009). It also has a knock-on effect via travel blog writing or interpersonal communication on social networks, especially the virtual social environment that creative tourists produce after their visits. These attractions and the resultant use of social media have a broad appeal for all who seek an indelible creative tourism experience.

References

Ahern, J. (2011). From fail-safe to safe-to-fail: sustainability and resilience in the new urban world. *Landscape Urban Planning*. 100(4), pp. 341–343.

Baloglu, S. and Mangaloglu, M. (2001). Tourism destination images of Turkey, Egypt, Greece, and Italy as perceived by US-based tour operators and travel agents. *Tourism Management*, 22(1), pp. 1–9.

Barcelona Creative. (2010). Creative experiences. [online]. Available at: www.barcelona creativa.info/category/creative-experiences/ [Accessed 10 May 2016].

Bowen, J.T. (1998). Market segmentation in hospitality research: no longer a sequential process. *International Journal of Contemporary Hospitality Management*, 10(7), pp. 289–296.

Brooks, D. (2000). *Bobos in paradise: The new upper class and how they got there*. New York: Touchstone.

Buchmann, A., Moore, K. and Fisher, D. (2010). Experiencing film tourism: Authenticity and fellowship. *Annals of Tourism Research*, 37(1), pp. 229–248.

Cheang, V. (2011). Angkor heritage tourism and tourist perceptions. *Tourismos*, 6(2), pp. 213–240.

Cheng, C. (2002). *Macau: A cultural Janus*. Hong Kong: Hong Kong University Press.

Chi, C.G.Q. and Qu, H. (2008). Examining the structural relationships of destination image, tourist satisfaction and destination loyalty: An integrated approach. *Tourism Management*, 29(4), pp. 624–636.

Coleman, S. and Crang, M. (2002). *Tourism: Between place and performance*. Oxford and New York: Berghahn Books.

Cracolici, M.F. and Nijkamp, P. (2009). The attractiveness and competitiveness of tourist destinations: A study of Southern Italian regions. *Tourism Management*, 30(3), pp. 336–344.

Creative France. (2013). Creative activity category. [online]. Available at: www.crea tivefrance.fr/en/category/visual-arts-arts-crafts [Accessed 4 May 2016].

Creative Life. (2008). Creative life products. [online]. Available at: http://creative.twfa rmcrop.com/ [Accessed 12 May 2016].

Culver, L. (2009). Sin city or suburban crucible? Searching for meanings in the new Las Vegas. *Journal of Urban History*, 35(7), pp. 1052–1058.

Garrod, B. and Fyall, A. (2001). Heritage tourism: A question of definition. *Annals of Tourism Research*, 28(4), pp.1049–1052.

Giovanardi, M., Lucarelli, A. and Decosta, P.L.E. (2014). Co-performing tourism places: The "Pink Night" festival. *Annals of Tourism Research*, 44, pp. 102–115.

Gordin, V. and Matetskaya, M. (2012). Creative tourism in Saint Petersburg: The state of the art. *Journal of Tourism Consumption and Practice*, 4(2), pp. 55–77.

Ivcevic, Z. and Mayer, J.D. (2009). Mapping dimensions of creativity in the lifespace. *Creativity Research Journal*, 21, pp. 152–165.

Jelinčić, D. A. and Žuvela, A. (2012). Facing the challenge? Creative tourism in Croatia. *Journal of Tourism Consumption and Practice Volume*, 4(2), pp. 78–90.

Kao, Y., Huang, L. and Wu, C. (2008). Effects of theatrical elements on experimental quality and loyalty intentions for theme parks. *Asia Pacific Journal of Tourism Research*, 13(2), pp. 163–174.

Kim, H. and Richardson, S.L. (2003). Motion picture impacts on destination images. *Annals of Tourism Research*, 30(1), pp. 216–237.

Lazzeretti, L., ed. (2012). *Creative industries and innovation in Europe: Concepts, measures and comparative case studies*. London: Routledge.

Ley, D. (1994). Gentrification and the politics of the new middle class. *Environment and Planning D: Society and Space*, 12(1), pp. 53–74.

Li, X.Y. (2005). Difficult expressed status: Macanese cultural identity, *21st Century*, 92(12), pp. 16–27.

Lindroth, K., Ritalahti, J. and Soisalon-Soininen, T. (2007). Creative tourism in destination development. *Tourism Review*, 62(3/4), pp. 53–58.

McCartney, G.J. (2005). Casinos as a tourism redevelopment strategy–the case of Macao. *Journal of Macau Gaming Research Association*, 2(2), pp. 40–54.

Mai, J.Z. (2006). Cultural creative industry and its development in Macao. *Administration*, 74(2), pp. 1139–1160.

Maitland, R. (2008). Conviviality and everyday life: The appeal of new areas of London for visitors. *International Journal of Tourism Research*, 10(1), pp. 15–25.

Murphy, P., Pritchard, M.P. and Smith, B. (2000). The destination product and its impact on traveller perceptions. *Tourism Management*, 21(1), pp. 43–52.

O'Dell, T. (2005). Experience-scapes. In: O'Dell, T. and Billing, P., eds., *Experiencescapes: Tourism, culture and economy*. Copenhagen: Copenhagen Business School Press, pp. 1–31.

O'Dell, T. (2007). Tourist experiences and academic junctures. *Scandinavian Journal of Hospitality and Tourism*, 7(1), pp. 34–45.

O'Dell, T. and Billing, P., eds. (2005). *Experiencescapes: Tourism, culture and economy*. Copenhagen: Copenhagen Business School Press.

Orbasli, A. (2000). *Tourists in historic towns*. London and New York: E & FN Spon.

Pappalepore, I., Maitland, R. and Smith, A. (2014). Prosuming creative urban areas. Evidence from East London. *Annals of Tourism Research*, 44, pp. 227–240.

Pinheiro, F. and Wan, Y.K.P. (2008). Urban planning practices and scenarios for Macao development: A Re-examination (2007–2008). In: Proceedings from the

International Conference on 13th Asian Real Estate Society Annual Conference. Shanghai, pp. 12–15.

Poria, Y., Butler, R. and Airey, D. (2001). Clarifying heritage tourism. *Annals of Tourism Research*, 28(4), pp. 1047–1049.

Poria, Y., Butler, R. and Airey, D. (2003). The core of heritage tourism. *Annals of Tourism Research*, 30(1), pp. 238–254.

Poria, Y., Butler, R. and Airey, D. (2004). Links between tourists, heritage, and reasons for visiting heritage sites. *Journal of Travel Research*, 43(1), pp. 19–28.

Raymond, C. (2003). Cultural renewal + tourism: Case study – creative tourism New Zealand. [online]. Available at: www.creativenz.govt.nz/assets/paperclip/publication_documents/documents/97/original/case-study-creative-tourism-new-zealand.pdf? 1322079829 [Accessed 1 Jan 2016].

Raymond, C. (2007). Creative tourism New Zealand. In: Richards, G. and Wilson, J., eds. *Tourism, creativity and development*. London: Routledge, pp. 145–158.

Richards, G., ed. (2001). *Cultural attractions and European tourism*. Wallingford: CABI.

Richards, G. (2005). Creativity: A new strategic resource for tourism. In: Swarbrooke, J., Smith, M. and Onderwater, L., eds. *Tourism: Creativity and development: ATLAS Reflections*, Arnhem, Netherlands: Association for Tourism and Leisure Education, pp. 11–22.

Richards, G. (2011). Creativity and tourism: The state of the art. *Annals of Tourism Research*, 38(4), pp. 1225–1253.

Richards, G. (2014). Creativity and tourism in the city. *Current Issues in Tourism*, 17(2), pp. 119–144.

Richards, G. W. and Raymond, C. (2000). Creative tourism. *ATLAS News*, 23, pp. 16–20.

Richards, G. and Wilson, J. (2006). Developing creativity in tourist experiences: A solution to the serial reproduction of culture? *Tourism Management*, 27(6), pp. 1209–1223.

Saint-Paul, G. (2015). Bobos in paradise: Urban politics and the new economy. *PSE Working Papers*, No. 2015–2034, pp. 1–43.

Simpson, M.C. (2008). Community benefit tourism initiatives – A conceptual oxymoron? *Tourism Management*, 29(1), pp. 1–18.

Tan, S.K., Kung, S.F. and Luh, D.B. (2013). A model of 'creative experience' in creative tourism. *Annals of Tourism Research*, 41, pp. 153–174.

Tapachai, N. and Waryszak, R. (2000). An examination of the role of beneficial image in tourist destination selection. *Journal of Travel Research*, 39(1), pp. 37–44.

Toffler, A. (1980). *The third wave*. New York: Bantam Books.

UNESCO. (2006). Towards sustainable strategies for creative tourism: Discussion report of the planning meeting for 2008 international conference on creative tourism. Santa Fe, New Mexico.

Vargas-Sánchez, A., Porras-Bueno, N. and de los Ángeles Plaza-Mejía, M. (2013). Clustering industrial heritage tourists. In: Staiff, R., Bushell, R. and Watson, S., eds. *Heritage and tourism: Place, encounter, engagement*. London and New York: Routledge, p. 274.

WTO. (1995). *What tourism managers need to know: A practical guide to the development and use of indicators of sustainable tourism*. Madrid: WTO.

Wu, T.C.E., Xie, P.F. and Tsai, M.C. (2015). Perceptions of attractiveness for salt heritage tourism: A tourist perspective. *Tourism Management*, 51, pp. 201–209.

Xie, P.F. (2015). *Industrial heritage tourism*. Bristol: Channel View Publications.

Xie, P.F., Wu, T.C. and Hsieh, H.W. (2012). Tourists' perception of authenticity in indigenous souvenirs in Taiwan. *Journal of Travel & Tourism Marketing*, 29(5), pp. 485–500.

Yeung, Y.M., Lee, J. and Kee, G. (2008). Hong Kong and Macao under Chinese sovereignty. *Eurasian Geography and Economics*, 49(3), pp. 304–325.

Zukin, S. (2010). *Naked city: The death and life of authentic urban places*. Oxford: Oxford University Press.

7 #travelselfie

A netnographic study of travel identity communicated via Instagram

Ulrike Gretzel

Introduction

Consuming modern tourist experiences has always been intricately linked with photographic practices, and sharing travel photographs with others is an important way of processing, remembering and prolonging these experiences (Gretzel, Fesenmaier and O'Leary, 2006). For many, travelling without taking photographs is unimaginable; indeed, the prototypical tourist is portrayed with a camera around their neck. Shanks and Svabo (2014) further stress the important role of travel photography by describing the making and sharing of images as a way of experiencing and enacting a place. What tourists take photographs of is shaped by the tourist gaze (Urry and Larsen, 2011), which is driven by the need to delineate travel experiences from everyday life by seeking out the exotic and extraordinary.

Travellers nowadays increasingly share their travel photographs on social media (Lo et al., 2011), a phenomenon that is fuelled by smartphone ownership, fast Internet connections and the prominence of social media in people's lives. Shanks and Svabo (2014) refer to this as a fluid, individualized connectivity and illustrate how it has recast photographic practices by enabling constant photo-taking and immediate sharing. Through this engagement with social media, and as a result of the prominence of mobile digital photography, the tourist gaze is transformed. The focus is increasingly on photographs as communicative devices that are taken not only for oneself or a small social circle, but as something that is instantaneously available for a potentially large and ever expanding audience. This audience scrutinizes posted photographs for their "social media share-worthiness", and only rewards posters with likes and positive comments if the photographs stand out. As a result, it is no longer enough to distinguish travel photographs from ordinary life, but also from the travel photographs of others, and even the photographs one has previously shared. In addition, Dinhopl and Gretzel (2016) suggest that the tourist gaze is increasingly directed away from destinations and attractions and toward the self in the process of producing the ultimate social media image, namely the selfie.

In academic discourse Dinhopl and Gretzel (2016, p. 127) define selfies as being "characterized by the desire to frame the self in a picture taken to be shared with an online audience". They also acknowledge that selfie-taking practice is constantly evolving (e.g. through the emergence of selfie sticks and selfie drones) and does not necessarily have to be taken by oneself or show a close-up of the self. Selfies taken in the travel context and shared on social media are a significant reflection of one's travel identity. The link between tourism consumption and self-identity has been established in the literature as direct and important (Desforges, 2000) and social media posts have been identified as central ways in which travellers construct narratives of themselves (Bosangit, Hibbert and McCabe, 2015).

Photographs take on a crucial role in providing evidence, but are even more important in relation to communicating the essence of one's travel identity. Lo and McKercher (2015) describe tourist photography as not only a performance of tourism, but also a performance of the self and argue that tourist photographs are therefore an essential element of online self-presentation. Similarly, Van House (2011) emphasizes the role of vernacular photography not only for memory and social relations but also as vehicles for self-representation and self-expression. While Lo and McKercher (2015) have examined specific practices connected with posting travel photos on social media, including the extent to which travellers engage in impression management online, very little is currently known about the content of travel-related self-presentations. Therefore, the goal of the research presented in this chapter is to investigate how travellers represent and express their identities in social media posts, with a specific focus on selfies.

Background

The travel selfie is a particular genre of the generic selfie and has to be understood in the broader context of selfie-taking, technological affordances and the creation and posting of user generated contents on social media. The following sections provide a brief introduction to the backdrop against which the research was conducted.

Selfies

Although historically grounded in self-portraiture and snapshot photography (Iqani and Schroeder, 2015), selfies are a relatively recent social media phenomenon, but have had a significant social impact as 2014 was named the Year of the Selfie by Twitter (Ng, 2014). Dinhopl and Gretzel (2016) claim the emergence of the front-facing camera represents the single most important technological affordance that spurred selfie-taking, and this has complemented the general need in social media to produce images of the self in order to complete one's profile. Indeed, as Wendt (2014) emphasizes, social media encourages selfie-taking, and animates users to create infinite versions of themselves. However, selfies have long graduated from being a functional necessity and have been incorporated into a number of complex psychological and social practices. For example, Rettberg (2014) suggests that we use selfies to see and shape our online and offline identities and Rokka (2015) has proclaimed that selfies do not just portray identities but are performances of the self that regenerate and transform identities.

Selfies come in all forms and shapes. Miller et al. (2016) identify several selfie genres. Groupies or groufies, for example, are selfies of more than one person. The latter have been found to be rather prominent and defeat claims that selfie-taking is a purely narcissistic pursuit. There are also selfies that only feature part of the self, for instance, the so-called footies. Rokka and Canniford (2016) have investigated another selfie type: the brand selfie, which prominently features the self in relation to or consumption of a particular brand. What selfie genres dominate within the travel context is currently not known.

Despite their prominence, selfies have been largely ignored in the travel literature. The few papers specifically dedicated to studies of travel selfies that have been produced include the conceptual paper on the selfie gaze by Dinhopl and Gretzel (2016), a paper by Lyu (2016) that investigated travel selfie manipulation for the purpose of impression management in Korea, a conference paper by Paris and Pietschnig (2015) that tried to link personality traits and travel selfie-taking, a conference paper by Magasic (2016) that more generally looks at how traveling with an imaginary social media audience shapes experiences and photo-taking as well as sharing, and, finally, a paper by Flaherty and Choi (2016) that addresses the often hazardous nature of travel selfie-taking. There is thus a great need for additional research into the representational and non-representational aspects of travel selfies and the social media practices surrounding them.

Instagram

Social media has recently experienced a visual turn (Gretzel, 2016), as visually dominated platforms have grown in number and ever more users are flocking to use them. This is especially so for younger users who are increasingly communicating, almost exclusively, in visual ways on social media. One of the most prominent and successful platforms in the visual social media category is Instagram. Instagram currently boasts 500 million active monthly users, an increase of 100 million users over the previous year (Statista, 2016). Over 90 per cent of Instagram users are younger than 35 and 32 per cent of US teenagers indicate that it is their most important social media platform (Brandwatch, 2016). These users have, to date, shared 40 billion photos and post on average 95 million photos and videos to the platform every day (Hootsuite, 2016). Engagement is very high on the platform, with 60 per cent of users logging in daily and 3.5 billion *likes* being logged every day (Brandwatch, 2016).

Until very recently, Instagram only supported the posting of photos taken on mobile phones, but it now provides programs that enable the alteration of photographs and uploading of short videos. Instagram's popular reputation is based on its provision of filter technology that allows its users to manipulate photographs in semi-professional ways. As a result, Instagram posts are in many ways more artistic and visually pleasing than photographs posted on other platforms. In response to this trend, popular magazine *Marie Claire* (2014, n.p.) has suggested: "in the world of Instagram, aesthetics matter". The platform also has a more ephemeral and self-focused flair than others; for instance, it does not allow users to organize their photographs into albums, and does not afford the tagging of others in photographs. The way users discover content on Instagram is through hashtags, and by following accounts. At the time of writing, Instagram featured over 136 million posts tagged with #travel and over 279 million posts with the hashtag #selfie.

Miller (2015) reports that on Instagram, photos are not posted to document, but are rather deployed to elicit likes and comments. He further notes that Instagram is the platform on which selfie-heavy profiles are the norm and that Instagram users perceive creating and posting Instagram photographs as a craft. It seems that Instagram users extensively engage in the types of editing and curating described by Lo and McKercher (2015), which is central to the impression management instigated by travellers. Through posting photographs on Instagram, users also craft their representation of self. This actually includes the deletion of previous posts if they did not receive enough likes, or do not fit within the current narrative to be portrayed (Business Insider, 2016). Scott Dadich, editor-in-chief of *Wired* magazine, has written about the way he uses his travel photographs to chronicle his experiences and represent himself. He has also noted how central curating is to Instagram use because, "since I post so many of them to social media, they're also a version of who I am. I edit and design my Instagram feed ... well, I'd say 'carefully,' but 'obsessively' might not be wrong" (*Wired*, 2016, p. 16). Miller (2015) suggests that while Instagram celebrates the mundane and users often post pictures of ordinary life, there is also a need to, "include something a bit special and distinct" (p. 14). This is achieved through crafting, for instance the careful composition of objects, the application of filters, the use of unexpected angles or perspectives and the performance of interesting looks, expressions or poses.

Methodology

Understanding social media creation behaviours and conventions requires a cultural understanding that is in-depth and holistic. It demands an approach that is open to seeing not only what is there, but also what is not there: what is obvious and what is implied. It calls for data collection and its analysis and skills that can understand and interpret the socio-technical context in which these behaviours occur. This includes the specific social media platform and its technological affordances, as well as its particular interaction culture, and the abilities of smartphone cameras and selfie-sticks to visualize and frame experiences, etc. Social media are social, and posting on social media platforms is a complex communicative act that addresses a variety of real and imagined audiences (Miller et al., 2016). At the same time, social media make such social communication publicly visible in unprecedented ways and offers rich field sites for exploring the representations of travel experiences (Kozinets, 2002).

Netnography is a research approach that was specifically designed to address the above considerations (Kozinets, 2012). Building on the principles of ethnographic research, it employs a mix of methods like observation, participant observation, research websites and interviewing. It strives to collect a variety of data that, together with field notes, are analysed in a qualitative way to derive rich insights into a cultural phenomenon. However, it is not just digital ethnography, i.e. ethnographic research done online. Kozinets (2015) explains that netnographic research takes advantage of social media affordances in accessing and archiving data (e.g. the ability to conduct searches on hashtags) and therefore offers opportunities to observe much more broadly and system-atically than conventional ethnographic research approaches. As a result, its findings can capture wider perspectives and trends through a macroscopic lens, while also allowing the researcher to zoom in on the individual level when desired. This combination of observational levels is neither available through quantitative content analyses nor traditional qualitative research.

Netnographic research also acknowledges the particular ethical concerns involved in conducting this kind of research: the ease with which observations can occur without participants' knowledge; the means of extracting and archiving large quantities of often very personal data; the level of intertwining of a researcher's personal and research-related social media personas; and the role of platforms as gatekeepers that provide rules specific to interactions on the platform as well as use of platform contents. Further, netnography is concerned with the selection of the particular online sites on which the research is to be conducted, suggesting that considerations regarding rich data and relevance for the research at hand are particularly pertinent. While originally applied to consumer culture research, netnography has been applied across many dis-ciplines, including tourism (see for example: Shao, Scarpino, Lee and Gretzel, 2011; Wu and Pearce, 2014; Mkono and Markwell, 2014).

As stated, the research presented in this chapter used netnography as a research methodology. Specifically, it focused on Instagram as the main research site due to the increasing prominence of Instagram use and its parti-cular focus on visual content. The study goal was to identify themes from the representational end products of touristic photographic practice, and this was difficult given the limited interactions on Instagram. The observational part of the study was also restricted to lurking, which meant that interactions with Instagram users were not initiated and the data collected was therefore com-prised of photographs posted with the respective hashtags/descriptors added. The data sampling encompassed searches for all posts with the hashtag #tra-velselfie and up to a hundred of the most recent pictures were captured during each engagement with the platform. Such a specific search was deemed appropriate as Miller et al. (2016) had identified relatively low incidence rates of selfies within general streams of social media posts, and searching for #selfie would have led to challenges in identifying the selfies that had been taken in a travel-context. Although there were a few videos besides the typical still photographs, they were not considered for the research. The data collection further involved only those photographs that were selfies according to the definition by Dinhopl and Gretzel (2016). In addition, comments by users responding to the selfies were ignored because the research question aimed at understanding self-presentation rather than understanding others' reactions to the photographs. This also allowed the research to include photographs irre-spective of the language used by the Instagram users. Only public data was considered and captured via screenshots. In 20 cases (selected to include a large variety of selfie types and user nationalities), the travel selfie was analysed in context of other trip-related posts by clicking through to the user's account and capturing posts that occurred immediately before and after the travel selfie.

Following ethnographic, and thus also netnographic, principles of researcher immersion, the research involved intense and long-term immersion in the subject area through participant observation of travel photography, travel photograph posting on social media and Instagram use in particular. While the latter has been occurring in systematic form since 2013, a focused obser-vational data collection period on Instagram was conducted from August to November 2016 to specifically inform the current research. At the time of data collection, over 16,000 posts on Instagram were tagged with the hashtag #travelselfie.

Analysis of the data involved hermeneutical cycles of reading and rereading; coding emergent themes; informing the identification of themes with the researcher's personal experiences; news articles and adding data until theore-tical saturation was reached (Schwandt, 2000). Hermeneutics is an inter-pretive methodology that requires reflective inquiry of the researcher in which understanding rather than explanation is sought (Laing and Moules, 2014). The analysis was also not aimed at understanding all types of travel selfies, but rather emphasized the most prominent themes, with travel identity pre-sentation serving as the backdrop.

Findings

A general observation based on the selfies collected for this research, is that the conceptualizations made by Dinhopl and Gretzel (2016) about travellers redirecting their touristic gaze onto themselves and presenting the self in very stylized ways, were largely confirmed. While the traditional "I was here" photograph of the self in front of an iconic tourist attraction (e.g. Big Ben, the Tower of Pisa, or the Lincoln Memorial in Washington, DC) exists, it is not very common. And even when it appears, it often includes the stylized perfor-mance of the self that was discussed by Dinhopl and Gretzel (for example, realized through duck face or other poses). In most travel selfies, the destina-tion does indeed only serve as the background, or prompt, or completely disappears into the location tag or hashtags. Without looking at the meta-data for the selfie, it is impossible to know where the picture was taken. However, one has to consider that these selfies are probably not isolated posts but part of a larger travel narrative in which the destination might or might not be featured in other ways. Some of the selfies actually took advantage of being able to post collages of multiple pictures, as this added narrative dimensions directly onto the selfie. When clicking through to some of the personal pages to confirm this, the travel selfies were indeed part of a series of travel-related posts. However, the aesthetics of the posts were so similar to everyday posts that it was difficult to determine where a trip started and ended.

Another important insight derived from the travel selfies collected, as well as observations of general Instagram use behaviour, is the large number of hashtags used. In many cases, these hashtags explicitly frame the travel identity that is to be communicated. Hashtags such as #solotraveler, #digitalnomad, #traveladdict, #globetrotter, #wanderlust, #freedomjunkie, #welltraveled and #adventureseeker are examples of how travellers try to present themselves as specific types of travellers because they wish to stress that they are not just regular tourists. These travel identities were sometimes mixed with other identities, for example #makeupartist, #entrepreneur, #ginger and #vegan. Further, the genre of the groufie or groupie that was identified as prominent in everyday Instagram photography by Miller et al. (2016) is evident in the travel selfie context. Camaraderie, friendship, fellowship, and romance are extensively portrayed in these group selfies. The research was able to identify these general characteristics as well as specific travel selfie themes, and a number of genres associated with travel selfies. A discussion of some of these genres follows:

Mundane travel selfies

A remarkably large number of the travel selfies observed on Instagram are selfies taken 'travelling' to, rather than consuming the destination. A common way in which Instagram users portray themselves when travelling include selfies taken in airplanes, trains, buses, subways, in front of airports or train stations, with passports and luggage, waiting, arriving and departing. They also often refer to the hardship that is being endured, a yearning to be there, or a regret that they have to leave. Mundane activities undertaken in destinations, such as walking through streetscapes are another popular theme in such selfies. These selfies seem to fit with social media posters' apparent need to be seen as travellers rather than as tourists. They also hint at the possibility that this photographic practice and use of selfies fill a void, help overcome awkwardness, or assist in staving off boredom.

Aesthetic/artistic selfies

Instagram affords the use of filters that help make posted photographs look professional or interesting, because it is expected that Instagram users will produce visually stunning pictures. While filters are certainly used in travel selfies, they do not represent the only way in which travellers seek to beautify their selfies. Interesting angles and perspectives are extensively used to capture the audience's eye. Travel selfies also often only portray parts of the self, something that would have been frowned upon in traditional travel photography. Poses and lighting effects are perfected, which is very different from the usual travel snapshot. The culture of selfies means that one can take endless pictures of the self until the perfect shot is achieved without making others hold their poses or wait. In many ways, these selfies hint at the very selective posting on Instagram and the careful curation of online identities mentioned in the literature. This could also be the reason for why there is a lack of so-called 'action shots'. Only a few selfies showing travellers while paragliding or zip-lining were found. Another possible explanation is that many action shots are probably portrayed on video and are shared on other platforms (Dinhopl and Gretzel, 2015).

Animal selfies

Animals such as camels, kangaroos, deer, whale sharks, and dogs sometimes provide the necessary twist in the selfie that allows it to be different from others. This especially relates to cute or especially rare animals. For some destinations, animal selfies have become iconic, such as the genre of Quokka selfies from Rottnest Island in Australia (Nationalgeographic.com, 2015) where Quokkas are now being described as "selfie-loving animals". Sometimes these animal selfies include animal sculptures/stuffed animals (for example a giant moose or bear displayed at the destination). These selfies represent continuity in earlier conventions of tourist photography as being portrayed with local wildlife is a traditional way of consuming animals as attractions, and self-portraits with animals have of course become formulaic and institutionalized (for example paying extra to get a picture of oneself cuddling a koala).

Sunglass selfies

Sunglasses are essential travel accessories and often used in stereotypical portrayals of tourists. However, these selfies are not of people who happen to wear sunglasses, but are rather self-portraits in which the sunglasses are emphasized. This is often the case for aesthetic reasons as the often-colourful sunglass surfaces add specific colour tones to the selfies, or enable one to display interesting perspectives gained through the reflections visible in the glasses. Sunglasses further add a coolness factor that is desirable when portraying the self on Instagram. Sunglass selfies are often accompanied by hashtags that refer to the specific brands or #glasses, #sunglassselfie, and #cool.

Panoramic selfies

When destinations appear in selfies, they often appear in the form of panoramic landscapes and grand, unidentifiable vistas. These panoramas serve as ideal backdrops for featuring the self. The destination is used as the 'wallpaper' that elevates the self, which is presented in the foreground (see Figure 7.1). While traditional lookout points were compositionally constructed to direct the touristic gaze into the distance, the panoramic selfie focuses the gaze onto the selfie-taker. This is true for the selfie-taker (who has his/her back to the view) as well as the social media audience that consumes the selfie.

Drinks selfies

A surprising finding of the research is the absence of food in travel selfies. Kozinets, Patterson and Ashman (2016) provide a possible explanation for this phenomenon in their netnographic research on foodporn posted on social media: this is the development of social norms that food is to be displayed on social media in pristine conditions and without any reference to those consuming it. The personal Instagram pages confirmed this assumption: food was included but never featured the self or any other people in it. In contrast, travel selfies often portray their subjects in the act of consuming or holding drinks. These drinks are either local specialities or champagne, cocktails or coffee (especially Starbucks) and allow travellers to perform certain identities. According to Rokka (2015, p. 114), social media images, and especially selfies, "express social-material-bodily configurations and ideologies … [and] effectively perform, generate and project potentialities of the self", and this is very evident in this type of travel selfie.

Figure 7.1 Groufie with grand vista taken at Praça do Papa in Belo Horizonte, Brazil
Source: Author

Ironic selfies

Dinhopl and Gretzel (2016) suggest that parodies of travel selfies are another way in which to make one's selfie stand out. The Instagram data shows this is achieved in a number of different ways. First, there are travel selfies that display the act of selfie-taking, either through mirrors or reflective surfaces. Second, there are selfies of selfies ('selfies squared') that show others taking selfies within the selfie, or have someone take a picture of oneself while taking a selfie. One Instagrammer describes her selfie-selfie as follows: "I call this one: Selfie within a selfie within a torii … within a dream". Third, there are selfies in which explicit mugging for the camera occurs. Last, there are critical selfies that mock the constructedness and increased institutionalization of selfie-taking. For instance, one selfie shows the feet of a traveller (a so-called footie) standing on a plaque that marks the spot with "Best selfie of Edinburgh Castle".

Contemplative selfies

While Dinhopl and Gretzel (2016) argue that selfies redirect the tourist gaze away from the destination and onto the self, the Instagram data suggests that this is not always the case. Some of the selfies show the travellers gazing at the destination, often with their backs to the camera (which is facilitated by selfie-sticks, timers or asking others to take the selfie). At times in these versions the gaze is directed away to the side or the distance, featuring a contemplative look, or are occasionally accompanied by profound statements in the description of the selfie or the hashtags. Rather than directly engaging with the social media audience through eye contact, these selfies redirect the viewers' gazes to either consume the traveller as an object or to consume what the traveller is consuming. The self-portrayed in these selfies is therefore objectified to some degree, or is at least less immediate or directly engaged with the viewing subject.

Conclusion

While the popular press is full of stories about 'daredevil', 'killer' or 'ultimate' selfies gone wrong (for example Rolling Stone, 2016), there was no evidence in the Instagram #travelselfie data of travellers trying to make their selfies special by putting themselves into especially adventurous or dangerous situations. Instead, following the spirit of Instagram, their travel selfies often depict the mundane or are simply self-portraits, but these are made interesting through the use of alternative gazes, angles, filters, expressions, and compositions. They are clearly carefully curated representations of the self and are central elements in the travel-related narratives communicated via social media. These efforts in interesting self-representations is further supported by the many hashtags that are added to the selfie.

Travel selfies also seem to at least partly break traditional hermeneutic circles associated with touristic representations (Caton and Santos, 2008). Rather than depicting the iconic sites promoted by the travel industry and photo-graphed by other travellers, the quest for the extraordinary and the need to be different, in order to harness acceptable amounts of likes, appears to encourage creators to put a twist on selfies that they take at iconic destinations. This sensibility feeds into the form of ironic selfies that are essentially parodies of other travel selfies. Communicating a sense of individuality was definitely a central preoccupation in the selfies analysed.

The desire to be seen as cool was evident in the Instagram travel selfies studied. Whether in the form of the sunglass selfies, or the contemplative selfies that portray the traveller as so immersed in the experience that they cannot be both-ered to engage with their social media audiences, these travellers clearly want to be admired. In such cases, the self is often elevated through impressive backdrops. Hashtags that identified them as avid travellers also fit within this schema.

What is also important to note is that besides these interesting and unique aspects of Instagram travel selfies, there is also continuity with traditional travel photography. Pictures taken in front of attractions or signage as well as wildlife 'trophy' shots are very familiar ways in which travellers depict their experiences. It is also crucial to highlight the need to understand these selfies within larger contexts of social media photograph sharing (for example food photo conventions). While the research tried to examine the travel selfie's role as embedded in overall travel and self-narratives, it was only able to scratch the surface of this topic. Further research is clearly needed to provide a more holistic view of travel selfie-taking within larger self-representation/impression management projects.

References

Bosangit, C., Hibbert, S. and McCabe, S. (2015). *'If I was going to die I should at least be having fun': Travel blogs, meaning and tourist experience. Annals of Tourism Research*, 55, pp. 1–14.

Brandwatch. (2016). 37 Instagram Statistics for 2016. [online]. Available at: www.bra ndwatch.com/blog/37-instagram-stats-2016/ [Accessed 19 Nov 2016].

Business Insider. (2016). If you have over 25 photos on Instagram, you're no longer cool. [online]. Available at: www.businessinsider.com/teens-curate-their-instagram-accounts-2016-5. [Accessed 15 Aug 2016].

Caton, K. and Santos, C.A. (2008). Closing the hermeneutic circle: Photographic encounters with the other. *Annals of Tourism Research*, 35(1), pp. 7–26.

Desforges, L. (2000). Traveling the world: Identity and travel biography. *Annals of Tourism Research*, 27(4), pp. 926–945.

Dinhopl, A. and Gretzel, U. (2015). Changing practices/new technologies: Photos and videos on vacation. In Tussyadiah, I. and Inversini, A., eds., *Information and commu-nication technologies in tourism 2015: Proceedings of the International Conference in Lugano, Switzerland, February 3–6, 2015*. New York: Springer International Publishing, pp. 777–788.

Dinhopl, A. and Gretzel, U. (2016). Selfie-taking as touristic looking. *Annals of Tourism Research*, 57, pp. 126–139.

126   *Ulrike Gretzel*

Flaherty, G.T. and Choi, J. (2016). The 'selfie' phenomenon: reducing the risk of harm while using smartphones during international travel. *Journal of Travel Medicine*, 23(2), tav026. DOI: doi:10.1093/jtm/tav026.

Gretzel, U. (2016). The visual turn in social media marketing. *Tourismos*. [online] Available at: www.researchgate.net/publication/310797670_The_Visual_Turn_in_Social_Media_Marketing.

Gretzel, U., Fesenmaier, D.R. and O'Leary, J.T. (2006). The transformation of consumer behaviour. In: Buhalis, D. and Costa, C. eds., *Tourism business frontiers*, Burlington, MA: Elsevier/Butterworth-Heinemann, pp. 9–18.

Hootsuite. (2016). A long list of Instagram statistics that marketers need to know. [online] Available at: https://blog.hootsuite.com/instagram-statistics/ [Accessed 10 Nov 2016].

Iqani, M. and Schroeder, J.E. (2015). # selfie: digital self-portraits as commodity form and consumption practice. *Consumption Markets & Culture*, 19(5), pp. 1–11.

Kozinets, R.V. (2002). The field behind the screen: Using netnography for marketing research in online communities. *Journal of Marketing Research*, 39(1), pp. 61–72.

Kozinets, R.V. (2012). Marketing netnography: Prom/ot(ulgat)ing a new research method. *Methodological Innovations Online (MIO)*, 7(1), pp. 37–45.

Kozinets, R.V. (2015). *Netnography: Redefined*. London: Sage.

Kozinets, R.V., Patterson, A. and Ashman, R. (2016). Networks of desire: how technology increases our passion to consume. *Journal of Consumer Research*, 43(5). [online] Available at: http://dx.doi.org/10.1093/jcr/ucw061.

Laing, C.M. and Moules, N.J. (2014). Children's cancer camps: A sense of community, a Sense of Family. *Journal of Family Nursing*, 20(2), pp. 185–204.

Lo, I.S. and McKercher, B. (2015). Ideal image in process: Online tourist photography and impression management. *Annals of Tourism Research*, 52, pp. 104–116.

Lo, I.S., McKercher, B., Lo, A., Cheung, C. and Law, R. (2011). Tourism and online photography. *Tourism Management*, 32(4), pp. 725–731.

Lyu, S.O. (2016). Travel selfies on social media as objectified self-presentation. *Tourism Management*, 54, pp. 185–195.

Magasic, M. (2016). The 'selfie gaze' and 'social media pilgrimage': Two frames for conceptualising the experience of social media using tourists. In: Inversini, A. and Schegg, R. eds., *Information and communication technologies in tourism 2016: Proceedings of the International Conference in Bilbao, Spain, February 2–5, 2016*. New York: Springer International Publishing, pp. 173–182.

Marie Claire. (2014). How to make your Instagram stand out. [online]. Available at: www.marieclaire.com/culture/a11586/how-to-make-your-instagram-stand-out/ [Accessed 26 Aug 2016].

Miller, D. (2015). *Photography in the age of Snapchat. Anthropology and photography*, Volume 1. London: Royal Anthropological Institute, pp. 1–17.

Miller, D., Costa, E., Haynes, N., McDonald, T., Nicolescu, R., Sinanan, J., Spyer, J., Venkatraman, S. and Wang, X. (2016). *How the world changed social media*. London: UCL Press.

Mkono, M. and Markwell, K. (2014). The application of netnography in tourism studies. *Annals of Tourism Research*, 48, pp. 289–291.

Nationalgeographic.com. (2015). Quokka selfies: What's the deal with that cute Australian critter? [online] Available at: http://news.nationalgeographic.com/news/2015/03/150306-quokkas-selfies-animals-science-photography-australia/ [Accessed 1 Oct 2016].

Ng, N. (2014). Twitter declares 2014 year of the selfie. *CNN*. 12 December 2014. [online]. Available at: www.cnn.com/2014/12/12/tech/twitter-selfie-trend/ [Accessed 1 Dec 2016].

Paris, C.M. and Pietschnig, J. (2015). 'But first, let me take a selfie': Personality traits as predictors of travel selfie taking and sharing behaviors. Travel and Tourism Research Association International Conference: Advancing Tourism Research Globally. Paper 1. [online]. Available at: http://scholarworks.umass.edu/cgi/view content.cgi?article=1138&context=ttra [Accessed 17 Oct 2016].

Rettberg, J.W. (2014). *Seeing ourselves through technology: How we use selfies, blogs and wearable devices to see and shape ourselves.* New York, NY: Palgrave Macmillan.

Rokka, J. (2015). Self-transformation and performativity of social media images. In: K. Diehl and C. Yoon, eds., *Advances in consumer research*, Volume 43, Duluth, MN: Association for Consumer Research, pp. 111–116.

Rokka, J. and Canniford, R. (2016). Heterotopian selfies: How social media destabilizes brand assemblages. *European Journal of Marketing*, 50(9/10), pp. 1789–1813.

Rolling Stone. (2016). Death by selfie: 11 disturbing stories of social media pics gone wrong. [online]. Available at: www.rollingstone.com/culture/pictures/death-by-selfie-10-disturbing-stories-of-social-media-pics-gone-wrong-20160714/stay-away-from-the-bulls-20160714 [Accessed 10 Nov 2016].

Schwandt, T. (2000). Three epistemological stances for qualitative inquiry: Interpretivism, hermeneutics and social constructivism. In: Denzin, N.K. and Lincoln, Y.S., eds., *Handbook of qualitative research*, 2nd ed., Thousand Oaks, CA: Sage, pp. 189–214.

Shanks, M. and Svabo, C. (2014). Mobile-media photography: New modes of engagement. In Larsen, J. and Sandbye, M., eds., *Digital snaps: The new face of photography.* London: I.B. Tauris & Co., Ltd, pp. 227–246.

Shao, J., Scarpino, M., Lee, Y. and Gretzel, U. (2011). Media-induced voluntourism in Yunnan, China. *Tourism Review International*, 15(3), pp. 277–292.

Statista. (2016). Number of monthly active Instagram users. [online]. Available at: www.statista.com/statistics/253577/number-of-monthly-active-instagram-users/ [Accessed 13 Oct 2016].

Urry, J. and Larsen, J. (2011). *The tourist gaze 3.0.* Thousand Oaks, CA: Sage.

Van House, N.A. (2011). Personal photography, digital technologies, and the uses of the visual. *Visual Studies* 25(1), pp. 125–134.

Wendt, B. (2014). *The Allure of the selfie. Instagram and the new self-portrait.* Amsterdam: Notebooks.

Wired. (2016). How to see the world. December 2016. Boone, IA: Condé Nast, p. 16.

Wu, M.Y. and Pearce, P.L. (2014). Chinese recreational vehicle users in Australia: A netnographic study of tourist motivation. *Tourism Management*, 43, pp. 22–35.

Part III

Cultural precincts, events and managing tourist and community expectations

8 The creative turn

Cultural tourism at Australian convict heritage sites

Susan Carson and Joanna Hartmann

Introduction

In recent decades, tourism scholars have analysed tourism in the context of local, global and neoliberal economies. More significantly, they have drawn on a number of related fields such as business, psychology, information technology, the social sciences and social theory in the humanities, to expand their understanding of the cultural and social impact of this pervasive leisure activity. These new directions have been evidenced in the nomenclature used by tourist researchers that has recently emerged, including 'the critical turn' (Bianchi, 2009), and the 'cultural moment' (Smith, Waterton and Watson, 2012). The impact of sociological theory, for example, on tourism studies was examined in detail by Erik and Scott Cohen (2012) including a focus on 'performativity and actor-networks' and Kevin Hannam (2008) wrote about the turn towards 'mobilities'.

Here we wish to build on these directions to think about a 'creative turn' in cultural tourism that involves managers, tourists, hosts and resident communities that re-work or fictionalise aspects of the past for contemporary visitor consumption. In this process of heritage re-creation the power dynamics that exist between producers and consumers has been changing, as tourists seek to curate their own version of a tourist engagement, or at least use the infrastructure provided by locations and providers to tailor an individual response to a location or cultural tourism event. It is true that the creative experience is placed on 'offer' by a provider and increasingly made available by technologies controlled by global organizations, but today's visitor still perceives, and often demands, a higher degree of agency in this type of cooperative relationship.

Examining these curated relationships demands new methodologies and approaches to understand how contemporary cultural tourism operates. In this chapter we refer to Foucauldian approaches, among others, in relation to two World Heritage Sites in Australia to comment on the way in which new methodologies are emerging from the intersection of economic demands, governance and community. This chapter speaks to a methodological goal of recognizing and explicating the competing agendas that are associated with historic cultural tourism sites. In this context of rapidly shifting relationships, collaborations between provider and consumer are constantly being re-negotiated to meet changing expectations about tourism from consumers and communities. Although the sites under discussion are World Heritage listed the issues examined stray outside of the heritage framework. The mix of *overlapping, and often layered*, activities at Cockatoo Island (Sydney, New South Wales) and the Port Arthur Historic Sites (Tasmania), represent increasingly diverse cultural tourism programs that connect with 'cultural convenors' who are placed within government organizations, as well as the volunteers who watch entry to the sites, the artists and performers who use the spaces, and the tourists who visit the sites. In this ontological framing, attention is placed on the ways in which imaginative and material aspects of these tourism sites are both subject to, and an outcome of, a number of competing discourses.[1]

Methodology

The chapter combines qualitative analysis and semi-structured interviews. Given the emphasis on the broader cultural tourism issues at stake, the methodologies include selective cultural studies theories, as well as the work of tourism and heritage scholars. The interviews were conducted with representatives of the Sydney Harbour Federation Trust, which is the body responsible to the New South Wales Government in Australia for managing Cockatoo Island. The Port Arthur material is based on analyses of published plans and programs, as well as scholarly material published about Port Arthur. We also consulted 2016 *Trip Advisor* entries for the sites, accepting that the latter sources offer immediacy, but may represent a narrow visitor population, and bearing in mind that social media reports are themselves performative acts (as is the process of analysing the material). The interviews were conducted in early 2016 as part of a wider examination of the histories of Cockatoo (archival, cultural and political).

Cockatoo Island and Port Arthur are of interest because they represent a unique 'mix' of operations, agendas and expectations, with a substantial local community and political presence in their respective regions. Cockatoo Island is an important site that possesses nineteenth-century convict heritage and twentieth-century industrial heritage. The island contains built heritage from the convict era and extensive landscape and building remnants of its time as a shipbuilding centre. It is also a popular entertainment venue for an array of creative industries' performances, and is a stop on the Sydney Harbour ferry routes that tourists take to explore the harbour and the city of Sydney from a water vantage point. The island's position as a site of colonization and heritage, together with its position as a contemporary tourist location in a world-famous waterway, means the island sits figuratively, imaginatively and spatially at the conflux of contemporary politics and culture in that city.

Although Cockatoo Island and Port Arthur were included in the UNESCO Australian Convict Sites listing in 2010, the sites differ substantially in terms of convict ruins, post-convict histories and contemporary use. Port Arthur in

Tasmania is perhaps the best-known convict site in Australia and contains a greater number of buildings than the ruins found on Cockatoo Island. It is also the site of a 1996 gun massacre when a single gunman killed 35 people and a further 32 were injured. The massacre attracted international headlines and had profound political and cultural implications for Australia because the tragedy initiated a reform of gun law legislation. What has become known as 'the Port Arthur massacre' has not displaced the site as a premier tourism destination, or indeed the primacy of convict heritage for visitors, but it has irrevocably changed the nature of tourist engagement. Elspeth Frew states that:

> [T]he Port Arthur Historic Settlement reflects the multifaceted and complex connections between people and places whereby the site was initially an imperial penal establishment, then reconfigured as a bucolic rural village, and later embraced as a national memorial to the role of convict punishment, colonial exile, and unfree labour (Frew, 2012, p. 45).

In different ways, the sites discussed here are subject to a type of worldwide heritage culture that Tim Winter describes as "one that is expected to fulfil a multitude of ends" (Winter, 2013, p. 536). Winter and Daly argued for a deeper examination of such expectations, stating that the ascendency of this culture "needs to be read, in part, as an expression of contemporary social and political life and shifting modes of governance, and, in part due to the formation of identities and economies tied to new modes of post-industrial, globalised capital" (Winter and Daly, 2012, p. 536). These sites well illustrate these complexities in heritage management and the competing narratives that operate in the growing Australian cultural tourism sector.

Performativity in cultural tourism

At both Cockatoo and Port Arthur tourists, hosts and a string of inter-locutors jostle for recognition. In these tourism scenarios it appears that the balance of power has recently shifted to the tourist who seeks a tourism experience that meets their own expectations of the event or journey, whether it is becoming immersed in a creative production or moving between guided tours and self-guided travel. Foucault's ideas are of interest given his attention to uncovering the layers and direction of power in institutions and, in the context of this chapter, his examination of the structures of power in prisons. John Urry used Foucault to draw attention to the social and cultural relations of power in tourism in *The tourist gaze* (1990). Cheong and Miller (2000) extended the discussion to develop ideas about the importance of prominent 'agents' in touristic power (p. 386), while Bianchi writes about Urry's use of Foucault to contest the notion that "power is uni-directional or exclusively associated with the tourist" (Bianchi, 2009).

This chapter however is principally concerned with the 'performing' of cultural tourism, and argues that such performativity plays into the shifting relationships between stakeholders in a contemporary tourism venture that is part of a heritage location. Erik and Scott Cohen's distinction between 'performance' and 'performativities' is pertinent because the former implies a staged event, and the latter a dynamic act of public engagement in which power slides between the producer of an event and the tourist performer. For the Cohens, 'performativities' refers to both a "strategic means of self-representation" and the use of non-lingual symbolic acts such as gestures. Performativities are therefore important in the production of "destinations, attractions or events ... as dynamic products of the performative acts of the public" (Cohen and Cohen, 2012, p. 2182). This sense of 'performativity' is used as a framework in this discussion because it demonstrates the way in which power is attached to an individual's mobile engagement with a site. As David Crouch (2012) said "the idea of performativity positions our practices, actions, relations, memories, performative moments as emerging contexts too" (in Smith, Waterton and Watson, *The Cultural Moment*, p. 21).

At the convict sites the question of performativity is important as planners and managers compete with other cultural tourism sites for visitors. At Cockatoo Island we see a mix of 'performances' in staged displays and guided activities, and 'performativities' in the crowds at music and art festivals, or individuals who attempt to create their own response to the site. Michel de Certeau (1984) saw power in a different way to Foucault, insisting that the public will inevitably subvert an authorized use of space because individuals employ 'tactics' to create an unauthorized and personal route through a space. This reclamation of power is in operation at Cockatoo Island and Port Arthur as the following analyses reveal.

Cockatoo Island and Port Arthur Historic Sites (PAHS): An overview

Cockatoo Island is a 17.9 hectare sandstone outcrop in Sydney Harbour, and is located about a 20-minute ferry ride from the centre of Sydney, the capital city of New South Wales. It is the largest island in Sydney Harbour. Since European settlement in 1788, the island has hosted a convict prison, a reformatory for wayward girls, an industrial school for orphaned and neglected females, and a shipbuilding centre. It is also home to the only remaining convict-built dry dock in Australia and contains the nation's most extensive record of shipbuilding. Today, the shipbuilding heritage is growing in importance, not only for heritage managers, but also to the Sydney communities whose families once worked on the docks, and who have become key stakeholders in heritage planning. Over time the site has been characterised by a range of dominant narratives supported by different interest groups: the convict heritage, the shipbuilding yard, and Sydney-based arts festivals. Indeed, the physical profile of the island represents this cross-sectional history: the remnants of penal life at the top of the island sit overlooking a re-formed shipbuilding landscape that changed the geography of an island where the foreshore hosts 'glamping' tents for tourists who want the ultimate view of Sydney Harbour.

Port Arthur, described on the Port Arthur Historic Sites website as one of "Australia's most important heritage sites and tourist destinations" (Port Arthur Historic Site, 2016) is said to house the best-preserved convict heritage in the country. In this study, we refer to Port Arthur Historic Site as that which lies 16 kilometres south-east of Hobart, bearing in mind that the Port Arthur Historic Sites Management Authority, (PAHSMA), a government enterprise, also manages two other historic sites in Tasmania under the banner of PAHS. At Port Arthur there is an open-air museum, heritage buildings, and ruins, such as the Separate Prison, which represent different stages of site history that visitors see via guided walks, museum and a number of self-guided tours in which the visitor follows the story of a particular convict.[2] Port Arthur is of interest here because it possesses a discernible linear chronology similar to that of Cockatoo: a convict-era punishment facility (1830–1877), an industrial prison and a shipbuilding yard.

The PAHSMA website states that the Site has been represented in publications as the "successful marriage of conservation and tourism operations" (Port Arthur Historic Site Management Authority, 2016). The 1996 Port Arthur massacre dramatically amended the convict narrative of Port Arthur. Since 1996 Port Arthur is often associated with the massacre in both overt and covert ways, although the convict heritage is still the dominant rationale for most visitors to the site. The tragedy did not diminish tourist numbers (a record number of 306,750 visitors arrived in 2014–2015), but the nature of Port Arthur tourism was altered. Tourists continue to visit primarily to see the convict buildings and learn about that era in Australian history, but there are a substantial number of visitors who attend to memorialize the events of 1996 (Preece and Price, 2005). With the 'mix' of earlier uses, the more recent memorialization, and the tensions that this re-visiting of 1996 events generates in some sectors, the way in which tourism is 'performed' on this site has changed. Some visitors engage in a personal itinerary that deviates from the usual paths around the convict buildings by attending the partially screened Memorial Garden that provides a quiet space of contemplation for those wishing to remember the massacre.

At Port Arthur, there are a series of competing narratives that involve attempts to balance local community sensitivities. Many would prefer that the 1996 massacre be left behind; others express a desire to pay respect to a tragic event; and there are others who want to satisfy curiosity. In this scenario the physical and imaginary spaces of the sites are subject to competing discourses that circle and inform chronological layers of historic activity. At both Cockatoo Island and Port Arthur, the dominant discourse of convictism is altered as other histories are discovered or produced in the gaps between institutionalized knowledge, whether it is a discourse of reverence at Port Arthur (Preece and Price, 2005, p. 196), or less publicized discourses of resistance on Cockatoo Island.[3]

Cockatoo Island exemplifies Foucault's 'scopic eye' as it was chosen as a jail site for convicts by Governor George Gipps due to its proximity to Sydney Cove. It was a place where convicts could be 'under the eye of authority' as the then-isolated site "offered security for the people of Sydney while allowing easy supervision by the colonial administration" (Sydney Harbour Federation Trust, 2010, p.18). Today, many of the buildings constructed during this period, including the silos, a military guardhouse, solitary confinement cells and the mess hall are available for tourists to explore. This suggests that the buildings are now under the 'scopic eye' of tourism, or perhaps, as Keith Hollinshead and Vannsy Kuon argue, they belong to the scopic drive of tourism in which 'the gaze' becomes 'the act' and "the deed (praxis) of knowing" (Hollinshead and Kuon, 2013, p. 1).

In Tasmania, the Port Arthur Separate Prison offers a pertinent exemplar of the way in which ideas about surveillance are re-interpreted for contemporary consumption. This prison, which is part of the penitentiary complex, was based on a 'Model Prison' of isolation developed in the United States, later adopted in England, with a version subsequently built at Port Arthur in 1849–1850. The Separate Prison is based on isolation rather than surveillance, but demonstrates connections to philosopher and social reformer Jeremy Bentham's panopticon that was famously analysed by Foucault. Since 2003, the penitentiary buildings, including the Separate Prison, have undergone significant conservation in order to stabilize the structures and include interpretative works for contemporary tourism. While there are many interpretative installations in the complex, the digitized historical information about individual convicts represents an interesting excursion into the re-inscription of surveillance that speaks to Hollinshead's and Kuon's drive of tourist enactment.

Cockatoo Island

This Island is a site of overlapping discourses in which certain narratives are dominant. For instance, convictism and the shipbuilding history are important drawcards for visitors. There are, however, other histories and narratives that have been elided as attention has been understandably focused on priority areas for visitation and conservation. One such story is that of the 'Biloela girls', the inmates of the Biloela Reformatory for Females and the Biloela Industrial School for Girls who in 1871 occupied the by then disused prison. The Biloela girls' story provides particularly interesting narratives for contemporary tourist consumption, but this history has been subsumed by other tourist management priorities to date. The Biloela institution catered to girls deemed at risk of criminality, neglect or abuse in the colony. Girls were housed in the former prison barracks and mess hall, and in an old overseer's cottage, all of which were located on top of the island's steep sandstone knoll. There were many instances of dissident behaviour and unrest as girls physically resisted discipline by attacking staff, as well as their dwellings. Many of the Biloela girls were incarcerated because they were vagrants, street workers, or petty thieves, and assumptions were made about their morality, criminality and uncertain future role in the community. The administrators' attitudes to

Figure 8.1 Military guardhouse, convict precinct, Cockatoo Island
Photo: Zakarij Kaczmarek

the girls, particularly during the institutions' early years when conditions were especially harsh and there was severe overcrowding, resembled the brutalities of penal regimes.

In 2013, the stories of the girls became the basis of a performance at the island where visitors were able to access an interactive audio drama, called *Ghosts of Biloela*. This is now a story-telling app for visitors. Developed for an arts festival, the app uses geolocation to tie the girls' stories to the island. A creative team for the Underbelly Arts Festival developed an audio play using verbatim transcripts from a Royal Commission into Public Charities that investigated the Biloela institutions because "the visitor feels that they are hopefully participating in the story ... you can whisper in the listener's ear" (Australian Broadcasting Corporation, 2013). The play was recorded on location as well as in a studio to capture the natural sounds and reverberations based on the many riots and rebellions that appear in transcripts of verbatim interview records with the girls. The Biloela girls' narrative emerged as a marginal but viable history among its other heritage narratives, and was transferred into a performance for tourists who were expected to "become part of their story" (Australian Broadcasting Corporation, 2013) by walking around and inspecting the stone convict prison rooms that were used to house the girls. Listeners entered into their own relationship with the past and engaged with the girls' history as part of their 'Cockatoo performativity', their own Island experience. Visitors were encouraged to play the role of being a 'new girl' to the reformatory so they could actively participate in the narrative and choose their own path in a type of 'choose-your-own-adventure format'. For some visitors, this history is new and will provide an entry point to the "pain and agony, not the current story of pleasure and delight" one finds in other arts festival experiences (Australian Broadcasting Corporation, 2013). The original audio play now is now available on a phone app that "is more ghostly and a bit more like *Harry Potter,* and little less like *The Shawshank Redemption*" according to writer Que Minh Luu, after an earlier version was found to be "too bleak and dark" (Power, 2016).

Performing at the Port Arthur Historic Sites

The Port Arthur Historic Site is a collection of 30 convict buildings, restored houses and ruins situated on 40 hectares of land in south-east Tasmania. Port Arthur's tourism has focused on convict heritage, and the PAHSMA regularly wins national tourism and heritage awards. In this context, there is an array of 'performances' for tourists that can involve night tours or following the narrative of a convict (for example, a playing card is given to each visitor with the identity of a convict whose story can be accessed at various points on the site). Given the importance of Port Arthur to Australian colonial history, and the site's status as the best-preserved convict heritage in Australia, it is not surprising that it has attracted significant heritage funding for extensive conservation over a long period of time. It has a "multilayered history" in "its ongoing role as a popular tourist destination" (Frew, 2012, p. 45), but as Elspeth Frew acknowledges, the tragic events of 1996 "have added a significant dimension to the site" (p. 45).

After a period of community debate in which divergent stakeholders' opinions were expressed about how to memorialize the massacre on the site, and how to interpret the event in relation to convict history, the Port Arthur Memorial Committee decided to build a physical memorial as a living reminder of those who died "just as the remnants of the convict buildings are to be gleaned from reading a plaque or looking at a photograph" (Frew, 2012, p. 39). The Broad Arrow Café, where the majority of people were murdered, was partly demolished after the event, and the remainder of the building has been left to commemorate the site. The Port Arthur Memorial Garden was completed in 2000, and is dominated by a Reflective Pool. It is in a secluded place out of the direct line of sight associated with the heritage infrastructure. Indeed tour guides are requested "not to mention the massacre whilst on-site" (Frew, 2012, p. 43) and Frew notes how the heritage managers have "avoided making the site a voyeuristic dark tourism attraction" (p. 46).

Tourism managers play vital roles in determining the authoritative narratives in tourist sites, and these narratives often become the dominant modes of story-telling and guidance for visitors. As Edensor reminds us, tourist spectacles are "contextualized for visitors by the professional interpreters of 'customized' travel" (Edensor, 2000, p. 73). Guidebooks give clues as to what to look for, says Edensor, and function as a type of 'master script' for tourists (p. 73). As de Certeau mentioned, visitors sometimes tactically avoid or subvert this authorized performance of tourism, but it is also the case that the 'authority' can resist tourist demands that do not conform to the provider's notions of narrated heritages. At Port Arthur, the PAHMS website FAQ page answers the question "Why don't staff dress up in costume?" with an answer that stresses that dressing up staff in convict and other costumes would turn the experiences of those imprisoned into light entertainment, adding:

> Many visitors have enjoyed this style of presentation at other sites and say that they would like to see it at Port Arthur Historic Site. But Port Arthur is not a theme park. It is a real place with a dark and difficult history (PAHMS).

On the same page another visitor FAQ stated: "Will staff tell us about the massacre?" and the visitor is advised to read a plaque at the Memorial Garden or a brochure rather than ask staff because "Many of our staff lost close friends, colleagues and family members on that day, and understandably find it difficult and painful to talk about" (PAHMS). Some tourists, at least some who write on *Trip Advisor*, offer muted resistance to the PAHSM rationale regarding the massacre, but in the main visitors respect this directive. The performative acts of the public are expressed in their willingness to 'see' Port Arthur because the site is deemed to be important, even if the visitor has no particular interest in convict history, but because the site is a 'must see' on the Tasmanian tourism itinerary, as demonstrated in tourists' responses on *Trip Advisor* to questions about why they drive from Hobart to the site. Once at the site, visitors appear to engage with the staged representations of convict history, but also express surprise at the richness of the site and the beauty of the landscape. Their performativity swings from what might be described as passive destination tourist mode to a more active engagement with the site's narratives. Research by Tanaya Preece and Garry G. Price (2005) found that the "need to pay their respects to those affected by the tragedy became stronger once participants were actually on site, an outcome of affective learning" (Preece and Price, 2005, p. 194).

Tourism today

Port Arthur must manage the competing narratives of convictism and memorialization. In contrast, Cockatoo Island faces competition between the demands of event tourism and heritage conservation, as commentary from Cockatoo Island visitors and the interviews with Sydney Harbour Federation Trust (SHFT) staff indicate. The Island is now a destination location with a wide diversity of tourist and heritage activities, ranging from self-guided heritage tours, to art events staged in contemporary performance spaces. Apart from the original convict-built prison barracks, guardhouse and a dock, a large part of the island's physical area is taken up by the former naval dockyard and ship-building complex. The convict barracks and colonial housing sits on an upper plateau on the island while the industrial heritage, including docks and shipyards, is at sea level where the entertainment areas

Figure 8.2 Cockatoo Island campground
Photo: Zakarij Kaczmarek

and camping ground are located. The landform is marked by docks, silos and tunnels, which were cut into the sandstone in earlier times. This mix of uses has meant that visitors arrive for multiple reasons at different times of the year so that the performance of convict narratives or shipbuilding history exhibitions exists in conjunction with camping at sites where tourists can watch the annual Sydney Harbour New Year's Eve fireworks displays, get married in the convict workshops, or follow one of the convict or maritime trails.

Sydney Harbour Federation Trust management says that a co-production strategy between events and heritage meant that "events were our public awareness driver and enabler for many years" (Carson, Hartmann and Beashel, 2016). In 2008 the 'staged performance' aspect of Cockatoo's offering was initiated when SHFT partnered with the Biennale of Sydney, a major arts festival, to host some of the activities of the Sydney festival on Cockatoo Island. The inclusion of this type of festival event attracted an increase in visitation from to the Island from 14,000 visitors in 2006–2007 to 100,000 visitors in 2008. The challenge for the SHFT became one of juxtaposing the 'event' and the 'island' with its premier location:

[Event visitors] think [the island is] almost as interesting as the event itself. So when we do our research, when we have done it in the past on the island, and it has predominately been during events, the question will come back that people love the location as much as whatever is happening in it … It's a complicated place really when you start opening up pieces like this; there are just so many different parts that go into it … that's what makes it special as well and so intriguing … And where we're at now is we're definitely still committed to partnerships like the Biennale because they're able to bring in the professional workforce to be able to resource it. There's quite a big focus now just generally in the events sphere and the cultural events sphere, about compliance and risk, and it's completely changing from when we first opened the island ... but what we're really more focused on is interpretation and visitor experience (Carson, Hartmann, and Beashel, 2016).

The question of the mix of attractions at the island is critical to future management directions since research has indicated that the island is now a well-known destination, as stated:

It's the combination of the whole experience, so things like the convicts and the layers of history generally, but then also the combination of the campground and having the bar and café where you can eat and drink, you can have a little staycation near where you live or on Friday after work, it seems to be a combination (Carson, Hartmann, and Beashel, 2016).

Convict heritage remains a top priority for the island's heritage managers. Future planning involves a collaborative approach with other World Heritage sites in Sydney (Hyde Park Barracks and Government House, Parramatta) to position the location as part of a combined experience. This connectivity obeys economic as well as organizational and cultural imperatives that can be observed in many other countries. As Tim Winter notes, a linking approach is pursued "aggressively" in some countries, and "the tensions between community-based needs and the institutional need to preserve the heritage itself is apparent in fast growing regions" (Winter, 2013, p. 539). Countries such as Turkey, China or Abu Dhabi are now "connecting landed heritage 'properties' from museums to archaeological sites to national programmes of socio-economic development" (Winter, 2013, p. 539).

In Australia, convictism provides a powerful link between heritage and tourism. This site, like so many other heritage locations, is subject to the demands of a tourist requiring mobile experiences, as Melanie Smith argued (2009, p. 195). This time-pressured visitor is invested in escapism, entertainment, new technology and values integrating their own story with the dominant narratives of a site as an expression of performativity. The site has also been integrated into tours that feature other attractions such as Hobart's Museum of Old and New Art (now the premier attraction in Tasmania) and Bruny Island. At various historic locations at Port Arthur conservation works and archaeological excavations are in progress, and tourists follow signs, read spoken word and publications, and view plays, art, films about these activities.[4] Weddings can take place in the ruins of a convict-built church where only the outer walls remain. This mix of staged historical and contemporary personalized scripts dominates narratives of Port Arthur, while the event that achieved international headlines in 1996 sits eerily to one side of the tourist experience.

In 2002 Preece and Price began interviewing 24 visitors to the site who indicated their motivations were "earning, historical interest and fascination with the abnormal and bizarre" (Preece and Price, 2005, p. 193).[5]

The recent feedback about the site that has appeared on *Trip Advisor* indicates that visitors value the convict heritage and the landscape, and are positive about the designation of World Heritage status. Most visitors appreciated the restraint and quiet of the memorial about the massacre. Many noted that site staff did not speak about the massacre, and references to the 1996 event were rare. Some understood this reticence as a way of downplaying the event in the overall history of the site. Few considered, or at least referred to the pain the local community still feels in relation to this event. For both Cockatoo Island and Port Arthur, heritage tourism is implicated in shifting discourses at sites that symbolize changing events and their attendant power structures. With the advance of participatory tourism goals and post-tourist demands power appears to be increasingly negotiated between the 'prosumer', who takes part in the event of heritage and the heritage managers who are charged with supporting a particular selection of narratives. For example, residents of Sydney who were former employees in the Island's ship-building industry are now key stakeholders in Cockatoo Island conservation and exhibition activities. Many of the former employees and their families visit the Island and they encouraged SHFT to produce the 'Shipyard Stories' exhibition which presents stories and images of the island's dockyard and shipbuilding history. In this instance, power was shifted to the domestic tourist, both in terms of prompting SHFT to collect stories, photographs and memories from community members, and also because due to popular demand management later decided to make the exhibition a permanent fixture.

This is a win-win situation, as the economic returns from attracting a diverse tourist population can fund essential conservation works. Yet attracting different tourist populations to staged performances develops a tourist performativity that is somewhat diverse if the *Trip Advisor* responses are an indication. In the studies discussed here some institutions have preferred to invest in certain types of performance to signify heritage, (a front-stage activity) while recognising that there is a large tourist market in developing more individualistic relationships that may involve entertainment as well as learning experiences. Tensions over this type of clash of representations are of course global. For example, Jonathan Meades notes the global propensity for tourism authorities to present 'sightbites' of the past in UAE countries in which:

> [T]raditional garb has taken on businessy, corporate connotations; 'heritage villages' have sprung up across the region, acting as avatars of demolished cities. Ancient activities such as falconry have taken on second lives on Instagram, where young men have enthusiastically curated their identities by adopting the more prestigious sightbites of Bedouin life (Meades, 2015, p. 336).

Conclusion

The examination of the Port Arthur and Cockatoo Island sites show that each site demonstrates changing circulations of power between different stakeholders in the tourist experience but that this circulation of power is productive: the competing discourses extend what is known and understood about the sites. The visitor constantly moves between an array of heritage and entertainment possibilities. Sydney is a city that uses its harbour geography as a stage for spectacles, such as arts and the performance of past histories, to connect with the globalized centre of the city. In the case of Port Arthur, it has had to connect with new forms of tourism that link the 'dark history' of the convict era with a contemporary tragedy, although this connection may be unwanted and ill-advised from a community perspective.

Jack Bowring in a study of Hart Island (New York), Ripapa Island (Christchurch) and Cockatoo Island suggests that there may be an argument for a heritage site "flying just below the radar" to ensure heritage longevity. He argues that for Cockatoo Island:

> The darkness of the island's past is shuffled off, as it becomes gentrified as a new destination in Sydney Harbour … Cockatoo Island signals this very danger, where the reconceptualisation of the island as big, surprising and entertaining suggests such threats are imminent" (Bowring, 2011, p. 262).

However, at least in 2016, this threat does not seem to have yet eventuated, and it is possible to argue that the strengthening of community engagement, as in the case of the shipyard workers, and the integration of heritage conservation and arts communities in management decision-making provides a model for a new type of creative space that is open to emergent forms of power. A May 2016 *Trip Advisor* comment showed the appeal of the 'mix' of options on the Island in which the tourist went to the island to go geocaching, but in a 'completely unplanned' visit, took in the views of Sydney Harbour from a wine bar and cycled around the island, saying "the audio tour is cheap and very interesting, although admittedly after the wine bar stop, the tour became less interesting LOL" ('Sydney's own little Alcatraz'). As scholars have noted, tourism attracts powerful narratives with its own circulations of power. Tracing the way in which the creative space designed for entertainment co-operates with formal governance processes and heritage requirements demands attention to the changing operations of power within the cultural tourism framework.

Acknowledgements

The authors wish to express their thanks to the Sydney Harbour Federation Trust representatives for their assistance with this project.

Notes

1 The interviews with the Sydney Harbour Federation Trust were undertaken after application to the Queensland University of Technology Human Research Ethics Committee. The approval number is 1500000282.
2 The Port Arthur Historic Sites also includes the sites of the Coal Mines Historic Site at Saltwater Creek and the Cascades Female Factory Historic Site, in South Hobart. The three sites are managed by PAHSMA, hence the reference to 'Sites' to denote the multiple sites involved. All three sites are included on the World Heritage List as three of the eleven sites that constitute the Australian Convict Sites World Heritage Property. This chapter however focusses on the site 16 kilometres south-east of Hobart.
3 In 2005 research indicated that participants to the Port Arthur Historic Site were motivated by the following: first, a need to learn factual information; second, a need to sympathize with the 'underdog'; and third then a need to pay homage to the departed at the site of the 1996 massacre (Preece and Price, p. 194).
4 Between 1834 and 1849, 3000 boys were sentenced to go to the boys' prison at Point Puer. The youngest had just turned nine years old. Located across the harbour from Port Arthur, Point Puer was the first separate boys' prison in the British Empire. It was renowned for its regime of stern discipline and harsh punishment.
5 The authors results "indicated that of the 14 respondents who indicated learning as a motivational factor for visiting Port Arthur, eight (57 percent of participants) were largely motivated by the need to learn factual information while six (43 percent) respondents indicated that affective learning was also an important motivational factor. The results also showed that, of the respondents who claimed a desire to learn as the major motivation factor for their visit to Port Arthur, five (62.5 percent) were also motivated by a need to sympathise with the underdog … . It was also found that, of the participants who indicated a desire to learn, four (29 percent) indicated a need to pay homage to the departed at the site of the 1996 massacre. The need to pay their respects to those affected by the tragedy became stronger once participants were actually on site, an outcome of affective learning." (p. 194).

References

Australian Broadcasting Corporation. (2013). Ghosts of Biloela. *Life Matters*. Broadcast 31 July 2013. [Online] http://www.abc.net.au/radionational/programs/lifematters/ghosts-of-biloela3a-underbelly-arts/4853106 Accessed 20 January 2016.
Bianchi, Raoul V. (2009). The 'critical turn' in tourism studies: A radical critique. *Tourism Geographies*, 11(4), pp. 484–504.
Bowring, J. (2011). Containing marginal memories: The melancholy landscapes of Hart Island (New York), Cockatoo Island (Sydney), and Ripapa Island (Christchurch). *Memory Connection*, 1(1). [online]. Available at: www.memoryconnection.org/ [Accessed 2 May 2016]
Carson, S., Hartmann, J. and Beashel, E. (2016). Interview. Sydney Harbour Federation Trust, Cockatoo Island, Sydney. 18 February 2016.
Casella, E.C. (2001). Female convict prisons in 19th-century Tasmania. *International Journal of Historical Archaeology*, 5(1), pp. 45–71.
Cheong, S-M. and Miller, M.L. (2000). Power and tourism: A Foucauldian observation. *Annals of Tourism Research*, 27(2), pp. 371–390.
Cohen, E. and Cohen, S.A. (2012). Current sociological theories and issues in tourism. *Annals of Tourism Research*, 39(4), pp. 2177–2202. DOI: doi:10.1016/j.annals.2012.07.009.

Crouch, D. (2012). Meaning, encounter and performativity: Threads and moments of spacetimes in doing tourism. In: Smith, L., Waterton, E. and Watson, S., eds., *The cultural moment in tourism.* London and New York: Routledge, pp. 19–37.

de Certeau, M. (1984). *The practice of everyday life.* Rendell, S., trans., Los Angeles: University of California Press.

Edensor, T. (2000). Staging tourism: Tourists as performers. *Annals of Tourism Research,* 27(2), pp. 322–344.

Edensor, T. (2001). Performing tourism, staging tourism: (Re)producing tourist space and practice. *Tourist Studies,* 1(1), pp. 59–81.

Erickson, B. (2015). Embodied heritage on the French River: Canoe routes and colonial history. *The Canadian Geographer / Le Géographe canadien,* 59(3), pp. 317–327.

Foucault, M. (2016). Questions on Geography. In: Crampton, S. and Elden, J. eds., *Space, Knowledge, and Power: Foucault and Geography.* London and New York: Routledge, pp. 172–182.

Frew, E. (2012). Interpretation of a sensitive heritage site: The Port Arthur Memorial Garden, Tasmania. *International Journal of Heritage Studies,* 18(1), pp. 33–48.

Gapps, S. (2011). Review. Cockatoo Island, Sydney, Australia. Sydney Harbour Federation Trust. *The Public Historian,* 33(2), pp. 145–152.

Hannam, K. (2008). Tourism geographies, tourist studies and the turn towards mobilities. *Geography Compass,* 2(1), pp. 127–139.

Harrison, D. (2005). Introduction. Contested narratives in the domain of world heritage. In: Harrison, D. and Hitchcock, M., eds., *The politics of world heritage: Negotiating tourism and conservation.* Clevedon, UK: Channel View Publications, pp. 1–10.

Hollinshead, K. and Kuon, V. (2013). The scopic drive of tourism: Foucault and eye dialectics. In: Moufakkir, O. and Reisinger, Y., eds., *The host gaze in global tourism.* Oxfordshire: CABI, pp. 1–18.

Hook, D. (2005). Genealogy, discourse, 'effective history': Foucault and the work of critique. *Qualitative Research in Psychology,* 2(1), pp. 3–31.

Meades, J. (2015). GCC: Talk about "A wonderful world under construction". *Art Forum,* 54(1), pp. 336–340.

Milner, L. (2015). Cockatoo, the Island Dockyard: Island Labour and Protest Culture. *Shima: The International Journal of Research into Island Culture,* 9(1), pp. 19–37.

Pons, O.P. (2003). Being-on-holiday. *Tourist Studies,* 3(1), pp. 47–66.

Port Arthur Historic Site [PAHS]. (2016). [online]. Available at: http://portarthurorg.au [Accessed 5 Jun 2016].

Port Arthur Historic Site Management Authority, [PAHSMA]. (2016). [online]. Available at: http://portarthur.org.au/pahsma/about-us/ [Accessed 25 May 2016].

Power, J. (2016). Ghosts of Biloela app conjures ghostly tale of girls exiled on Cockatoo Island. *The Sydney Morning Herald.* [online]. Available at: www.smh.com.au/nsw/ghosts-of-biloela-app-conjures-ghostly-tale-of-girls-exiled-on-cockatoo-island-20160902-gr7i2e.html [Accessed 15 Nov 2016].

Preece, T. and Price, G.G. (2005). Motivations of participants in dark tourism: A case study of Port Arthur, Tasmania, Australia. In: Ryan, C., Page, S. and Aicken, M. eds., *Taking tourism to the limit: Issues, concepts and managerial perspectives.* Amsterdam: Elsevier, pp.191–198.

Smith, L., Waterton, E. and Watson, S. (2012). *The cultural moment in tourism.* London and New York: Routledge.

Smith, M.K. (2009). *Issues in cultural tourism studies.* London: Routledge.

Street, A.P. (2014). Cockatoo Island shipyard history unveiled in exhibition. *Sydney Morning Herald*. [online]. Available at: www.smh.com.au/entertainment/art-and-de sign/cockatoo-island-shipyard-history-unveiled-in-exhibition-20141003-10p9cx.html [Accessed 17 Jul 2016].

Sydney Harbour Federation Trust. (2010). Sydney Harbour Federation Trust Management Plan–Cockatoo Island. [online]. Available at: www.legislation.gov.au/Deta ils/F2010L02391 [Accessed 10 Jun 2016].

Trip Advisor. (2016). Sydney's Own Little Alcatraz. [online]. Available at: www.tripa dvisor.com.au/ShowUserReviews-g3668744-d258200-r370847573-Cockatoo_Isla nd-Cockatoo_Island_New_South_Wales. html [Accessed 21 May 2016].

Walby, K. and Piché, J. (2015). Staged authenticity in penal history sites across Canada. *Tourist Studies*, 15(3), pp. 231–247.

Wang, N. (1999). Rethinking authenticity in tourism experience. *Annals of Tourism Research*, 26(2), pp. 349–370.

Waterton, E. and Watson, S. (2013). Framing theory: Towards a critical imagination in heritage studies. *International Journal of Heritage Studies*, 19(6), pp. 546–561.

Winter, T. (2013). Clarifying the critical in critical heritage studies. *International Journal of Heritage Studies*, 19(6), pp. 532–545. DOI: doi:10.1080/13527258.2012.720997.

Winter, T. and Daly, P. (2012). Heritage in Asia: Converging forces, conflicting values. In: Daly, P., and Winter, T., eds., *Routledge handbook of heritage in Asia*. London: Routledge, pp. 1–35.

Urry, J. (2002). *The tourist gaze*, 2nd ed. New York: Sage.

9 Cultural tourism and the Olympic movement in Greece

Evangelia Kasimati and Nikolaos Vagionis

Introduction

The modern Olympic Games were first held in Athens in 1896, with subsequent Games held every four years thereafter. The Games have survived many trials, including wars and boycotts. In recent years, the interest of countries and regions in staging the Games has grown because of the perception that doing so will help attract tourists and generate income, as well as providing the opportunity to improve the infrastructure of host cities (Kasimati, 2003). Countries spend significant amounts of money in bidding and, if successful, in constructing the infrastructure and stadia required to host such events.[1] Economists Noll and Zimbalist (1997) and Siegfried and Zimbalist (2000) however have argued that the economic evaluation of sports venues is weak, which leads to the overestimation of the economic benefits and under-estimation of overall costs when making an argument in favour of such projects. Given the generally high costs associated with the Olympic Games, the perception that host cities and surrounding regions benefit economically from these events has therefore come under major scrutiny. As well, longer term community benefits, and indeed infrastructure promises, are often not forthcoming. For example, Lynn Minnaert's paper (2012) on the legacies of seven Olympic cities indicates that despite the positive effects of new infrastructure Olympic Games "generally bring few benefits for socially excluded groups" (Minnaert, p. 361) although recent experiences with refugees and immigrants to Greece as documented below (see Table 9.1) complicate this picture and indicate a re-purposing of infrastructure in times of need.

Greece's successful bid to host the 2004, Twenty-eighth Olympic Games was announced by Juan Antonio Samaranch, President of the International Olympic Committee, on 5 September 1997. This positive development, following an unsuccessful bid to host the 1996 Olympics, inspired the Greek public to welcome sports to the top of the national agenda when the benefits of sports were highlighted. There were however also complaints about the enormous drain on public funds that such a large-scale event would entail (Kissoudi, 2010). For critics, the Games were viewed as a problematic financial drain, and were met with hostility by citizens wary of corruption and the misuse of public funds.

Table 9.1 Post-Olympic use of the Greek Olympic venues

Facility	Olympics use	Current/proposed use
International Broadcasting Centre (IBC)	International Broadcast Centre	Was leased to the private company Lamda Development SA in August 2006 and has been converted to a shopping, retail, office and entertainment complex known as the "Golden Hall". Will also become home to the Hellenic Olympic Museum and the International Museum of Classical Athletics.
Main Press Centre (MPC)	Main Press Centre	Has been converted to the new headquarters of the Ministry of Health and Social Security, and the amphitheatre contained within has hosted numerous ceremonies and public events.
Olympic Village	Housing	2,292 apartments were offered at a reduced price to low-income workers, beneficiaries of the Workers' Housing Organization. A modern town of about 10,000 residents was envisaged.
Athens Olympic Stadium (OAKA)	Opening and closing ceremonies, Track and Field, Football	Home pitch for Panathinaikos FC, AEK FC (Football: Greek Super League, UEFA Champions League), Greek national football team (some matches), International football competitions; Track and Field events (e.g. IAAF Athens Grand Prix), 2005 Eurovision Song Contest.
Hellinikon Olympic Indoor Arena	Basketball, Handball	Home court for Panionios BC (basketball), Conventions and trade shows.
Hellinikon Canoe/Kayak Slalom Centre	Canoe/Kayak	Turned over to a private consortium (J&P AVAX, GEP, Corfu Waterparks and BIOTER), plans to convert it to a water park.
Hellinikon Olympic Hockey Centre	Field Hockey	Accommodation of refugees and immigrants.
Hellinikon Baseball Stadium	Baseball	Accommodation of refugees and immigrants.
Hellinikon Softball Stadium	Softball	Concerts.

Facility	Olympics use	Current/proposed use
Agios Kosmas Olympic Sailing Centre	Sailing	Turned over to the private sector (Seirios AE), will become marina with 1,000+ yacht capacity and will be part of Athens' revitalized waterfront.
Ano Liosia Olympic Hall	Judo, Wrestling	TV filming facility, future home of the Hellenic Academy of Culture and Hellenic Digital Archive.
Faliro Sports Pavilion	Handball	Converted to the Athens International.
	Taekwondo	Convention Centre, hosts conventions, trade shows and concerts, such as a concert by the guitarist Gary Moore, the Todo Latino Salsa Festival and a three-day international Salsa dance festival.
Galatsi Olympic Hall	Table Tennis, Rhythmic Gymnastics	After 2004, was the home court of AEK BC (basketball) before the team moved to the Athens Olympic Indoor Hall. Turned over to the private sector (Acropol Haragionis AE and Sonae Sierra SGPS S.A), being converted to a shopping mall and retail/entertainment complex.
Markopoulo Olympic Equestrian Centre	Equestrian	Horse racing, domestic and international Equestrian meets, auto racing (rally).
Markopoulo Olympic Shooting Centre	Shooting	Converted to the official shooting range and training centre of the Hellenic Police.
Nikaia Olympic Weightlifting Hall	Weightlifting	Has hosted fencing competitions in the years following the Olympics, but has recently been turned over to the University of Piraeus for use as an academic lecture and conference centre.
Schinias Olympic Rowing and Canoeing Centre	Rowing and Canoeing	One of only three FISA-approved training centres in the world, the others being in Munich and Seville. Hosts domestic and international rowing and canoeing meets. Part of the Schinias National Park, completely reconstructed by the German company Hochtief.
Pagritio Stadium	Football	Home pitch for OFI FC and Ergotelis FC (Football: Greek Super League). Hosted the 2005 Greek football All-Star game. Also home to various track-and-field meets.

Source: Kasimati (2015). Author's own elaboration

Greece was the smallest country to stage the Summer Olympics since Finland in 1952, and the organisers faced the challenge of delivering all the facilities on time in line with the required standards. After the event, the effect of the Games on the Greek economy received some academic attention. Kasimati and Dawson (2009) found that the Olympic Games appeared to have had a positive impact on the Greek economy. In particular, by developing a small macroeconometric model of the Greek economy, they found that for the period 1997–2005 the Games boosted economic activity by around 1.3 per cent of GDP per year, while unemployment fell by 1.9 per cent per year. The cumulative GDP increase attributed to the Games over the period 1997–2005 was estimated to be 2.5 times the total preparation cost. Veraros et al. (2004) found a positive and statistically significant impact on the Athens Stock Exchange following the announcement of the nomination of Athens to host the Games in 1997. Papanikos (1999) and Balfousia-Savva et al. (2001), through their impact assessment studies, calculated GDP growth of between US$10.1–15.9 billion, new tourist arrivals were predicted to increase from 4.8 to 5.9 million, and 300–445,000 new jobs were to be created.

The 2004 Games provided Athens with an opportunity to acquire world class sporting venues and accelerated the completion of major infrastructure upgrades in transportation, telecommunications and other sectors. This led some commentators (for example, Preuss, 2004) to draw parallels with the successful Barcelona 1992 Olympics. The cost related to the construction of sporting facilities was estimated at euro 3.0 billion (Galpin, 2005). An additional amount of euro 4.2 billion was invested in transportation projects (euro 1.2 billion), communication (euro 1.2 billion), Games security (euro 1.1 billion) and other infrastructure (euro 0.7 billion). In November 2004, the government announced that the Games' aggregate cost had topped euro 9 billion (Kasimati and Dawson, 2009).

The post-Games use of the above investments was a challenge for Greece. It was expected that the Athens Olympics would act as a catalyst for promoting modern sports and culture in Greece, and would thereby benefit the national economy. As such, the exploitation of first, the Games' legacy, and second, the urban infrastructure developed for it, needed to be carefully planned and incorporated into a long-term strategy that targeted cultural and economic developments that would have a beneficial impact on the country as a whole.[2] Consequently, the benefits offered by the Games, which would provide Athenians with a unique opportunity to upgrade the city infrastructure and acquire new sports facilities to enjoy for years to come, was intended to outlast the two-week celebration. Harry Hiller (2000) refers to research by Ritchie and Hall that argues that although a mega-event may be of short duration it has impact and meaning "far beyond the event itself" for the host city (p. 439).

However, soon after the 2004 Games, serious questions arose about the extent of real benefits that could be extracted from the Olympic facilities. These questions were well founded, as twelve years later some of Athens' post-Olympic facilities are still vacant and some of the promised parks and other infrastructure projects have not materialized. The recent recession and serious financial shortages that Greece has suffered during the last four to five years, together with some uncertainty about the future, has aggravated the process of usefully developing the Olympic facilities, either by the state, or by domestic and international investors. The plans and spaces however are still there, and these can be a starting point for integration into a new round of planning and development procedures for the city.

In the present context, we focus on examining the effects of the Olympic Games on Athens's cultural tourism, and the city's potential to leverage the Olympic movement in synergy with its rich heritage. For this purpose, the paper is developed as follows: a discussion of the new sports facilities and the urban infrastructure developed for the Athens Olympics, as well as the post-Olympic use of the precious Olympic legacy. Next, we examine cultural tourism in Greece, arguing for the importance of museums in particular to the Greek tourist product. Finally, we consider the contribution of the Athens Olympic Games to Greek cultural tourism and report our conclusions and reflect on policy implications.

Olympic movement in Greece

Athens summer Olympics: new sports facilities and urban infrastructure

There are two basic conditions that must be satisfied for a city to be eligible to host the Olympic Games, Firstly, the amount of investment for the city's development must be in line with Olympic standards. Secondly, investments must be in accordance with the urban development concepts of the specific city. The 2004 Olympic Games presented a great economic and urban improvement opportunity for the city of Athens. The Games inspired it to acquire world-class sport facilities, modernize and regenerate the city-centre and surrounding districts, create a modern transportation system, and develop projects for greater environmental protection (Synadinos, 2004). It was anticipated that these projects would generate a building boom around the metropolitan Athens area that would significantly boost the city's transport options and networks.

In Athens and the other Greek Olympic Games hosting cities the funding for infrastructure was provided by the public and private sector, and the government was responsible for the construction. The total cost was about 3 billion euros: 962 million was financed by the private sector, 1,800 million by the Greek government, and 242 million from the organising Olympic committee (Kasimati, 2008; 2015).

Since 1932 the construction of Olympic villages has required long-term business planning. The 1984 Los Angeles, and the 1996 Atlanta Olympics, were two exceptions because the student residences of UCLA and Georgia Tech served as Olympic villages, respectively. The Athens Olympic Village was designed with the aspiration to ameliorate environmental and accommodation problems. It was located at the foot of Parnitha Mountain and had the capacity to house 16,000 Olympic athletes and 6,000 Paralympic athletes. Other Olympic sites that are worth mentioning include the Media Village, which was built for housing the media and press representatives, and the International Broadcasting Centre (IBC) that televised the Olympics globally.

All these Olympic constructions were intended to offer world-class sporting venues for the benefit of the local community and athletes. The 2004 Olympics was a chance to transform previously-neglected sections of western Athens and elevate Greece's international image. The sports facilities that already existed in Greece and were used for the Olympic Games were the Olympic Sports Centre, including the Olympic Stadium that seated 72,000 spectators. The latter was used for the opening and closing ceremonies, and for track and field events. The Olympic Sports Centre also enclosed a small sporting hall and outbuildings, an aquatic centre (seating 22,500 people), a velodrome with a seating capacity of 5,000, a big sporting hall (seating 16,000 people) and a tennis court which could host 20,000 people. In the area of Faliro a large construction scheme was accomplished. It included a Sports Pavilion (Tae-Kwon-Do Hall), which could accommodate 4,000 people, and was perfect for hosting events such as concerts, exhibitions and conferences. An aquarium, a modern marina, Olympic beach volleyball courts, an open-air theatre, pedestrian streets and an esplanade were also constructed.

Figure 9.1 Athens 2004
Photo courtesy of Ms Roy Panagiotopoulou

The Canoeing and Rowing Centres were built in Schinias with the protection of the environment in mind as it reclaimed and highlighted the attractive landscape and natural springs in the area. Some facilities were also built in downgraded areas and the objective was to upgrade them for tourism, employment, culture and sports activities (Agios Kosmas Sailing Centre, Nikea Weightlifting Centre, Markopoulo Shooting and Equestrian Centre, Ano Liossia Centre, Peristeri Boxing Hall, Galatsi Hall). However, this infrastructural legacy remained largely unexploited after the Games due to a general inertia that characterized post-Olympic Athens, and a lack of coordination between the Olympic Games' organizers and government bodies (Singh and Hu, 2008).

The sports of Olympic fencing, basketball, baseball and softball were held in the renovated Hellinikon Olympic Complex (the old Athens airport). In that same site, a remarkable 2,250-metre-long artificial lake was added and hosted the Canoe Kayak Slalom. Additional sports facilities included Goudi Olympic Centre, a large hall for badminton, a renovated equestrian centre and two open-air spaces.

Athens might have gained more cultural outcomes from these Olympic development projects. Due to the uncontrolled construction growth that took place from 1950 to 1970, Athens shared the traffic congestion and air pollution problems that beset many large cities, and many of its residential areas had been developed in an uncoordinated manner. The city of Athens took advantage of the Olympic largesse and began working on a resourceful city regeneration plan. As a result of this plan a new airport was built, as was the Athens metro, tram and suburban railway. The road network was also upgraded. The European Union and the Community Support Framework were the main funders of these projects. The plan was realized by the Ministries of Culture and Environment, Physical Planning and Public Works, the Municipality of Athens, the Prefecture of Athens and Piraeus, the Technical Guild of Greece, the National Tourism Organisation and the Unification of the Archaeological Sites of Athens SA. The 2004 organizing Olympic committee, with the experience of working with other large cities that had previously hosted the Games, coordinated the whole project (Beriatos and Gospodini, 2004).

The city of Athens aimed to achieve tangible infrastructure improvements, such as construction works and inventive designs that could restore and rejuvenate the historic centre of the city. These improvements were to be accomplished by uniting the city's archaeological sites with pedestrian roads, renovating a number of neoclassical buildings, rebuilding some of the squares and streets of the historic Athens centre, and restoring old opens spaces and monuments (Kissoudi, 2008). Architects like Santiago Calatrava submitted innovative and pioneering architectural designs. 'Non-sporting' projects included transportation system renovation, such as the construction of new roads, junctions, a tram network, metro lines, and improvement and renovation of building and wall facades in the centre of Athens (Beriatos and Gospodini,

2004). As can be seen, Athens tended to focus more on the physical infra-structure changes to the city fabric, rather than more intangible, non-infra-structural cultural effects.[3]

The most important construction plan for easing traffic congestion was the revitalized transport infrastructure. The car ownership rate in Athens, a city with around five million residents, has a rate of 350 cars per 1,000 citizens, and only 30 per cent of the inhabitants use daily public transportation. This multiple construction project dedicated to transportation was in keeping with promises made during Athens's bid for the 2004 Olympics (Frantzeskakis and Frantzes-kakis, 2006). This was considered to be very important for the improvement of the city's quality of life. The modernization of the Metro public transport system, the construction of a new tram line linking the city-centre to the waterfront, the provision of motorways and slip roads to provide access to Athens International Airport, and finally the creation of footpaths linking the city-centre attractions were all implemented. Because of the large number of athletes, team escorts, judges, referees, media and press representatives, spectators, employees and volunteers that came to Athens, these road and railway network improvements were vital to the success of the Games (Kissoudi, 2008).

The 2004 Olympic Games played a crucial role in the urban development of Athens, accelerating changes that would have taken a longer time to be completed. According to a public opinion poll during the period 21 February 2003 to 10 January 2004, Greek people were proud of the Olympic Games and thought they were worth the cost. It seems that there was a strong emo-tional bond between national pride and the Olympic Games among people of different ages and political ideologies (Karkatsoulis et al., 2005). According to one survey the majority of the citizens polled believed that the 2004 Olympics were worthwhile despite the fact that the government had not taken enough advantage of the games which resulted in a missed opportunity (Kotrotsos, 2008). Despite the under-utilization of Olympic venues, research that sur-veyed spectators' attitudes (and focused mainly on opinions about the com-bination of sport and culture as a motivation for international mutual friendship and understanding), showed that 76.3 per cent of the respondents believed that through the marriage of sport and culture the Olympic ideals could be accomplished[4] (Messing et al., 2008).

The post-Olympic use of the Greek Olympic venues

After the Olympic Games ended a special legal framework, which was enacted by law in 2005, for the future use of all Olympic facilities was formulated (Offi-cial Gazette of the Government, 2005). According to the category of the venue the following uses were allowed: within basketball and fencing venues, cultural events and exhibitions, commercial shops and food courts were permitted. Within baseball, softball and hockey venues, athletic uses, cultural events and public assemblies were allowed. Within the existing installations of the canoe-kayak-slalom venue, shops selling or renting sports gear and public assemblies were allowed, also in the surrounding areas a theme (sports) park and a hydro park were legal (Milionis, 2010). Through the same legal framework, Hellenic Olympic Properties (HOP), a management authority established for securing the post-Olympic use of most of the Olympic properties, was legislated.

On the day of the opening ceremony of the Beijing 2008 Games the Greek newspaper *Kathimerini* reported:

> [A]s soon as the Athens Games were over, it was clear that without the International Olympic Committee's incessant carping and with Greeks no longer needing to display their best face to the world, there was no plan for the day after. Apart from the major transportation projects that have transformed the city, the purely Olympic projects were left in limbo like the fossils of white elephants, the decaying abandoned reminders of a collective dream that we could not translate into reality (Kathimerini, 2008, p. 10).

The foreign press, on the other hand, reported that:

> [E]conomic stagnation, widespread corruption, a troubled education system, rising poverty and unreliable security were all thrust to the fore as thousands of Greeks spilled into the streets to protest against the government. Many demonstrations turned violent, led by a relatively small group of anarchists (Kissoudi, 2010, p. 2,789).

HOP (Hellenic Olympic Properties) was criticized by the Greek and foreign press due to neglected and underused venues despite HOP publishing many press releases about its progress in the use of the post-Olympic assets. Table 9.1 depicts the current or proposed status of the 2004 Summer Olympic facilities. The sense of contestation over post-Olympic use of a city continues. One of the legacies of the criticism of the 2004 games has been perhaps a greater focus in more recent Olympiads on the needs of resident communities versus the needs of tourists during the event. The 2004 Olympics were criticized for the under-use of venues post the Games. The socio-economic critique of the impact of the Games has not lessened. In 2014 Michael Silk wrote that London became an unequal city (Silk, 2012 p.283) during the 2012 London Games, an event in which tourist images were nurtured in Olympic mode but the city itself was a space of 'elective belonging' for many of the city's socio-economic groups (p. 283).

By 2016 only some of the post-Olympic assets were in full or partial use. The reconstruction work on a number of facilities has been postponed due to the Greek economic crisis, some are being leased on short-term contracts, and others remain deserted. Some of the post-Olympic sports facilities that have been leased to businessmen have been transformed into shopping centres and recreation places, which has had a limited cultural benefit for society, and no particular provision for the protection of the environment has been made. These issues caused conflict and debate between the municipal authorities and

HOP (Kissoudi, 2010). Some other post-Olympic sports venues, like the Hellinikon Olympic Hockey Centre and the Hellinikon baseball stadium have found unexpected uses, such as accommodating refugees and immigrants, mainly from Syria, Afghanistan, Iraq and Pakistan, who are waiting for a doorway to open into the rest of Europe. Even if the refugees and immigrants could be described as a new type of 'community' who are re-purposing existing structures and bringing new cultural concepts to the city of Athens, this is occurring against the backdrop of discussions about racism and xenophobia in Greece that suggest any integration of these migrants into Greek society will proceed very slowly (Lianos, 2004).

Cultural tourism in Greece

Identification and definitions of cultural tourism

Cultural and sports tourism constitutes a specific form of tourism that, as defined below, can provide a boost to Greek tourism. The broad definition of Cultural Tourism is a:

> kind of tourism where the cultural heritage – old and contemporary – lies in the center of the activity. The multi-cultural meeting, which constitutes an essential characteristic of this type of tourism, has consequences to both the tourist and the reception society (Baud and Ypeij, 2009, p. 3).

Cultural tourism includes sporting events that primarily satisfy the human need for physical and cultural development and improvement, and has strong resonances in Greek culture. The Greek community unanimously regards the Olympics as a kind of spiritual child, and some believe that they should be permanently held in Greece. And of course there is a profound integration of the tourist business with the Olympics in this country. The marble stadium where the first Olympics of the modern times in 1896 were held is one of the most visited cultural resources in Athens. The national air-carrier of Greece carries the name Olympic Airways, and the biggest sports club in the country is called Olympiacos.

In Greece, according to the above definitions, the charms that attract cultural tourists include a broad spectrum of categories. Cocossis et. al. (2011) identified the primary cultural tourism resources including those related to history (locations, built environments, parks, landscapes and farms); material articles; the intangible characteristics of local traditions; the physical characteristics related to the natural environment; festival and event tourism; and large or small sports events as well as the routes that connect resources or themes across regions.

Table 9.2 shows the detailed classification of selected countries for 2013 with respect to their cultural resources. As illustrated, Greece is highly

Table 9.2 Competitiveness of cultural resources of selected countries, according to the TTTCI Index (2013)

	Greece		Italy		Spain		France		Turkey		Portugal	
	Nr	Rank	Nr	Rank	Nr	Rank	Nr	Rank	Nr	Rank	Nr	Rank
14 Pillar Cultural resources	4.3	25	6.1	7	6.6	1	6	8	5.2	19	5.7	13
Number of world heritage monuments	18	14	47	3	53	2	45	4	20	12	14	20
Stadium seats per mil inhabitants	65,737	38	52,072	52	99,938	23	50,213	55	25,008	83	133,368	12
Number of international exhibitions	133	28	410	6	472	3	423	5	163	20	216	15
Exports as percentage of world	0.2%	42	6%	5	1.3%	18	4.2%	8	1.4%	16	0.3%	31

Source: World Economic Forum (2013): Calculations by the authors

competitive in the number of World Heritage Monuments considering its size. Moreover, if we account for the global importance of monuments like the Acropolis and Delphi, then Greece is particularly competitive. The data on the spatial analysis of archaeological sites are of special interest. Most archaeological sites are located in Attica, in the Dodecanese, Heraklion, Argolida and Lassithi. The total traffic per area does not necessarily depend on the number of archaeological sites. The Treaty for the Protection of the World Cultural and Natural Heritage (1972) was ratified by Greece in 1981, and to date 17 Greek World Heritage Monuments have been listed.

The cultural tourism industry in Greece is not negligible. Its archaeological sites have been receiving from 6 to 8.2 million visitors every year during the last 15 years, with an average annual growth of 1.4 per cent. In 2014, annual revenues from the above visits amount to some 30 to 43 million euros. Of course, apart from cultural relics contemporary Athens is also a lively city with many entertainment options, including theatre, music of all kinds, and a range of amusements for tourists and inhabitants. Archaeological sites are scattered over almost all the regions of Greece. For example, in 2014 Attica received some 2.7 million visitors to 15 archaeological sites. The Dodecanese received 1.1 million visitors to seven sites. Heraklion, in Crete, hosted about 0.9 million to eight sites; while Argolida received 0.7 million visitors to five sites (Cocossis et al., 2011, and Moira and Parthenis, 2011). Tourism is however very seasonally dependent as some 50 per cent of visits occur in just three months: July, August and September.

Greece's museums are the second most popular attraction for cultural tourists. During the last 15 years, museum visitors have varied from 2 million annually, to 3.37 million in 2014. This trend for visits to Greek museums amounts to an average increase of 2.8 per cent annually since 1998. All regions in Greece have at least one museum. In Attica, for example there are 20 major museums catering to some 1.75 million visitors, while in Dodecanese there are 13, with 300,000 visitors, and in the Cyclades there are 16, with 122,000 visitors.

Museums are not as reliant on seasonality as open archaeological sites. The months of July, August and September account for about one third of the annual visits, rather than the half recorded at open sites. This also shows that museums are a very useful business asset for promoting cultural tourism. Of course the economic imperative is not always the main motive, as both state and private resources operate all-year round. These enterprises may run at a loss during certain periods of the year, but they serve important educational and cultural purposes.

Contribution of the 2004 Olympics to Cultural Tourism

The 2004 Games also supported a Cultural Olympiad that took place between 2001 and 2004. During this time, 110 programs consisting of more than 250 events or performances were held (Aggelikopoulos, 2004). The core idea was to emphasize the multicultural and international character of Olympic cultural activities by hosting major cultural events in Athens and some smaller events in the Greek periphery. Greece, the Balkans and other Mediterranean countries also held a number of major cultural programs.[5] The cost of the four-year program was 143 million euros, from which only three million euros were recovered as revenue (Panagiotopoulou, 2008). During the Games the Athens Organising Committee also organised the *Athens 2004–Culture*, a cultural-events program (of 422 events) that took place throughout the Greek periphery and along the Olympic Flame's route. The campaign began with the torch's lighting in Ancient Olympia on the 25 March 2004, and ended on the 30 September 2004 with the completion of the Paralympic Games.

The 2004 Olympic Games played an important role in the development of cultural tourism in Greece. During the preparation for the Games, the Ministry of Culture funded the restoration of many museums in Athens, such as the Acropolis Museum, the National Archaeological Museum and the Christian and Byzantine Museum. A number of new museums were also built in Athens: the Glyptotheque, Museum of Islamic Art and the New Benaki. Museums at Delphi, Olympia and Marathon (outside of Athens) were also renovated. With the Cultural Olympiad, this construction activity helped to raise the number of foreign and domestic travellers to museums and archaeological sites, which turned out to be a very positive investment that further enhanced Greece's cultural tourist products. It is beyond question that great athletic events belong to the wider cultural sector of sport and social activities. Athletics unite countries in fair competition, improve tolerance of varying religious beliefs, contribute to the equality of rights between men and women, and of course create their own history. Athletic mega-events like the Olympic Games also rely on heavy infrastructure. Not only infrastructure required for athletic contests, but also infrastructure in the fields of transport, tourist accommodation and services, telecommunications, safety and health. And of course, all of these have economic and marketing dimensions, which under normal conditions can work positively for the cultural tourism of the hosting region for long periods.

Conclusion

For a contemporary city seeking global recognition and status, the Olympic Games offer a unique opportunity to present a dynamic profile. Those cities bidding for the Olympics aspire to boost their economies and presence in the global tourism market, and use such events to upgrade urban areas, transport infrastructure and create new venues that can provide a basis for future bids for major global events. The ambitions of Athens included all aforementioned arguments and prospects.

In the post 2004 Olympic Game era it seems that there was inadequate planning for this period, and consequently, Athens failed to realize its ambitions of maximising the Olympic legacy for the joint development of sport and cultural tourism. Athens focused heavily on winning the bid, building the infrastructure and staging successful games, but the post-Games period was poorly planned. In a public opinion poll held four years after the games, and on the accession of the Beijing Olympics, Greek citizens were asked to declare whether their government had fully taken advantage of the Athens Games (Kotrotsos, 2008). Eight out of ten citizens answered that they thought their government had failed in this regard. However, it was also evident that citizens had strong feelings of pride and nostalgia about the Games. According to the survey the majority of citizens polled believed that the games had benefited the country in general, and Athens in particular, despite the huge cost and the failure to immediately exploit the opportunities the games had offered (Kotrotsos, 2008).

Athens did realize some of its aspirations; others, however, still await realization. This has occurred because there was lack of coordination between public governing bodies, commercial providers, and community representatives on what should be done with the Games infrastructure. This was particularly the case in relation to the new venues that were created for the games. HOP, the government-controlled company that was responsible for making use of each of the Olympic venues after the games was extremely slow and inefficient in its utilization of assets, and its annual financial statements consistently revealed negative bottom lines. More attention needed to be paid to securing an ongoing return and community benefit from Olympic precincts and venues. It also failed to implement realistic planning that maintained state of the art Olympic venues after the games and making them cost effective, even under the weight of the Greek economic crisis.

These outcomes are the subject of continuing scholarly consideration. Minnaert makes clear that although the regeneration of urban areas often serves the economic goals of attracting new investment and stimulating the local economy, "there are associated social benefits" (Minnaert, 2012, p. 361). Quoting Lenskyj (2008) on arguing for a "fourth pillar" of social responsibility for the Olympic movement, Minnaert concludes that skills (volunteering), employment and sports participation are necessary to promote benefits for socially excluded groups (Minnaert, p. 363). In relation to Athens, Minnaert states that the infrastructure benefits of the Games were unlikely to 'trickle down' to communities and there was no evidence of participation by 'socially excluded groups' in the planning process (Minnaert, p. 367).

To the extent that most of the infrastructural facilities have not had meaningful post-Games use means they have become 'white elephants' that are a burden on Greek taxpayers, and the cost of the Olympics has been blamed as a major contributing factor to the current economic crisis. As most European countries were coming out of recession at the end of 2009, Greece was entering a tumultuous period. The slowdown in global economic activity in 2008, and the recession in OECD countries in 2009 were however the prelude, rather than the cause, of the Greek crisis. When the global financial crisis struck, Greece was badly prepared after years of profligacy, which included the cost of the Olympic Games in 2004, but it had also failed to rein in its spiraling public debt.

In terms of culture, the 2004 Summer Olympic Games provided an extraordinary opportunity for the host city, region and country through the *Cultural Olympiad*, the organization of the *Athens 2004–Culture* and various cities that hosted cultural events such as music festivals, arts, literature and photography exhibitions. The hosting of the 2004 Athens Games helped upgrade Athens's image from an unfriendly urban landscape to a European tourist destination. The successful organization of the 2004 Olympics reshaped Athens with improved infrastructure and an enhanced urban aesthetic status that was recognized internationally. However, the post-Olympic heritage remained mostly unexploited due to lack of adequate strategic planning and management, and Athens has yet to find a path towards fully reaping benefits from its cultural heritage. In order to succeed here, there is a need to develop cross-leveraging synergies between the Olympic legacy and cultural tourism for the city of Athens. The future integration of Olympic resources into successful tourist products and community benefits remains an important priority. This may require increased cooperation between public administrators, private entrepreneurs and local and international communities.

Notes

1 Economists, see Noll and Zimbalist (1997) and Siegfried and Zimbalist (2000) have argued that the economic evaluation of sports venues is weak which leads to an overestimation of the economic benefits and an underestimation of the overall costs in order to make an argument in favour of the project.
2 There are various areas of the beneficial impact in the society: (1) changes in city's design; (2) alterations to the built and physical environment; (3) improvements in air, sea, rail and road transport; (4) presentation of the city and country and their culture; (5) alterations in public decision-making and governance; (6) transformations in political relationships and politics; (7) potential greater business activity and tourism; (8) new sporting venues; (9) the potential of increased community participation, discussion and even protest; (10) the participation of the community as torch-bearers and volunteers.
3 The academic literature mentions, as intangible impacts of hosting the Olympics, the city's image promotion and marketing; human-related effects (education, volunteering, skills expansion, knowledge creation); aggregate memory and spirit (civic pride, feel-good factors, shared values); culture (cultural aspects, recognition) or network effects (virtual and/or physical).
4 This survey included the Summer Olympic Games from Barcelona 1992 to Beijing 2008. Concerning the Athens Olympics, 1,519 questionnaires were completed by international and domestic tourists and by Athenians attending the competitions of modern Pentathlon. The sample covered 21 per cent of the spectators.
5 For this aim, the following four programs were implemented that called *Major Programs*:
     The New Balkans (2001–2004). It referred to inter-Balkan activities in arts, science (e.g. paintings, music festivals, literature and photography exhibitions, etc.) intending to counteract Balkan 'marginalization' and suspicion and to foster the co-existence of people in the European war zones.

Agora (2002–2004), built cooperation between local community organizations and stated as its main focus, the artistic revitalization of a city's street or a city's square giving the opportunity to the citizens to 'explore' their own city and artists. This program involved 45 various towns.

Harbors of Mediterranean (2003). From Barcelona to Smyrna and from Marseille to Alexandria, port towns engaged in various cultural activities in order to reveal the never-ending cultural exchanges of the Mediterranean cities and their link with the sea.

Cultural Routes (2003–2004). There were small arts groups traveling abroad and creating small Greek festivals by performing or presenting characteristic achievements of Greek cultural productions (Panagiotopoulou, 2008).

References

Aggelikopoulos, V. (2004). The achievements and failures of the cultural olympiad. *Kathimerini*, 28 Nov 2004, p.2 [in Greek].

Balfousia-Savva, S., Athanassiou, L., Zaragas, L. and Milonas, A. (2001). *The economic effects of the Athens Olympic Games*. Athens: Centre of Planning and Economic Research, KEPE.

Baud, M. and Ypeij, A. (2009). Cultural tourism in Latin America: An introduction. In: Baud, M. and Ypeij, A., eds., *Cultural tourism in Latin America, the politics of space and imagery*. Boston: Leiden.

Beriatos, E. and Gospodini, A. (2004). "Glocalising" urban landscapes: Athens and the 2004 Olympics. *Cities*, 21(3), pp. 187–202.

Cocossis, H., Tsartas, P. and Grimpa, E. (2011). *Special and alternative forms of tourism*. Athens: Kritiki (in Greek).

Frantzeskakis, J. and Frantzeskakis, M. (2006). Athens 2004 Olympic Games: transportation planning circulation and traffic management. *ITE Journal*, 76(10), pp. 26–32.

Galpin, R. (2005). Greece lays out post-Olympic plan. *BBC News*. [TV programme]. 30 Mar.

Hiller, H.H. (2000). Mega-events, urban boosterism and growth strategies: An analysis of the objectives and legitimations of the Cape Town 2004 Olympic bid. *International Journal of Urban and Regional Research*, 24(2), pp. 449–458. DOI: doi:10.1111/1468-2427.00256.

ICOMOS. (1997). Charter for cultural tourism. In: Csapo, J., Kasimoglou, M. and Audin, H., eds., *Strategies for Tourism Industry*. Rijeka, Croatia: InTech.

Karkatsoulis, P., Michalopoulos, N. and Moustakatou, V. (2005). National identity as a motivational factor for better performance in the public sector. The case of the volunteers of the Athens 2004 Olympic Games. *International Journal of Productivity and Performance Management*, 54(7), pp. 579–594.

Kasimati, E. (2003). Economic aspects and the Summer Olympics: A review of the related research. *International Journal of Tourism Research*, 5(6), pp. 433–444.

Kasimati, E. (2008). *Macroeconomic and financial analysis of mega-events: Modelling and estimating the impact of the 2004 Summer Olympic Games in Greece*. Saarbrucken: VDM Verlag.

Kasimati, E. (2015). Post-Olympic use of the Olympic venues: The case of Greece. *Athens Journal of Tourism*, 2(3), pp. 167–184.

Kasimati, E. and Dawson, P. (2009). Assessing the impact of the 2004 Olympic Games on the Greek economy: A small macroeconometric model. *Economic Modelling*, 26(1), pp. 139–146.

Kissoudi, P. (2008). The Athens Olympics: Optimistic legacies – post-Olympic assets and the struggle for their realization. *The International Journal of the History of Sport*, 25(14), pp. 1972–1990.

Kissoudi, P. (2010). Athens' post-Olympic aspirations and the extent of their realization. *The International Journal of the History of Sport*, 27(16–18), pp. 2780–2797.

Kotrotsos, P. (2008). From national pride to regret of missed opportunity. *Eleftheros Typos*, 10 Aug., p. 3.

Lenskyj, H.J. (2008). *Olympic industry resistance: Challenging Olympic power and propaganda*. Albany, NY: SUNY Press.

Lianos, T. (2004). *Report on immigration to Greece*. Athens: European Migration Network-Greek National Contact Point-Centre for Planning and Economic Research.

Kathimerini. (2008). Life after the Games. 8 Aug., p. 10 [in Greek].

Messing, M., Mueller, N. and Schormann, K. (2008). Zuschauer beim antiken Agon und bei den Olympischen Spielen in Athen 2004 – anthropologische Grundmuster und geschichtliche Figurationen. In Mauritsch, P., Petermandl, W., Rollinger, R. and Ulf, C., eds., *Antike Lebenswelten. Konstanz – Wandel – Wirkungsmacht. Festschrift für Ingomar Weiler*, Wiesbaden: Harrassowitz, pp. 211–237.

Milionis, S. (2010). City marketing in Greece: The post-Olympic use of Hellinikon former airport site. *Regional Science Inquiry*, 2(2), pp. 151–172.

Minnaert, L. (2012). An Olympic legacy for all? The non-infrastructural outcomes of the Olympic Games for socially excluded groups (Atlanta 1996-Beijing 2008). *Tourism Management*, 33(2), pp. 361–370.

Moira, P. and Parthenis, S. (2011). *Cultural and industrial tourism*. Athens: Nomiki Vivliothiki [in Greek].

Noll, R.G. and Zimbalist, A. (1997). *Sports, jobs and taxes: the economic impact of sports teams and stadiums*. Washington, DC: Brookings Institution Press.

Official Gazette of the Government. (2005). Statute no. 334. *National Press*, 131(1) A, pp. 1955–1982 [in Greek].

Panagiotopoulou, R. (2008). The cultural Olympiad of the Athens 2004 Olympic Games: A tribute to culture, tradition and heritage. In: Messing, M. and Mueller, N., eds., *Olympismus – Erbe und Verantwortung*, Kassel: Agon Sportverlag, pp. 316–337.

Papanikos, G. (1999). *Tourism impact of the 2004 Olympic Games*. Athens: Tourism Research Institute [in Greek].

Preuss, H. (2004). *The economics of staging the Olympics: A comparison of the games 1972–2008*. United Kingdom: Edward Elgar.

Richards, G. (1996). *Cultural tourism in Europe*. Walingford: CAB International.

Siegfried, J. and Zimbalist, A. (2000). The economics of sports facilities and their communities. *Journal of Economic Perspectives*, 14(3), pp. 95–114.

Silk, M. (2014). The London 2012 Olympics: The cultural politics of urban regeneration. *Journal of Urban Cultural Studies*, 1(2), pp. 273–293. [Accessed 15 Sep 2016].

Singh, N. and Hu, C. (2008). Understanding strategic alignment for destination marketing and the 2004 Athens Olympic Games. Implications from extracted tacit knowledge. *Tourism Management*, 29(5), pp. 929–939.

Synadinos, P. (2004). *O agonas mias polis*. Athens: Kastaniotis Publications [in Greek].

UNWTO. (1985). The states' role in protecting and promoting culture. Madrid: UNWTO.

UNWTO. (1993). Recommendations on tourism statistics. Madrid: WTO.

Veraros, N., Kasimati, E. and Dawson, P. (2004). The 2004 Olympic Games announcement and its effect on the Athens and Milan stock exchanges. *Applied Economics Letters*, 11(12), pp. 749–753.

10 Local/global

David Walsh's Museum of Old and New Art and its impact on the local community and the Tasmanian tourist industry

Mark Pennings

Introduction

In this era of global tourism some national governments and corporations are investing billions of dollars to construct glamorous starchitect-designed art museums and stunning experiencescapes to seek nourishment from this lucrative leisure industry. Projects such as Abu Dhabi's Saadiyat Island and West Kowloon's M+ epitomize the grand ambitions of governments seeking market reach. However, one does not require a massive enterprise to succeed, as illustrated by Tasmania's Museum of Old and New Art (MONA) in Australia, which has achieved a high-profile place in the global tourist marketplace as a much smaller 'boutique' experiencescape. MONA is owned by gambling entrepreneur David Walsh, and is an independent entity that does not rely on a top-down government or corporate-driven agenda to determine its role.

MONA is distinctive in a number of ways. Walsh has described it as "a subversive adult Disneyland" (Pennings and Walsh, 2016), which alludes to his immersive experiencescape that offers cultural experiences, including art viewing, digital interaction with a museum collection, cultural events and festivals, wine and food banquets, and markets. The museum has gallery spaces for function hire, a café, wine bar, restaurants, and luxury apartments. MONA is particularly distinctive in the way it encourages its audience to participate in a *democratization of experience* when engaging with art and culture; that is to say, audiences are not 'talked down' to, and are encouraged to express their opinions about art via digital technologies like the 'O' device that the museum provides, as well as sharing an egalitarian community sensibility in MONA's festivals. In the process, the museum has "re-defined cultural tourism from a Tasmanian perspective at least, and probably also on a national perspective. And that is because it is more of a complete experience. It's attracting a visitor that is looking for that immersive experience" (Pennings and Wilsden, 2016).

Having established its reputation MONA must sustain its distinctive place in a competitive global market without losing its links with the local community. While an increasing number of interstate and international tourists are visiting MONA (which brings in greater revenue, allowing this institution to buy more art, hold more events, and employ more local people), it is struggling to secure repeat visits from the local population. Attracting repeat visitors is a common problem for many museums, and MONA is maintaining interest in its art and culture from local inhabitants by persisting with its commitment to the democratization of experience via festivals whose carnival spirit is inclusive and embraces universal themes. This chapter considers MONA's place in the global market of tourist experiencescapes, reports on its economic impact on Tasmanian tourism, describes the qualities that make it unique in its local community, and examines the means by which it is seeking to expand its external audience while sustaining local interest, with particular attention to the sociological dimensions of festivals such as Dark Mofo. This study employs qualitative analysis as its primary methodology as interviews were conducted with key personnel at the Museum of Old and New Art, and with its owner David Walsh.

Global tourism: a mega-business

In this neo-liberal era there are concerns about rising economic inequality, stalling economic growth, and the terrorist threat, but this has not prevented tourism from becoming one of the fastest growing industries in today's global market. The industry's expansion has outpaced financial, health, and automotive industries, and is only bettered by information technologies. The

Figure 10.1 Exterior view of MONA (on the left) approaching the MONA ferry terminal from the Derwent River, Hobart

Photograph courtesy of Stephen Haley

numbers speak for themselves, as around 1.3 billion people have undertaken tourism annually in recent years. Given that the global population is around 7.4 billion people, tourists represent a sixth of the world's population, which is quite a market.

Tourism has been a resilient and lucrative economic activity, and the World Travel and Tourism Council's (WTTC) economic impact report in 2014 claimed that it generated US$7.6 trillion, or 10 per cent of global GDP. It also produced 277 million (or one in eleven) jobs (UNWTO, 2015). Tourism is therefore extremely important for global economic activity, and has led United Nations World Tourism Organisation's Secretary-General Taleb Rifai to declare

> The robust performance of the sector is contributing to economic growth and job creation in many parts of the world. It is thus critical for countries to promote policies that foster the continued growth of tourism, including travel facilitation, human resources development and sustainability (Statista.com, 2016).

It is anticipated that there will be nearly 1.8 billion global tourists by 2025, which would represent a 58 per cent increase on 2014 figures. This staggering growth in traveller numbers demonstrates that global tourism is in the midst of a boom, and as transport costs continue to decline, and those with disposable incomes continue to invest in travel experiences to enhance and enrich their lives, tourism will continue to be a vital sector in many economic planning ventures.

Investing in 'Catwalk' global markets, and the role of experiencescapes for tourism

With so much at stake, governments engage in intensive planning to capture their share of a lucrative tourist market. As a consequence, this era has seen the rise of what has been referred to as 'geo-economics', where there is rivalry between global cities to attract corporate investment and revenue from tourists. This is because such revenue can be vital for fostering infrastructure development, economic growth, and employment prospects (Ek, 2005, p. 73). Those that are fully engaged in this fight for tourist capital have been referred to as participants in a 'Catwalk Economy' where they act like

> models showing off clothing on a catwalk at a fashion show [where] businesses, cities, regions and nations all have to compete for the attention of the surrounding world … this is a crowded market, and it is not always easy to be heard above the cacophony (O'Dell, 2005, p. 28).

Tourism is a persuasive economic force, and many of the larger projects are top-down enterprises driven by governments and corporations to gain advantageous access to the tourist market. This can involve the construction of massive experiencescapes, or securing rights to host global mega-events like the Olympic Games and the Football World Cup.

Japan for example is using the Olympic Games in 2020 as part of its strategy to profit from global tourism to assist an economy that has been in recession for several decades. The Olympics is to be the springboard for a range of government initiatives to expand tourist facilities. Prime Minister Abe has recently stated:

> Tourism is an important pillar of our country's growth strategy, and a trump card for regional revitalization. It is also an engine to boost growth to achieve Y600 trillion GDP goal ... To establish a tourism-based country, I'm determined to take any political measures in advance to be fully prepared (Murai, 2016).

Along similar lines, Brazil's Rio de Janiero hosted major global sporting events to attract tourists. The government believed the acquisition of rights to host the football World Cup and Olympic Games would boost the economy. Brazil spent around US$1 trillion in public and private funds on public works and infrastructure to support these global events. Despite a range of problems associated with the Zika virus, law and order, and government corruption Brazil's investment in tourism was a success, for 650,000 people visited Rio during the 2016 Olympics.[1]

Experiencescapes such as M+ in West Kowloon and Saadiyat Island in Abu Dhabi are specially designated urban and cultural precincts driven by government and corporations. They generally contain distinctive starchitect-designed buildings that give cities profile branding in the global Catwalk Economy.[2] To enhance a city's global reputation, governments stake massive investments in attracting tourist revenue to help grow retail sales, business investment, and employment. The complex on Saadiyat Island typifies the scale and kind of investment some governments are prepared to outlay to appeal to tourists. This project will cost US$27 billion and is part of a broader plan to turn the United Arab Emirates into a global cultural hub. The island will contain branches of the Louvre and the Guggenheim, as well as an NYU campus. Kanish Tharoor has claimed that Saadiyat Island will be:

> a highbrow and high-rolling amusement park, a place to park your yacht or toddle from green to green in close proximity to some of the world's most celebrated art. Its additional frills are a performance space designed by Zaha Hadid, a marina, a golf course, exclusive villas and luxury hotels (Tharoor, 2016, p. 26).

This experiencescape is a vital instrument in Abu Dhabi's plan to be a global entrepôt for cultural tourists.

Hong Kong's West Kowloon cultural precinct, known as M+, is another billion-dollar investment in creating a high-profile cultural experiencescape. The government has furnished a US$2.7 billion budget (with supplementary funding from private donations) to construct this precinct on reclaimed harbour land. It will accommodate 17 arts and cultural venues, including the distinctively T-Shaped M+ Museum for visual culture (designed by TFP Farrells and starchitects Herzog & de Meuron). It is hoped that these venues and events will attract enough tourists to have long-term beneficial impacts on the cultural and economic well-being of the local population.

Abu Dhabi and West Kowloon are massively scaled, top-down, government-driven projects. Their power and scope suggest they will be major global precincts in the tourism and leisure industries in years to come, but there is room for other players. MONA is a case in point. It is a popular experiencescape that is making a major contribution to its tourism sector, yet it operates by very different principles than those manifested in the larger zones. Indeed, MONA is not the product of top-down development, but is the work of a single entrepreneur in a remote island off the south coast of Australia. It is an independent enterprise that occasionally works with, but is not reliant on government. It is also immersed in its local community, as opposed to the distinctly internationalist posture maintained by some of its larger rivals.

MONA's contribution to Tasmania's tourist industry

The Museum of Old and New Art (MONA) in Tasmania, Australia was designed by Nonda Katsalidis and opened in 2011. It is a boutique art museum in an experiencescape that is set in the working class Hobart suburb of Berriedale. It has achieved global recognition due to its unique character, attitude, and type of cultural activities it offers.

Australia, like so many other countries is benefitting from the tourism boom. From August 2015 to August 2016, 7.99 million tourists visited the country (Tourism Australia, 2016). In addition, the overall financial contribution of tourists to the Australian economy in 2015 was a record AUS $34.8 billion. Many of these visitors found their way to Tasmania, in large part due to MONA's profile. Although in June 2016 only about 1 per cent of international visitors to Australia went to Tasmania, yet this was worth AUS $2 billion to that state, and contributed 8 per cent of its GDP (which was tourism's highest contribution to a state's GDP in the nation). Tourism in Tasmania also directly supports 15,000 jobs, and indirectly 38,000 jobs, which is 16.2 per cent of employment in the state. This is once again the highest ratio in Australia (Tasmanian Government, 2016).

MONA has played a pivotal role in this success. Tourism Tasmania's *Visitor Survey* (July 2011) stated that MONA "quickly became a significant attraction for visitors in the State", and by mid-2012 MONA was attracting 25 per cent of all visitors to Tasmania, which made it the second most visited tourist attraction in the state [Table 10.1, Column 2]. Surveys from 2013 to 2015

Table 10.1 MONA visitor numbers

Year	Total tourist visitors to Tasmania	Visitors to MONA as a per cent of the total	Local visitors to MONA	International visitors to MONA	Visitors who came just to see MONA	Money spent in Tasmania by MONA visitors
2013	280,700	28 per cent	76 per cent	14 per cent	6 per cent	$AUD 549 million
2014	300,900	28 per cent	73 per cent	15 per cent	16 per cent	611 million
June 2015	330,700		75 per cent	14 per cent	5 per cent	
December 2015	340,000	29 per cent	72 per cent	16 per cent	4 per cent	741 million
June 2016	335,127	29 per cent	70 per cent	16 per cent	3 per cent	738 million

Source: Author

continued to chart MONA's consistent growth as a tourist attraction. By September 2013 this museum was attracting 28 per cent of all tourists coming to Tasmania, and 6 per cent of those came directly to visit MONA. The percentage of those who visited the state just to see MONA jumped from 6 in 2013 to a record high 16 in 2014 [Table 10.1, Column 4]. By 2015–16, 29 per cent of tourists going to Tasmania were visiting MONA. In 2013 these travellers spent $549 million during their trip, and by the end of 2015 were spending AUD$741 million, a 21 per cent increase on earlier figures [Table 10.1, Column 5]. Numbers of actual visitors to MONA rose from 210,300 in June 2012 to 340,800 by June 2016, which was about a 60 per cent advance on attendances during this period [Table 10.1, Column 1].

MONA's value to Tasmania's tourism industry in economic terms is substantial, and in the process it has captured the attention of global media. In 2013 Tasmania's capital, Hobart, was ranked seventh in the top ten global cities that *Lonely Planet* travel guide recommended for visitation. *Lonely Planet* cited MONA as the major tourist attraction in this small city, and compared it to the Guggenheim's impact in Bilbao (ABC News, 2012). MONA owner David Walsh has also advised, "The *New York Times* and *New Yorker* have done something on us. Particularly in Europe just about every major magazine and newspaper has done something on us" (Pennings and Walsh, 2016).

MONA's uniqueness and the democratization of experience

A range of factors has made MONA a distinctive destination. These include the museum's design and art collection, both of which are owned by gambling entrepreneur David Walsh. The museum has dramatic interior (rather than exterior) architectural features, including Triassic sandstone walls; and the building is sunk into the ground, so visitors begin viewing the *objet d'art* in an underground basement. It also contains theatrically lit exhibition spaces suggestive of a theme park entertainment complex. There are no wall labels to describe its exhibits, instead,

Figure 10.2 Interior view of MONA showing Julius Popp's *Bit.Fall* (2005)
Photo courtesy of Stephen Haley

an iPhone device called an 'O' is provided for use and contains basic information about the art, opinion pieces, and options for visitors to express their own judgments about the art. MONA's experiencescape also offers luxury accommodation, a winery, a brewery, and a variety of music, film, and art events.

MONA's distinctive reputation derives from Walsh's idiosyncratic approach to this venture. He built the museum to house a private collection of art and *objet d'art*, which had been stored on his residential estate. MONA was designed by an architect-friend, and was built on a whim to display his collection. Walsh was not as interested in making a profit as he was in having complete control over the nature and direction of the museum. In the process, he has rejected a didactic or authoritative museological and curatorial approach, choosing instead to give visitors the freedom to view his art collection on their own terms (Pennings and Walsh, 2016).

A fundamental characteristic of MONA's approach is what I call its commitment to a *democratization of experience* when engaging with art and culture. Museum visitors do not see wall labels next to the art objects because Walsh believes these are too dictatorial and elitist. The visitor is not obliged to follow an institutionally prescribed interpretation of the art rather the 'O' device contains data about each work, Walsh's opinions of his art, and a love or hate option that the visitor can select. Walsh has stated, "I removed the preaching from the exposition. I allowed them to form their own opinions ... they feel good about being able to form an opinion and express it" (Pennings and Walsh, 2016). Mark Wilsden, MONA's business manager has elaborated upon this commitment, saying that MONA is:

> about the complete experience ... we don't tell people how they should think about things, right down to no wall labels on the art. The 'O' let's you choose if you wish to engage in that or not. You can hate stuff, and this is liberating for some people ... You spend more time reading the label than looking at the work some times, and half the time you don't understand it ... here, everyone is treated on an equal footing where everyone can have an opinion ... We are inclusive (Pennings and Wilsden, 2016).[3]

This egalitarian and populist philosophy encourages visitors to back their own judgment when interacting with art and culture, and by refusing to determine a right or wrong answer MONA embraces the value of anyone's opinion whether or not they are educated in the arts.

MONA's use of digital technology has proved to be very popular. The nature of the 'O' device is compatible with social media formats and brings visitors closer to the art by enabling them to register opinions others can read. This is a central element in the democratization of the cultural experience, for as Mark Wilsden has argued:

> What the 'O' does is gives visitors more control, it is powerful and liberating ... and allows them to decide how much knowledge and information they get. There is a need to feel you have some control of your experience, rather than being hustled along (Pennings and Wilsden, 2016).

Justin Johnston, Manager of Guest Services, has also explained that with the 'O' device people can:

> click on our website, visit the blog, or they can see YouTube, or Twitter ... [with] the 'O' device ... people will soon have some kind of live feedback ...The growth in social media (like Facebook) in the last five years or so has coincided with how people engage with MONA ... MONA uses the same kind of approach to social media (Pennings and Johnston, 2016).

Events: successful experiential initiatives

A crucial element in MONA's democratization of experience is embedded in the nature of its public festivals. The first significant event it held was MONA FOMA (Museum of Old and New Art: Festival of Art and Music). This annual festival was initiated in 2008, and soon became the state's largest contemporary music festival, and it has featured a number of headline performers, such as Philip Glass, John Cale, and Nick Cave. Dark Mofo is a recent festival developed by MONA that has boosted its popularity with tourists and local denizens. It is an art, performance, and music festival that celebrates the winter solstice and provides public rituals and ceremonies, such as a nude swimming event in the Derwent River. Dark Mofo has entrenched MONA's reputation as a producer of popular and innovative experiences that are universal and inclusive, and bring local and external communities together. It was instigated after consultation with the Tasmanian government, as the latter was keen to attract more tourists to the state during the quiet winter season. Accordingly, Dark Mofo was first developed to appeal to outside tourists, rather than locals, and "80 per cent of all the tickets are sold to residents from somewhere else other than Tasmania" (Pennings and Walsh, 2016). The festival however has also proven to be very popular with local residents, and has purportedly re-energized MONA's relationship with its community due to its open and inclusive perspective.

Dark Mofo offers a diverse range of activities, but perhaps what resonates most for visitors is participation in universal collective ceremonies, which at the same time enrich a sense of local place. Dark Mofo celebrates a venerable celestial event – the winter solstice – and does so by drawing on ancient traditions such as ritualistic ceremonies with bonfires. In this sense, it resembles events like Burning Man, the annual festival held in the Nevada Desert that promotes inclusion, self-expression, participation, and community cooperation. The ritualistic carnivals that characterize Dark Mofo are devised to entertain tourists, but they are also community events based on egalitarian principles. People are encouraged to lose themselves in the crowd with local inhabitants and indulge in cathartic experiences and temporary relief from the rigid conformity of everyday life. Mary Lijnzaad, MONA librarian, and one of Walsh's earliest colleagues, believes Dark Mofo's success is due in part to the fact that there are "very few opportunities in everyday society to maybe give out that primal scream, so I think that is where the *carnivalesque* comes in … These kinds of carnival-like events act as safety valves" (Pennings and Lijnzaad, 2016).

The concept of the *carnivalesque* was notably examined by theorist Mikhail Bakhtin who traced it to medieval festivals such as the "Feast of Fools", which allowed a transitory discombobulating of ecclesiastical and social hierarchies. Carnivals are playful, celebratory and anti-authoritarian, and often provide an undertone of carnal sensuality that is enacted in theatrical and symbolic terms. Sociologist Adrian Franklin identified the *carnivalesque* as one of the key reasons behind Dark Mofo's appeal to broad audiences.[4] An inclusive, collective and democratic experience pervades Dark Mofo, which for David Walsh is more about theatre, and that:

> the key component of it is the *carnivale* … where people come together and forget all their values and all caste and structural systems evaporate, so MONA is more a 'coming together', a democratization of art and an accidental public institution" (Pennings and Walsh, 2016).[5]

Events such as Dark Mofo have provided MONA with a new direction that extends its commitment to democratising the visitor experience. MONA's success has been built on its egalitarianism, on its rejection of elitist pretensions, and with providing audiences with a sense of *equality before art* that does not privilege the view of the cognoscenti over the non-art trained visitor. This democratic spirit has in turn become a kind of methodology in MONA's museological procedures and attitudes. Moreover, by organising festivals that are often held in Hobart and surrounding areas (as well as in its home base at Berriedale) MONA is in some respects instigating an outreach program in which its inclusive philosophy is extended into the broader community; for these events provide opportunities for communities – consisting of both local and tourist – to perform their own engagement with culture. In this sense, as with the use of the 'O' device, the local inhabitant and tourist acquire the agency to undertake a self-organized experience as their own cultural performer. MONA may arrange the performance, but it is the participant that undertakes the act of 'performativity', and in this sense, it is almost as if it is the participant in these festivals who provides MONA with backstage access to the participant's experience. Therefore, rather than being a guest of MONA, MONA becomes a guest of the local denizens and the tourists that engage in these activities.

That Dark Mofo has struck a chord with this outreached audience is demonstrated by Tasmania Tourism's statistics, which recorded 174,000 visitors to Hobart over the festival's ten-day period in 2015. Dark Mofo included a range of activities including a Winter Feast that catered to 43,000 people, as well as performances at Hobart's Odeon Theatre, and an after-hours Blacklist party that attracted around 1,500 people a night. Hundreds of others participated in the naked Winter Solstice Dip in the River Derwent. The Premier of Tasmania, Will Hodgman, reported that Dark Mofo drew AUS$46 million into the economy in 2015, and created about 400 full-time and short-term jobs. He also claimed that this festival has:

> rewritten attitudes about winter in Australia's southernmost and coldest state and shaped how we define ourselves … Dark Mofo has embraced all that makes Tasmania quirky and unique … No one can copy it and nowhere can replicate it, making the event and Tasmania very difficult to compete with (Smith, 2016).

This statement demonstrates the government's reliance on MONA, and its recognition that it represents the character of the community in an inimitable manner. The museum has also become the stellar events organizer in the state with the power to lift the entire state's tourism industry. Yet this is not undertaken as part of a massive top-down venture, rather MONA is a partner or stakeholder that has assisted government.

MONA's emphasis on the local

Dark Mofo and the other attractions MONA's boutique experiencescape offers have been embraced by the local community, and in a very short time the museum has had a profound impact on this community on economic, cultural, and social levels.[6] Many of its economic benefits have already been noted, but the museum also directly employs:

> at least 120 with fine arts degrees that might otherwise have migrated out of Tasmania, and now I'm seeing people migrating into Tasmania. There are now people making art in Tasmania than wouldn't have otherwise have been, which arguably has something to do with MONA, perhaps as the main circumstance (Pennings and Walsh, 2016).

There has been a beneficial impact on local businesses, and many in the hospitality sector, for example, owe their continued existence to MONA's visibility.[7] MONA has significantly enhanced Tasmania's reputation as a clean environment with organic foods, for it has hosted banquets managed by celebrity chefs, which have attracted national recognition, and:

> has become the experience that everyone is seeking. It becomes the new cultural fad, the food fad ... That and MONA are the two things that are being marketed now, and MONA essentially expanded that, so more visitors came, people opened more restaurants – there are good Tasmanian restaurants with good Tasmanian experiences in that they use high quality, organic paddock to plate ingredients, and ... there are more tourists ... It's a place everyone has heard of now ... I didn't mean it, but I am glad I've been a part of it (Pennings and Walsh, 2016).

MONA has brought many cultural and social benefits to its local community. Walsh and staff regard the museum and its experiencescape as integral to the community, and it is situated in the suburb where Walsh grew up, which means that MONA has not strayed far from its owner's roots. In the process, the museum has given the community a sense of pride and a shared sense of ownership, and it offers local people access to new ways of cultural life. In relation to this role, Mark Wilsden has stated:

> These are very much working class suburbs around here, where there is high unemployment, low socio-economic areas, and we want to see kids come up here, to walk around ... In the early days when we opened I spoke to someone about community benefit, and I said "If it changes one teenager's life significantly. If it put them on a different path then it has achieved something" ... That is why it is free for locals because [Walsh] wants locals to have the opportunity because art and that experience changed his life. The generosity of public space to provide opportunities for this kind of experience is critical. Although we are private land, we don't have any fences or gates ... anyone can come here and just hang out ... We want it to be their MONA, that they'd be proud of it. David's on record as saying that is one of the biggest kicks he got out of MONA

was when people started calling it "Our MONA". That's the ultimate affirmation – that is engaged with it, proud of it, and is touching the community (Pennings and Wilsden, 2016).

The inflow of tourists has also deepened the community's personal and socio-cultural contact and exchange with outsiders. This has brought new awareness, appreciation, and increased understanding of others. It has also generated a stronger sense of cultural identity, and the belief that this local community matters, and that it has the capacity to host a globally significant cultural institution (Besculides, 2002, 306). This impact on community attitudes has been noted by Mofo's Creative Director, Leigh Carmichael, who says:

> [L]eading the charge in a cultural sense is a thing of pride, and it has lifted our confidence, and we can do well, and we can achieve ... It's gone right through the community – a sense of purpose, a sense of pride. I think MONA provides some leadership in that direction (Pennings and Carmichael, 2016).[8]

These phenomena are connected to another critical element in MONA's relationship with its local community: a sense of authenticity. MONA has been able to tap into, and is indeed, a product of a local sensibility. Tasmania has not been one of Australia's most prosperous states, and has historically been looked down on by some mainlanders. Being a small and remote region fostered a strong sense of community identity, and a down-to-earth attitude that Carmichael described when explaining MONA's place in the community: "It's earthy and it's grounded in community and it's very real, and we are very connected to our environment so I think that people who are visiting feel that is a huge part of it" (Pennings and Carmichael, 2016). MONA's success is therefore dependent on articulating local values while providing community leadership as a prestigious conduit between the cultures of Tasmania, Australia, and the world.

Conclusion

Most museums confront the challenge of balancing the needs of local communities with the expectations of national and international tourists. In 2006 Hans Belting discussed the positive and negative impacts that art museums can have on local communities and visitors, and noted the difficulties of seeking to satisfy both audiences:

> [M]useums need to attract global tourism, which means claiming their share in a new geography of world cultures ... On the other hand, they need acceptance and support from a local audience. Culture ... is specific in a local sense, even if minorities demand their own visibilities in art institutions (Belting, 2006, p. 5).[9]

MONA has been very successful in this regard, mainly due to Walsh's astute instincts, but also because the museum is very much attuned to these issues. These considerations are integral to MONA's association with authenticity. Justin Johnston has explained the different way in which MONA has approached the task of building an experiencescape predicated on local values:

> [W]e are doing similar things to these large-scale precincts with our hotel and other things … but they tend to work best if there is still some kind of integrity around the experience. That is a difficult thing to manage and maintain because you need to provide something for locals, as well as the tourists – it still has to have some kind of cultural sense, but it's not just forcing art down people's throats and trying to make a buck out of them (Pennings and Johnston, 2016).

Recent changes to visitor statistics however suggest a significant shift in the origins of MONA's primary audience. The overall number of visitors to MONA is increasing, but the percentage of those who are local inhabitants is declining. Walsh has claimed, "About 15 per cent of our guests are international. Less than 20 per cent from Hobart" (Pennings and Walsh, 2016). These contentions are supported by Wilsden who has stated, "Half the population of Hobart came in the first year to have a look. Probably only about 10 per cent of them have really come back" (Pennings and Wilsden, 2016). Johnston has explained that MONA currently receives around 400,000 visitors a year, but in 2011 "it was 50 per cent Tasmanian and 50 per cent interstate, mostly Sydney and Melbourne, and a small percentage from overseas, but within five years it's about 80 per cent from interstate" (Pennings and Johnston, 2016). This trend is concerning to an institution that is attached to its local community, but it has been able to mitigate this drift away from local visits to the actual museum by attracting more local people to festivals and events. MONA is also supporting activities like a local market, and these are attracting audiences that are purported by MONA staff to be proportionally 90 per cent local.

MONA, like other global museums, is strongly connected to a broader art world community. It is a large organization in a small town and needs to maintain its reputation by being an active member of a global museum circuit that exhibits major global artists who are in effect high-profile brands. MONA might not be a franchised branch of the Guggenheim, but it does show global celebrity artists such as Matthew Barney who produce spectacular events that sustain the reputation and profile of this institution as a global player. In 2017 Walsh is planning to build a museum extension to house artwork by the perennially popular global artist James Turrell, and this may spark renewed interest from locals, as well as catering to a growing audience from beyond Tasmania.

These activities keep the museum up to date with contemporary art and culture, and the festivals continue to attract government funding and bolster

Tasmanian tourism. However, the danger that MONA is turning into a tourist-only destination persists, and this jeopardizes an institution that wants to stay connected to its community. This balancing act has been described by Leigh Carmichael:

> It's good that everyone wants to be a part of it … but it's important not to get too caught up in that. We can't be too many things to too many people, as that would dilute our energy across too many areas.… Do we keep doing what we are doing, or do we go through some kind of re-birth? … Do something completely different? (Pennings and Carmichael, 2016).

MONA has achieved a great deal for a museum that cost only AUS$75 million to build, contains a AUS$30 million art collection, and requires about AUS$8–10 million a year to run. Its success has been built on a distinctive identity in a competitive marketplace while maintaining its links to the local community. However, as it entrenches its place in the global art museum circuit, it risks becoming a generic experiencescape, rather than a unique, boutique version of the same that is rooted in local community. It is a difficult balancing act, and Carmichael has summarized the challenges facing MONA, when he states that it is:

> prepared to take great risks. It's not doing things the way they would be normally done. It has the ability to break the rules, to go against them, to live on the fringes, and I think the greatest challenge going forward is to remain there. Once you are open, for some reason, there is a pull back to the centre because it is a safe place to be – it worked last week, let's do it again. I don't know if that's the way we should go. Maybe better to say: "It worked last week, so let's do it different". The big danger for us is feeding the market what it wants, and that's not how we started (Pennings and Carmichael, 2016).

MONA's use of festivals in particular point to the manner in which it is trying to maintain a balance between its local orientation and sensibility, while catering for increasing numbers of interstate and international visitors. Festivals like Dark Mofo have enabled MONA to maintain its community nexus by moving out of the museum and going directly into the community, rather than waiting for its community to come to them. As mentioned earlier, MONA's philosophy relating to the democratization of experience as illustrated in the universalist and non-expert access to the 'O' device, and the egalitarian tenor of its festivals provide a platform for acts of cultural performativity that is maintaining the interest of local and visitor, and in turn points to the enabling of individual agency within a community ethos that may help sustain MONA in the immediate future.

Notes

1 Brazil was also troubled by protests against a government that it was claimed had invested in these global events at the expense of its own citizens. *The Guardian's* Jonathan Watts reported, "massive spending on stadiums at a time when the government can barely afford wages for doctors and teachers, a huge security presence that protected rich foreigners at the expense of poor residents, dismal crowds that suggested most locals were uninterested in most sports, and massive inequality between the $920 a day payments to International Olympic Committee executives and the $13 a day earnings of cleaners in the Olympic village" (Watts, 2016, p. 5).

2 As Anna Klingmann has suggested, for "politicians, investors, citizens, and tourists, architecture is successful when it provides an operational value that improves the image, experience, and field of interaction between people … architecture serves … as a catalyst for cultural and economic change, thus enabling it to surpass its use value and attain brand equity" (Klingmann, 2007, 317).

3 Wilsden has also stated in relation to this matter: "You can say, 'This is shit', but some other galleries don't provide you with a mechanism to feed back this kind of thing. You can say it, and take that opinion away with you, but you can't feed it back, and you get stuck into this gallery guilt where if you are not reading the essay next to the artwork then you are not really appreciating the work." – interview, Hobart, 13 April 2016.

4 Adrian Franklin, "MONA and the *Carnivalesque*". School of Social Sciences Seminar, University of Tasmania, 23 May 2014.

5 This sense of communal conviviality was remarked upon by journalist James Valentine in his report on his attendance at a Dark Mofo festival: "And then there are the fires. Lots of them. Standing around them are groups of people warming their hands. There's no barriers around the braziers. You can walk right up to them. It's fantastic because what happens at a fire? You greet everyone and everyone greets you. You immediately comment on the cold and then go straight to talking about what you've just seen" (Valentine, 2016).

6 This claim is supported by Australian Council research, as reported in the *Sydney Morning Herald*: "Tasmania has the highest per capita rate of people working in the arts sector and attending arts events, based on figures provided by the Australia Council compiled before the Museum of Old and New Art was opened last year" (Taylor, 2012).

7 Mary Lijnzaad has stated, "There are a lot of businesses in Hobart that say … that visitors brought to Hobart by MONA have saved their business. So, particularly in hospitality, hotels that would ordinarily be almost shut at certain times of year, but now have bookings … There's a sense of responsibility with that" (Pennings and Lijnzaad, 2016).

8 Mark Wilsden has also commented on this phenomenon: "Experiences like MONA … make the locals proud about what they have got. That's where 'Our MONA' comes from, and undeniably in the last five years I have seen a strut in the step of Hobart in general, whether that's seen in our bars and restaurants, or other retail, and other galleries. More confidence" (Pennings and Wilsden, 2016).

9 MONA is making a major contribution to tourism in the state and to the pride of local people. Wilsden says, "We are fairly active in many sectors of the community, and I think that gives us buy-in, and we have helped build a tribe. We have advocates everywhere for what we do. The strongest advocate you can have for any business is the local people. You want the taxi driver saying 'You've got to go to MONA', or 'I took my kids there last week' or the person serving you coffee in your hotel to say a similar, and that's a personal testimonial that visitors take on its merits, and are less inclined to listen to marketing or advertising … You have to build the trust and support and buy-in from your local people. Whether it's a

festival, an experience like MONA, or a business, or a restaurant in a small town. If you don't have your locals who are prepared to go there and support it you're losing your best advocates" (Pennings and Wilsden, 2016). David Walsh has also stated, "Between September and December 2015, 85 restaurants opened. They call it the 'MONA effect' and it is certainly promoting business" (Pennings and Walsh, 2016).

Griselda Murray Brown has also proposed, "As public art institutions attract new visitors, they must strike a balance between treating them as an audience and as a community. Fail to adapt to their changing desires and habits, and you risk obsolescence. But lose sight of the fact that you are a place of culture and expertise, and you might as well be an ace caff without the museum attached" (Brown, 2013).

References

ABC News. (2012). MONA helps Hobart make top 10 cities list . 22 Oct 2012. [online]. Available at: www.abc.net.au/news/2012-10-22/hobart-makes-top-10-cities-list/4326384) [Accessed 16 Feb 2015].

ABC News. (2015). Dark Mofo declared a winner as Tasmania looks to leverage off its success. [online] Updated 23 June. Available at: www.abc.net.au/news/2015-06-23/dark-mofo-a-success-the-state-wants-to-leverage-off/6568142 [Accessed 15 Oct 2016].

Bailey, S. (2015). Monira Al Qaadiri. *Art Forum*, 53(9), p. 361.

Bakhtin, M. (2009). *Rabelais and his world*. Bloomington, Indiana: Indiana University Press.

Belting, H. (2006). Contemporary art and the museum in the Global Age. In: *L'Idea del Museo: Identita, Ruoli, Prospettive*. [online] Available at: www.forumperma nente.org/en/journal/articles/contemporary-art-and-the-museum-in-the-global-age-1 [Accessed 10 Nov 2015].

Besculides, A., Lee, M.E. and McCormick, P.J. (2002). Residents' perceptions of the cultural benefits of tourism. *Annals of Tourism Research*, 29(2), pp. 303–319.

Brown, G.M. (2013). The global art goer. *Financial Times*, [online] May 11. Available at: www.ft.com/content/d25f8602-b894-11e2-a6ae-00144feabdc0 [Accessed 5 Apr 2016].

Cuthbertson, D. (2014). Creating a $2 billion cultural project for Hong Kong. *Sydney Morning Herald*, [online] May 16. Available at: www.smh.com.au/entertainment/a rt-and-design/creating-a-2-billion-cultural-project-for-hong-kong-20140516-38fhw. html [Accessed 15 Jan 2016].

Daily Mirror. (2015). FIFA World Cup 2014 leads to record number of foreign visitors to Brazil. [online]. July 20. Available at: www.mirror.co.uk/news/world-news/fifa-world-cup-2014-leads-6106072 [Accessed 12 Sep 2016].

Degen, M.M. (2008). *Sensing Cities: Regenerating public life in Barcelona and Manchester*. London and New York: Routledge.

Ek, R. (2005). Regional experience-scapes as geo-economic ammunition. In: O'Dell, T. and Billing, P., eds., *Experience-scapes: tourism, culture and economy*. Copenhagen: Copenhagen Business School Press.

Franklin, A. (2014a). MONA and the Carnivalesque. School of Social Sciences Seminar. Tasmania: University of Tasmania. 23 May 2014.

Franklin, A. (2014b). *The making of MONA*. Australia: Viking/Penguin.

Fuggle, L. (2015). Rio 2016: How the Olympic Games will affect Brazil's tourism industry. *TREKK SOFT*. [online] 19 Nov. Available at: https://www.trekksoft.com/en/blog/rio-olympics-2016-tourism-impact [Accessed 15 Aug 2016].

180   *Mark Pennings*

Goncalves, R. (2015). Tourists spend a record amount in Australia. *SBS News*, 30 Jul. [online]. Available at: www.sbs.com.au/news/article/2015/07/30/tourists-spend-record-amount-australia [Accessed 11 Mar 2016].

Hirsch, N., Aranda, J., Wood, B.K. and Vidokle, A. (2015). Editorial – "Architecture as Intangible Infrastructure". *E-flux Journal* 66(2), October. [online]. Available at: www.e-flux.com/journal/66/60734/editorial-architecture-as-intangible-infrastructure-issue-two/ [Accessed 3 Aug 2015].

Hospitality Net. (2015). Travel & tourism in 2015 will grow faster than the global economy – WTTC reports. *World Travel and Tourism Council*, 30 March. [online]. Available at: www.hospitalitynet.org/news/4069673.html. [Accessed 3 Sep 2016].

Klingmann, A. (2007). *Brandscapes: Architecture in the experience economy.* Cambridge, Massachusetts: MIT Press.

Louisiana Museum of Art. (2015). Between the DISCURSIVE and the IMMERSIVE: a symposium on research in 21st-century art museums. Copenhagen [online]. Available at: http://research.louisiana.dk/ [Accessed 16, 17, 24, Jul 2016].

Murai, S. (2016). Japan doubles overseas tourist target for 2020. *Japan Times*, 30 Mar, p. 2.

O'Dell, T. and Billing, P., eds, (2005). *Experience-scapes: Tourism, culture and economy.* Copenhagen: Copenhagen Business School Press.

O'Dell, T. (2005). Experiencescapes. In: O'Dell, T. and Billing, P., eds., *Experience-scapes: tourism, culture and economy.* Copenhagen: Copenhagen Business School Press, pp. 11–29.

Peltier, D. (2015). International Tourist Arrivals Will Top 1.7 Billion Per Year by 2025. *Skift* [online] 25 Mar. Available at: https://skift.com/2015/03/25/international-tourist-arrivals-will-top-1-7-billion-per-year-by-2025/ [Accessed 22 Aug 2016].

Pennings, M. and Carmichael, L. (2016). Interview about the Museum of Old and New Art. Hobart.

Pennings, M. and Johnston, J. (2016). Interview about the Museum of Old and New Art. Hobart.

Pennings, M. and Lijnzaad, M. (2016). Interview about the Museum of Old and New Art. Hobart.

Pennings, M. and Walsh, D. (2016). Interview about the Museum of Old and New Art. Melbourne.

Pennings, M. and Wilsden, M. (2016). Interview about the Museum of Old and New Art. Hobart.

Smith, M. (2016). Dark Mofo's $10.5 million cash feast to help the even expand and boost visitor numbers. *Tasmanian Mercury*, [online]. 17 Jul. Available at: www.themercury.com.au/entertainment/events/dark-mofos-105-million-cash-feast-to-help-the-even-expand-and-boost-visitor-numbers/news-story/f31191530bda5df4134e74cecbe8f357 [Accessed 29 Jul 2016].

Statista.com. (2016). Global tourism industry – statistics & facts. [online]. Available at: www.statista.com/topics/962/global-tourism/ [Accessed 22 Aug 2016].

Stylianou-Lambert, T. (2011). Gazing from home: Cultural tourism and art museums. *Annals of Tourism Research*, 38(2), pp. 403–421.

Tasmanian Government. (2016). A world-leading destination of choice – Tasmania. [online]. Available at: www.cg.tas.gov.au/__data/.../INVEST_14182_TD_Tourism_En_20160401_Web.pdf [Accessed 2 Sep 2016].

Taylor, A. (2012). Tasmania is the arts end of Australia. *Sydney Morning Herald*, [online]. May 13. Available at: www.smh.com.au/entertainment/art-and-design/tasmania-is-the-arts-end-of-australia-20120512-1yjd4.html [Accessed 4 Sep 2016].

Tharoor, K. (2016). The Louvre is reimagined in Abu Dhabi. *The Guardian Weekly.* 1 Jan., pp. 26–30.

Tourism Australia. (2016). Visitors arrival data. [online]. Available at: www.tourism. australia.com/statistics/arrivals.aspx [Accessed 14 Oct 2016].

Tourism Tasmania.(2011–2016). Museum of Old and New Art – visitor statistics. [online]. Available at: www.tourismtasmania.com.au/research/reports/mona_statis tics [Accessed 5 Jul 2016].

UNWTO, World Tourism Organisation. (2015). Over 1.1 billion people travelled abroad in 2014. [online] Jan. 27. Available at: http://media.unwto.org/press-release/ 2015-01-27/over-11-billion-tourists-travelled-abroad-2014 [Accessed 22 Aug 2016].

UNWTO, World Tourism Organisation. (2016). International tourist arrivals up 4% reach a record 1.2 billion in 2015. [online]. Jan. 16. Available at: http://media.unwto. org/press-release/2016-01-18/international-tourist-arrivals-4-reach-re cord-12-billion-2015 [Accessed 22 Aug 2016].

Valentine, J. (2016). Hobart's Dark Mofo leave vivid in the dark. *Sydney Morning Herald*, [online] 14 Jun. Available at: www.smh.com.au/comment/hobarts-dark-m ofo-leaves-vivid-in-the-dark-20160614-gpimwl.html [Accessed 15 Oct 2016].

Watts, J. (2016). Were the Olympics worth it for Rio? *Guardian Weekly*, 26 Aug, 195(12), p. 5.

World Travel and Tourism Council. (2016). *Travel & tourism. Economic impact 2016 world*. London: World Tourism & Travel Council.

Conclusion

Susan Carson and Mark Pennings

The major themes in this book evolved while listening to national and international conference presentations in the field of cultural tourism and talking to colleagues about what it means to research 'cultural tourism'. We welcomed the inter-disciplinary nature of this field, and as researchers, we appreciated the ways in which cultural tourism scholars consistently stimulated the broader field of tourism studies by bringing expertise from their diverse backgrounds to the fold. *Performing cultural tourism* therefore bears the traces of dialogues that began when preparing papers for journals and conferences and the discussions undertaken at conferences, and now presents the work of colleagues who have so readily entered into the spirit of the project.

Given the range of the authors' scholarly interests, the chapters in this collection offer a diversity of subject matter and approach that emphasises a polyvocal sensibility. The spirit of the project was always to include the voices, and the stories, of a broad range of participants who engaged with the field of cultural tourism. Our rationale was to bring together new ideas about how communities, creative producers, and visitors can productively engage in an increasingly complex tourist environment in which there are competing notions about experience and authenticity. We wanted to explore methodologies that prioritize how community interests intersect with the desires of tourists who want to engage more fully with what has been called the 'backstage', including the 'brokers' in this ecology. We felt that whereas experiential 'staging' is well documented in tourism studies, there is less written about the diverse types of experiences and expectations that visitors bring to the tourist space and how host communities can respond to, or indeed challenge, these expectations. For us the term 'community' could relate to a specific geography, social, or cultural practice, or a virtual landscape, as all of these sites enable the sharing of experiences between communities of producers and consumers in tourist cultures.

The chapters in this collection represent these aspirations and have brought new concepts and methodologies to this round table of ideas. Some chapters directly represent the voice of a community participant and observer, such as Patricia Santiago, who is engaged in the daily challenge of protecting local cultural traditions while attempting to boost tourism opportunities, or a scholar such as Tim Middleton, who interrogated his own position as an academic researcher and the nature of the academic scholarly practices he undertook when pursuing literary tourism. In general, the authors in this collection provide a range of new insights with a refreshing awareness of their own position. In this context, the story of the land, as well as of the tourist who traverses new territory, is of prime concern to many Indigenous communities. Several contributors, such as Sally Butler, propose ideas about what it is to undertake cultural tourism in Indigenous communities, while others such as Ulrike Gretzel and Hilary du Cros examine the new frontiers of tourist engagement with sites (and the tourist notion of self) via social media platforms.

As contributors have elaborated upon their research experience a number of insights have been brought to key areas; such as, an increasing emphasis on tourism as a co-learning experience; the need to establish a cultural profile that pays attention to community spirituality and the role of temporary or elective belonging to a community; a reappraisal of 'creative tourism' in developing cultural tourism; the role of a democratization of experience in contemporary tourism; a changing global geo-economic framework that includes renewed attention to China in which Eurocentric assumptions about the operation of cultural tourism are shifting; the increasing focus on the 'self' in both digital and non-digital modes of representation in tourism; and the potential for creative tourism to boost tourism sectors by allowing creative workers, and tourists, to innovate and 'twist' understandings of conventional tourist behaviour. In brief, the research depicts the evolution of the cultural tourism market as independent tourism competes with package tourism, niche markets emerge, independent tourism is increasingly dispersed, and virtual worlds complement the physical. In this complex scenario for instance there is a growing demand for self-expression that does not necessarily focus on destination as such, as Ulrike Gretzel discovers in her research on 'selfies'.

One of the most persistent themes of the various chapters in this collection is an emphasis on cultural tourism as an educative process in which both consumers and providers negotiate the terms of this experience. If the historic desire of the cultural tourist often has been to simply learn about other places and cultures that assumption may no longer hold true: there is today instead an equally powerful desire to learn from and about oneself in negotiation with another community or site, and to place oneself in that location or event in an act of self-representation that out-performs 'gazing' or even 'doing'. This drive to individualization can be mediated by digital platforms: the need to go 'off the beaten track' is often concomitant with sharing the track instantly and globally with like-minded individualists. As Ulrike Gretzel points out, such behaviours are contemporary innovations of long-established tourist practices (such as travel photography). In arguing for a 'visual turn' to tourism via social media Gretzel focuses on the way in which cultural understandings should be a part of methodologies such as netnography, a concept that connects to du Cros's argument for a greater emphasis on the 'why' in tourism research. Gretzel's study of immersion through participant observation speaks, as well, to Middleton's interest in the process of capturing imaginative contexts in self-guided travel.

For communities where local traditions and cultures are perceived to be under threat there is a greater emphasis on community organization and the development of appropriate management plans that begin with community involvement rather than following a top-down regional or national approach determined by other/outside parties. Authors such as Buzinde, Vandever and Nyaupane, and Santiago document the way in which engaging with spiritual aspects of a community can either promote or hinder effective management. In this situation, intra-community tensions over tourism are aggravated by the disruptions facilitated by ineffective regional or national programs. There is an increasing awareness of the damage that can be wrought by mass tourism, and cultural tourism is therefore seen as a way of achieving economic benefit without losing local identity, working as it were, from the ground up. Communities are seen to be attempting to envisage a new type of relationship with 'outsiders' in order to increase benefits to local regions, but also to *educate* as Buzinde et al., Santiago, and Butler make clear in their chapters. The debates over being inside or outside the tourist enterprise points to a community concern over categorizing visitors who may be for a time, inside a community or, in the case of residential stakeholders, both inside and outside of their community. Sally Butler pays attention to such oscillation of activity and positioning and argues for an alternative model of 'temporary belonging' to replace 'authenticity'.

This sense of inclusion/exclusion is also evident in major tourist cities, which can also suffer from a process of exclusion when top-down management of events that are major tourism draw cards do not work in favour of local interests. One of the insights of the study of the post-2004 Olympic Games in Athens is the way in which buildings designed for Olympic use have been re-purposed for the housing of refugees. The stories of immigrants who are seeking, and often denied, integration are framed by the structures of an event that offered a Cultural Olympiad, and was intended to operate as an assertion of national identity as well as an international sporting mega-event.

In many of the studies herein the role of 'creative tourism' is of increasing interest. As Yang Zhang and Philip Xie note, creativity is a loaded word and it follows that the concept of creative tourism is similarly challenging. However, many of these chapters note the pervasive impact of creative artifacts, performances, and performers that are appropriated in the service of enhancing heritage or bringing tourist populations to sites to engage in cultural exchange. These authors argue for further research on cultural tourism from the tourist perspective and draw attention to the way in which creative tourism is a unique learning and participative experience.

In all chapters a shift in the power structures of tourism dynamics is detected. Consumer-to-consumer, consumer-to-provider, and peer-to-peer negotiate their touristic role in locations and at events that offer visitors a stake, whether authentic or not, in the process. Managers of major tourism sites must now operate across these sectors and find ways of incorporating contemporary events as leisure activities without diminishing the heritage, historic, or cultural value for which they are responsible. In this context, UNESCO World Heritage Sites, such as Cockatoo Island in New South Wales, Australia, and Port Arthur Historic Sites in Tasmania, Australia, demonstrate ways in which placating visitors' desire for 'performativity' means developing open narratives that include events that may have a traumatic impact on the site (and, in the case of Port Arthur, an event that had national political and social impact), as well as protecting an environment that supports a World Heritage listing. The role of spectacles as a mechanism of cultural tourism development appears in the studies of Macau and that city's vernacular heritage, as well as in the analysis of former convict sites in Australia.

Many of the narratives that have emerged in recent tourism phenomena develop increasingly through a methodology of negotiation and cooperation with stakeholders and community. At the Museum of Old and New Art (MONA) in Hobart, Tasmania, the art museum, an institution that normally celebrates individual originality, is reconfigured in today's realignment of tourist interests to be both a site of art and a means of democratizing high culture in a manner that both enhances and is nourished by the cultures of local and global tourists. MONA sets out to be subversive and this 'anti' stance has proved to be enormously popular. The technologies and methodologies employed by this museum asks visitors to "back their own judgement" in a museum-scape, and in so doing, contests the habitual way in which museums have become business assets for promoting cultural tourism.

The rise of Chinese tourism, across independent/package/mass sectors now has a significant influence on Asian tourism in general, according to Zhang and Xie. The scholarship presented here examines the way in Eurocentric frameworks of tourism are becoming diversified in the face of Chinese tourism where the development of vernacular tourism has a major role to play in tourism development. Hilary du Cros calls for research that discloses the difference in Asian and Anglo-American use of social media in order to better establish a sense of collective identity for tourists seeking a new experience in another land and culture.

Finally, the arguments developed around the digital are critical for understanding many trends in contemporary tourism and point to a need to develop a greater understanding of the way in which mobile technologies offer tourists and providers extraordinary opportunities in the consumption and delivery of tourism services. With social media firmly in the foreground, Hilary du Cros argues for an embrace of new approaches and makes the point that issues such as trust, expertise, and reliability are central to the future way in which tourists will use peer-to-peer networks rather than rely on hospitality sites. Her research suggests that there are hidden anxieties (in this case, of Asian youth) that may be revealed in further research, and that such studies might complicate the accepted picture of narcissistic tendencies and self-representation in this demographic sample. The methodologies proposed therefore are open and focused on the cultural, some would even say philosophical, tendencies that appear to lie at the heart of practices of cultural tourism that move forward in an era of what Marc Augé has called *supermodernity* in which we live on global (and digitized) highways while dipping in and out of localized experiences. It is this concentration of highways, byways, new communicative trajectories, and new modes of cultural cognizance that facilitate terms such as cooperation, exchange, creative tourism, negotiation, and temporary belonging in contemporary forms of cultural tourism, and it is these that constitute the conceptual schema of this text.

References

Augé, M. (2009). *Non-places: An introduction to supermodernity*, Howe, J., trans. New York: Verso.

Index